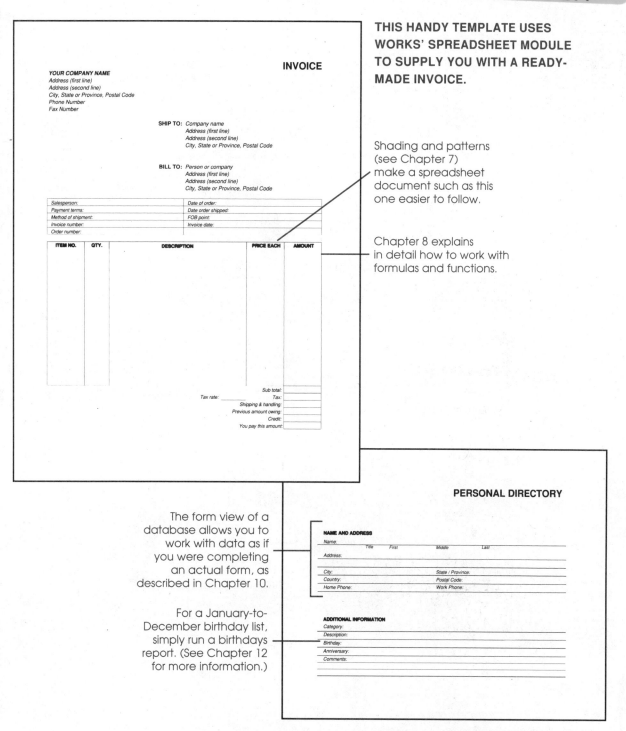

THIS HANDY TEMPLATE USES WORKS' SPREADSHEET MODULE TO SUPPLY YOU WITH A READY-MADE INVOICE.

INVOICE

YOUR COMPANY NAME
Address (first line)
Address (second line)
City, State or Province, Postal Code
Phone Number
Fax Number

SHIP TO: Company name
Address (first line)
Address (second line)
City, State or Province, Postal Code

BILL TO: Person or company
Address (first line)
Address (second line)
City, State or Province, Postal Code

Salesperson:	Date of order:
Payment terms:	Date order shipped:
Method of shipment:	FOB point:
Invoice number:	Invoice date:
Order number:	

ITEM NO.	QTY.	DESCRIPTION	PRICE EACH	AMOUNT

Sub total:	
Tax rate: Tax:	
Shipping & handling:	
Previous amount owing:	
Credit:	
You pay this amount:	

Shading and patterns (see Chapter 7) make a spreadsheet document such as this one easier to follow.

Chapter 8 explains in detail how to work with formulas and functions.

The form view of a database allows you to work with data as if you were completing an actual form, as described in Chapter 10.

For a January-to-December birthday list, simply run a birthdays report. (See Chapter 12 for more information.)

PERSONAL DIRECTORY

NAME AND ADDRESS
Name:
　　　　Title　　First　　Middle　　Last
Address:

City: State / Province:
Country: Postal Code:
Home Phone: Work Phone:

ADDITIONAL INFORMATION
Category:
Description:
Birthday:
Anniversary:
Comments:

IT'S EASY TO KEEP YOUR PERSONAL DIRECTORY CURRENT WITH THIS DATABASE TEMPLATE.

For Micah and Sara

May you live to see your world fulfilled,
May your desire be for worlds still to come,
And may you trust in generations past and yet to be.
May your heart be filled with intuition
and your words be filled with insight.
May songs of praise ever be upon your tongue
and your vision be a straight path before you.
May your eyes shine with the light of holy words
and your face reflect the brightness of the heavens...

Talmud, Berachot 17A

RUNNING

Microsoft®
WORKS 3

FOR WINDOWS™

JOANNE WOODCOCK
REVISED BY NEIL J. SALKIND

PUBLISHED BY
Microsoft Press
A Division of Microsoft Corporation
One Microsoft Way
Redmond, Washington 98052-6399

Library of Congress Cataloging-in-Publication Data
Woodcock, JoAnne.
    Running Microsoft Works 3 for Windows / JoAnne Woodcock and Neil
J. Salkind.
        p.   cm.
    Includes index.
    ISBN 1-55615-584-0
    1. Integrated software.   2. Microsoft Works for Windows.
    I. Salkind, Neil J.   II. Title.
    QA76.76.I57W67   1993
    005.369--dc20   93-36475
                                                       CIP

Printed and bound in the United States of America.

    5 6 7 8 9 AG–M 9 8 7 6

Distributed to the book trade in Canada by Macmillan of Canada, a division of Canada Publishing Corporation.

A CIP catalogue record for this book is available from the British Library.

Microsoft Press books are available through booksellers and distributors worldwide. For further information about international editions, contact your local Microsoft Corporation office. Or contact Microsoft Press International directly at fax (206) 936-7329.

Acquisitions Editor: Lucinda Rowley
Project Editor: Maureen Williams Zimmerman
Manuscript and Technical Editors: Benchmark Productions, Inc.

Chapters at a Glance

Table of Contents

Table of Contents

Table of Contents

Acknowledgments

There was once an elephant who had a cold, but still wanted to go out and play with his friends. His mother told him that "just because your trunk is packed, doesn't mean you're ready to leave." This logic is equally applicable to producing a book. Words are only characters on a page until a book production team can apply their unique experience and skills to prepare for the reader a book. I was fortunate enough to work with such a team in the creation of this book.

I want to thank Lucinda Rowley, Acquisition Editor, for giving me the opportunity to revise an already good book authored by JoAnne Woodcock. Special thanks go to Maureen Zimmerman, Project Editor, for her attention to detail and high standards. Maureen guaranteed that what needed to get done, got done. Thanks also to Andrew Williams from Benchmark Productions, who supervised the production of this book. He well understands that writing can be fun as well as demanding, and he helped to ensure that my style of teaching was not edited out.

As did JoAnne Woodcock, in her acknowledgments to the second edition, I too have to thank the team of developers at Microsoft for putting together a wonderful set of integrated applications in Microsoft Works 3 for Windows.

Neil J. Salkind
November 30, 1993

Introduction

You may already be aware that Microsoft Works has been around for years, operating on a variety of platforms such as MS-DOS, AppleDOS, the Macintosh, and more. The most recent version is Works for Windows. This book covers Works 3 for Windows. As you will see, the combination of Works and Windows provides you with a complete integrated software package, which runs on a graphical user interface. Works gives you the power to do everything from write this week's shopping list using the word processor to figure out how the national debt will be settled using the spreadsheet. And Windows allows you to do all of this in an easy-to-use multi-tasking environment.

While Works 3 for Windows contains modules that offer the capabilities of several applications, you may not know how well they can all work together. The main modules—the word processor, spreadsheet, and database—are integrated with one another so that information stored in or generated by one can easily be used by another. That means no retyping! Data can be easily copied from module to module. The other parts of Works, such as Draw, also provide you with tools that have many of the features that the best graphics and communications modules on the market offer. In all respects, Works is a complete package of computer applications. I hope you're reading this before you go out and spend $500 on a word processor and another $500 on a spreadsheet, and so on. Unless you're a high-powered turbo user, Works is really all you will need.

Who This Book Is For

Almost anyone who is more concerned about getting a letter to the IRS or Aunt Gussie than recovering a lost file cluster will love Works and (I hope) this book. Throughout this book, you will find the kind of information you need to understand the process of creating several different types of documents and then modifying them to fit your particular computing needs. Works 3 for Windows has plenty of advanced features, and this latest version introduces enough new tools to make any one module competitive with dedicated word processors, spreadsheets, and databases. But, its most important feature is its ease of use. With WorksWizards, WordArt, and the user friendly interface, you'll be up and running with Works in minutes. Really!

What's in This Book

Running Microsoft Works 3 for Windows is organized into seven parts, each of which takes you through the beginning and advanced features of a particular aspect of Works 3 for Windows.

In Part 1, *Getting Started with Works,* you will learn about how to start Works and about some of the built-in features, such as WorksWizards and toolbars. You will learn how these features make Works 3 for Windows such an easy and powerful tool to use.

Part 2, *Using the Word Processor,* introduces you to the word processor and starts by showing you how to create a simple document. From there, the part goes on to describe more advanced features, such as formatting text and incorporating graphics into your pages.

Part 3, *Using the Spreadsheet,* begins with the creation of a simple spreadsheet. It then shows you how to manage cell entries, design formulas, and work with functions. Finally, it ends with a startling display of charts. (How *did* you do that?)

Part 4, *Using the Database,* takes you through the steps of designing a database form, using the form and list views to display your records, and creating reports to customize your printouts. If you've ever lost your first edition of *One Flew Over the Cuckoo's Nest,* your database of first editions will help you locate it and not lose it again.

Part 5, *Using Graphics,* shows you what Works can do with graphics, including special features such as WordArt that allow you to transform ordinary characters and words into interesting shapes and presentations. Here, you will also be introduced to the Microsoft Draw program.

Want to know the weather in Tokyo? How much one share of Marvel Comics is worth (about $30 today), or how to buy a perfume bottle from the Museum of Modern Art? In *Using Works Communications* (Part 6) you'll find out how to use Works 3 for Windows and the communications tools it comes with.

Part 7, *Working Together*, shows you the true power of integrated applications. Create a chart using the spreadsheet, place it in a word-processed document, and then change the numbers the chart is based on two weeks later. Guess what? The chart you created in the spreadsheet changes as well. Applications and files can be connected in Works 3 for Windows so everything stays nicely in touch.

Whatever you want with Works 3 for Windows you can have. I had fun writing this book and I hope you have fun using it to learn how to use Works. I welcome e-mail from you and suggestions, ideas, criticisms, or whatever else will make the next edition of this book even better. Good works to you!

Neil J. Salkind
Internet: njs@ukanvm.bitnet
CompuServe: 70404,365

Getting Started
with Works

1

Works and Windows

You're about to learn how to use Microsoft Works 3 for Windows, the most powerful integrated set of computer applications available for the personal computer. Even better, Works operates with Microsoft Windows, a working environment that allows you to perform complex operations with a simple click or two of a mouse button. That's why the official name of Works is Works *for* Windows—the name says it all.

You don't have to be a Windows expert to learn how to use Works. But you should be familiar with how to use Windows and what the Works menus are all about.

If you are new to Windows, or even new to computers, take the time to read this chapter. You'll find that the skills you learn will be used throughout *Running Microsoft Works 3 for Windows*.

We assume that both Windows and Works for Windows (which we'll call Works from here on) have already been installed on your hard drive. If they have not, turn to Appendix C, page 541, for instructions or see your Windows or Works for Windows documentation.

Say Hello to Windows

Windows is a working environment that surrounds MS-DOS, or DOS, the operating system that controls your computer's basic functions.

Why add another system on top of MS-DOS? In other words, why do you want or need Windows? There are many reasons; most of them relate to how efficiently your programs can run. In your daily work, however, you'll find that the most compelling reason for using Windows is how easily it can execute complex MS-DOS commands without the confusion introduced by character-based operating systems such as MS-DOS.

For example, you may be familiar with this famous MS-DOS prompt:

```
C:\>
```

When you see this prompt on your computer monitor's screen, MS-DOS is waiting for you to enter a command such as

```
C:\> xcopy e:\workswin\*.* /s a:
```

This command tells MS-DOS to copy all the files in the directory named *Workswin*, including subdirectories, to the disk in floppy drive A. Remembering such cumbersome commands can be difficult.

With Windows, such elaborate commands are not necessary. Rather, you interact with a graphical interface. Symbols and words on the screen represent operations, and you simply select the symbol that represents the operation you want to perform.

If you haven't started your computer, do so now. If Windows doesn't appear, type the following at the MS-DOS prompt:

```
C:\>win
```

TIP: If Windows does not start, you may be in the wrong directory. Look at your MS-DOS directory (use the DIR command) to find out where Windows is and switch to that directory. The command to switch to another directory is CD\(directory name).

You might need to type

```
CD\WINDOWS
```

and press Enter. Then type

```
WIN
```

Within a few seconds, you see a display like the one in Figure 1-1, on the next page.

TIP: Unlike a character-driven system, Windows allows you to use symbols and simple mouse clicks to perform complex commands.

You've just entered the world of *graphical user interfaces,* where a mouse becomes your friend and the MS-DOS prompt gives way to pictures. Working with your computer now changes from typing strings of characters to using a far more visual approach. Windows presents you with various options and waits patiently until you make a choice. If you haven't used Windows before, you'll find the experience like riding a two-wheeler bike for the first time or getting up on water skis or acing that final exam—all exhilarating experiences.

FIGURE 1-1.
A typical opening screen display in Windows.

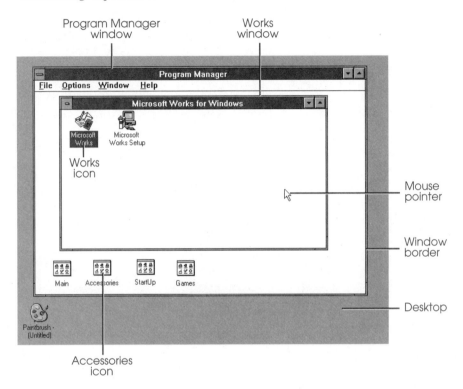

Four characteristic features of Windows are labeled in Figure 1-1: one or more open *windows,* an open area called the *desktop,* the *mouse pointer,* and several graphics called *icons.* You are going to learn a lot more about icons, but for the time being, you should know that icons are the small pictures or graphics that represent various types of applications and files in Windows.

 TIP: If you computer display does not look exactly like Figure 1-1, do not worry. You have done nothing wrong. You will soon learn how to adjust the elements you see on your screen so it looks like this screen.

What Is a Window?

What is a window, aside from being a feature from which Windows takes its name? A window is a rectangular portion of the screen framed in a doublelined border. It is a part of the screen that is reserved for displaying a particular program (such as a word processor) or, within a program, a particular document, such as a letter.

One of Windows' great strengths is its ability to allow you to keep track of two, three, or more open programs at the same time. To avoid chaos, Windows runs each program in its own *application window*. Similarly, if you want to work with one program but several different documents, Windows (and Windows programs) displays each document in its own *document window*. Windows is designed to make available as many documents as your computer's memory can handle. In Works, document windows can hold text files, spreadsheets, or databases. For example, in Figure 1-2, you can see three different Works documents, all open and accessible.

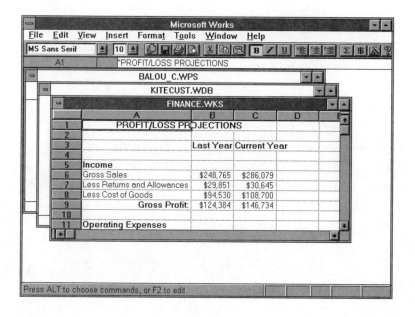

FIGURE 1-2.
Three different and open Works windows.

7

The Desktop

All of the work you do in Windows takes place on the *desktop*. This is the area Windows occupies on your computer screen (see Figure 1-1). Windows uses a desktop as a metaphor to help you visualize your screen as the electronic equivalent of the desk on which you work. You can arrange several types of "objects" on the desktop—a clock, a calculator, a letter, a budget, and so on. Unlike on a real desktop, each of these objects appears in a separate window. And just as with a real desktop, you can move these items around to suit your preferences.

The Mouse and How to Use It

When you use a mouse, the small pointer on your screen moves as you move the mouse on your desktop. When you move the mouse, the pointer moves the same relative distance, in the same direction, on the screen. The mouse pointer can change to a different shape depending upon the task or work you are doing.

We assume that you have a mouse and that it will be your primary way of communicating with Windows and Works. If keyboard equivalents are faster or more efficient, we'll tell about those when we discuss a specific feature. You can also find a list of keyboard equivalents for certain mouse operations in Appendix B, page 527.

Once you've positioned the mouse pointer, you use the left mouse button to carry out one of three basic mouse actions.

- *Clicking* is done by (really!) quickly pressing the left mouse button once. Clicking is used to select objects on the desktop.

- *Double-clicking* is done by pressing the left mouse button twice in rapid succession. Double-clicking is used to activate an icon or open a window. If you double-click too slowly, you will simply select and then de-select an object. In other words, you will be clicking once, then clicking again, rather than double-clicking.

■ *Dragging* is done by placing the mouse pointer on an object (such as an icon or a window), pressing down and holding the left-hand button, and then moving the mouse pointer to a new location on the desktop. When the object is in its new location, release the mouse button.

TIP: Is your mouse pointer off the desktop? Do this: Use the mouse to place the pointer in the middle of the screen, then pick up the mouse and place it in the middle of your mouse pad or mouse area.

Moving Around with Scroll Bars

If you've had any experience with other Windows applications, including Windows itself, you are already familiar with scroll bars and what they do. You can see a horizontal scroll bar here.

Scroll box

Scroll arrow   Scroll arrow

Any scroll bar consists of the following elements:

■ Two scroll arrows (pointing in opposite directions) that you click on to move a short distance—one line with a vertical scroll bar

■ The light gray scroll box inside the scroll bar that you drag to move to a different part of the document .

■ The scroll bar area outside the scroll box that you click in to move one screen's worth

TIP: Scoll bars are often horizontal in Windows applications. You can scroll your documents left or right by clicking on the left or right arrow, just as you can move up or down by clicking on the up arrow or the down arrow.

Moving around a document using the mouse means using the mouse and the scroll bars as follows.

To move in the document...	Place the mouse pointer...
one line up	on the up scroll arrow and click once
one line down	on the down scroll arrow and click once
up one window of text	above the scroll box and click once
down one window of text	below the scroll box and click once
anyplace in the document	on the scroll box in the scroll bar and drag the scroll box to the approximate location in the document you want to move to

These moves can be used on the vertical and horizontal scroll bars.

For example, if you wanted to move to the middle of the document using the mouse and scroll bars, you would follow these steps.

1. Place the mouse pointer on the scroll box in the scroll bar.

2. Drag the scroll box to the middle (or as close as you can get it) of the scroll bar.

The text in your window will be the text located at approximately the middle of the document.

The Program Manager

The Program Manager is Windows' central control. From it, you can start the applications that help your computer become a productive part of your life. Because the Program Manager is so useful, its window is the one you normally see whenever you start Windows. And because it's so important, closing the Program Manager window is the first step in ending a Windows session.

Here's a closer look at a typical Program Manager window.

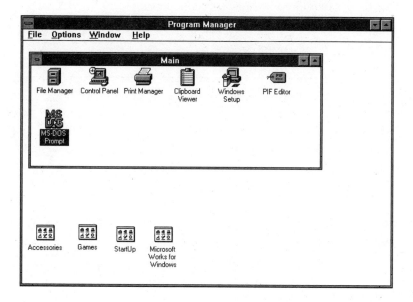

Within the Program Manager window in the illustration (and, probably, on your own screen), you see a second, smaller window. This second window represents a *program group* that contains a set of programs, each of which is represented by its own *icon*. Windows organizes programs into groups to keep order and to enable you to find your programs quickly. Within the program group window, you see several icons—small graphic images that Windows uses to represent the programs available on your personal computer.

When Windows is installed, it creates four program groups:

- The *Main group*, which gives you access to a set of Windows utility programs, including one called File Manager that allows you to manage programs and files

- The *Accessories group*, which includes a set of useful application programs such as Write (an elementary word processor), Paintbrush (a drawing program), and Terminal (a computer communications program)

- The *Games group*, which offers potentially addictive amusement in the form of Solitaire, Hearts, and Minesweeper

- The *StartUp group*, which contains programs that Windows runs automatically when it is started

 TIP: If you are not an expert at using your mouse, take some time to play both of the games included with Windows. To win at the games, you must use your mouse. These games will quickly build your basic mouse skills.

You might also see groups named Windows Applications and Non-Windows Applications or others such as WordPerfect, dBASE, or Clipper.

Program groups can be displayed as open windows or as a small icon, like this:

Accessories

Let's look at some of the things you can do with Program Groups.

Opening a Program Group

The icon representing the Accessories group (shown above) is said to be *minimized.* The program group is available, and you can open it whenever you want. Because the program group is not currently active, Windows has tucked it away at the bottom of the Program Manager window to eliminate clutter on the screen.

You probably have more than one minimized program group window on your desktop. Open them one at a time by placing the mouse pointer on the icon that represents the group and double-clicking.

Moving Among Group Windows

The group windows you've opened should be overlaid like shingles on a roof, as you can see in Figure 1-3. Notice that only the window on top of the stack has any color to its border. This color (dark shading on a non-color screen) indicates the current, or active, window—the one that will be affected by any commands you issue. More than one group can be open, but only one window or group can be active.

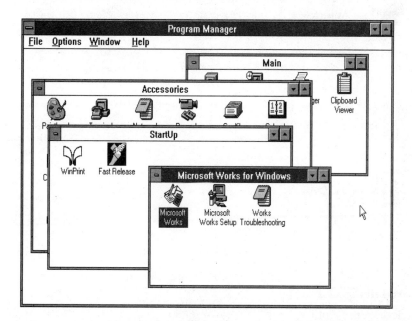

FIGURE 1-3.
Several open windows; only the top one is active.

You can change to a different group window in any of three ways. Try one or all of them to see which best suits your style of working.

- Place the mouse pointer anywhere in a window that is not active and click.

- Hold down the Ctrl key and press the Tab key repeatedly to cycle from group to group.

■ Open the Window menu by clicking on it or by pressing Alt and the W key (notice the underlined letter W in the menu name.) The menu shows you a numbered list of open windows. Just select the one you want by clicking on its name or by pressing the number key indicated by underlining.

TIP: If you want, you can use key combinations to perform certain operations. In this book, such combinations are joined by a plus sign (for example, Ctrl+Tab for the key combination mentioned above). When you see these combinations, remember to press and hold down the first key while you press the second key.

Whichever method you choose, notice that the new window comes to the front of all the open windows.

Starting a Program

One of the main reasons for using the Program Manager is to start programs. To see how it's done, start the Windows accessory called Clock. It's interesting to look at and easy to manipulate. Here's how to do it.

1. Find the Accessories group and make it the active window.

2. Double-click on the Clock icon you see here.

Clock

The clock appears on your rather crowded desktop. Just for fun, change the Clock's face from analog to a more computer-appropriate digital display by following these steps.

1. Open the Clock's Settings menu by clicking on it or by using the Alt+S key combination.

2. Choose the Digital command by clicking on it or by pressing D. The digital display appears as you see here.

Managing Windows

When you have more than one window open, you want to be able to use them efficiently: by closing them, changing their sizes, rearranging them, and moving them out of the way by turning them into icons at the bottom of the screen. Windows lets you do all this with the help of a mouse and several different window elements.

The following illustration labels the window elements that most concern you.

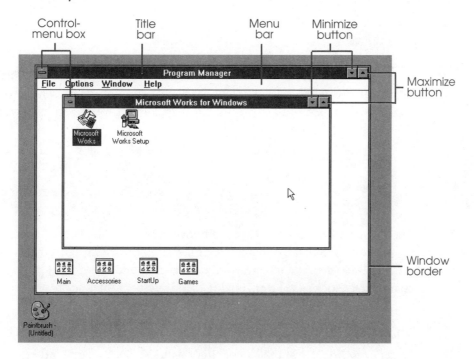

Let's take a quick tour of Windows' high points. Grab your mouse and let's go.

Sizing a Window with Borders

Many windows can be sized. In other words, you can change the size of the window, making it larger, smaller, thinner, or wider. A window that can be sized always has a double-lined border, which frames the window on the desktop. (When you see a window with a solid border, it is a window that you cannot adjust or change in size. It can be moved, however.)

You can change the size of a window by moving either a side or a corner. When you are sizing a window, the mouse pointer changes shape and appears as a double-headed arrow on the side or corner you are pulling or pushing into position. You can see how the mouse pointer looks at the bottom of this window:

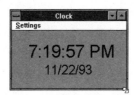

To change the height of a window, you move the top or bottom border. To change the width of a window, you move the left or right border. To change both dimensions of a window—to make it shorter and narrower at the same time—you move a corner.

Be sure that the Clock is the active window. Follow these steps to make the Clock smaller.

1. Place the mouse pointer on the bottom right corner. The mouse pointer should change shape.

2. Press and hold the left mouse button and push the corner up and to the left until the outline of the Clock is about the size of a business card.

3. Release the mouse button.

Moving a Window with the Title Bar

The *title bar* appears at the top of every window. As its name indicates, the title bar identifies the program or document in the window. The title bar is also the key to moving a window around on the desktop.

The Clock is now a handy size for displaying the time in an out-of-the-way corner. Here's how to move it to another location on the desktop.

1. Place the mouse pointer anywhere on the title bar of the window. (On the word Clock is a useful place.)

2. Press and hold the left mouse button and drag the grayish outline to the bottom right corner of the desktop.

3. Release the mouse button, and the Clock appears in its new location.

Now let's tinker with the Program Manager's display, so click in the Program Manager window.

Selecting Commands from a Menu

A *menu bar* appears just below the title bar in any window in which a program is running. Each program has its own set of menus, as you can see by comparing the menu bars in the Program Manager window with the one in the Clock window. Menus always contain lists of commands to choose from. In many respects, these menu commands are equivalent to typing commands at the MS-DOS prompt.

Earlier you saw how the Window menu was used to change to a different group window. The same procedure applies to choosing any menu or command in either Windows or Works. Either click on the menu name or press the Alt key and the key for the underlined letter in the menu name (such as Alt+F for the File menu).

Let's use the Window menu to rearrange the group windows in the Program Manager.

Point to the Window menu and click. Notice that the first two items on the Window menu are Cascade and Tile. When windows overlap, as they do now in the Program Manager, they are cascaded like shingles on a roof. If you tile the open windows (which you'll do next), windows are arranged side by side so that the content of each is visible.

Before you begin tiling the windows, notice the key combinations Shift+F5 and Shift+F4 to the right of Cascade and Tile menu options. These are the keyboard shortcuts we mentioned earlier. You are welcome to use them instead of clicking with the mouse to select the menu option.

Now place the mouse pointer on the Tile option and click, or press the Shift+F4 key combination. Almost immediately, the screen changes to look like Figure 1-4.

Return to cascaded windows by using the keyboard shortcut, Shift+F5.

FIGURE 1-4.
Active windows
when they
are tiled.

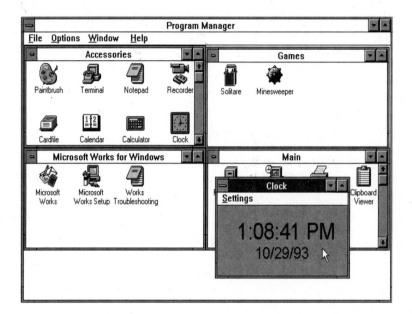

Controlling a Window with the Control-Menu Box

A Control-menu box appears in the upper left corner of every application and document window and looks like this.

If you use a mouse, the Control-menu box offers a quick way to close a window. You don't need to have so many windows open in the Program Manager. To close a window, follow these steps.

1. Point to the Control-menu box in the active group window.

2. Double-click.

Now, close one or two other group windows, including the Accessories group. The Clock won't stop running. You can return to the Clock window by clicking on it or by pressing the Alt+Esc key combination to cycle through all the open windows.

TIP: To get to a buried window, restore the maximized window (for instructions, see "Growing and Shrinking Windows," this page) and then choose the window you want by pressing Alt+Esc to cycle through all open application windows.

Growing and Shrinking Windows

The Maximize and Minimize buttons can have a profound effect on the size of a window. Looking like side-by-side Scrabble tiles in the top right corner of the Clock window title bar, the Maximize button is identified by an upward-pointing triangle (▲), and the Minimize button by a downward-pointing triangle (▼). You can use these buttons only if you have a mouse.

Let's practice by minimizing the Clock window. Be sure it's the active window and follow these steps.

1. Point to the Minimize button.

2. Click.

    The Clock becomes an icon in the lower left corner on the desktop.

    When the Clock, or any other application, is minimized, it is out of the way, yet it remains available for you to access or use. You don't have to stop and start an application and then stop again each time you want to switch to another application and then switch back again.

TIP: Even though a window is minimized, it still uses up valuable computer memory. If you are finished with an application or a document, close it. Minimize windows when you want to continue to have access to them but don't need them at the moment.

After you've minimized an application, you'll probably want to restore it to its former size at some point. To do this, just point to the minimized Clock and double-click.

To maximize a window, place the mouse pointer on the maximize button and click once. The window will then take up the entire screen. Do that now with the Clock window and it will appear as in Figure 1-5.

FIGURE 1-5.
The maximized
Clock window.

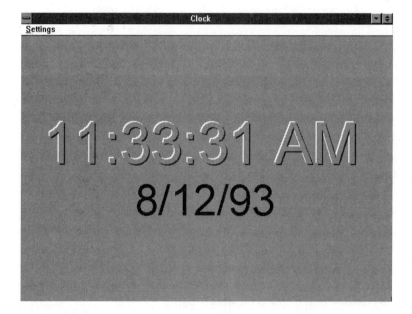

Although this display is too big for a simple clock, you'll find that a full-screen display is very useful when you're working with even a moderately long document in an application window.

When a window is maximized, as the Clock is now, notice that the Maximize button changes to display two triangles, one pointing up and the other down.

You have no need for a Maximize button now, so Windows has changed it to a Restore button. To use the Restore button and return the Clock to its former size, follow these steps.

1. Point to the Restore button.

2. Click.

That concludes your whirlwind tour of Windows. Next, we'll turn our attention to some important information on how to start Works.

Welcome to Works

It's time to begin what you're really here for! In the remainder of this chapter, you'll learn how to start Works, take a look at the various parts of the program, and learn how to set up Works so that your screen resembles those illustrated in later chapters.

Along the way, you'll see how the look of Windows extends to applications designed to work with it, and you will come to view Work as a set of valuable tools that help you define a productive way of working. That's what computers and good applications like Works are all about: providing the tools that let you concentrate on what you want to do, rather than on how you're supposed to do it.

Starting Works

When you install Works, Windows creates a program group named Microsoft Works for Windows. Check your desktop for the Microsoft Works for Windows group and make it the active window, as you see in Figure 1-6, on the next page.

When you install Works, the Setup program creates two icons, one for Works itself and one for setting up Works.

Start Works by double-clicking on the Works icon. In a moment, you will see a licensing message, followed by the Welcome to Microsoft Works screen, as shown in Figure 1-7, on the next page.

FIGURE 1-6.
The contents of the Microsoft Works for Windows group.

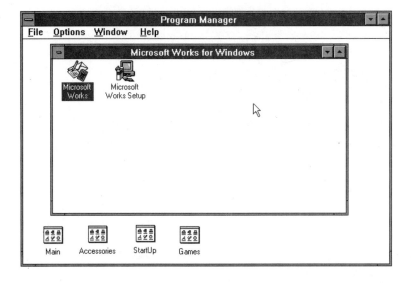

To make you feel comfortable from the start, the Works opening screen lets you choose to take a guided tour of Works (in a working tutorial) or to Start Works Now and get right down to business. You'll soon find this display unnecessary, perhaps even a little bothersome, so the third button, Skip Welcome Screen, lets you choose to skip this opening screen altogether.

FIGURE 1-7.
The Welcome To Microsoft Works screen.

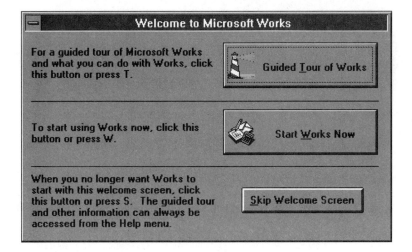

The Guided Tour of Works is a self-contained and self-explanatory look at major attractions, so it's a good idea to try it out at some point. Skip the tour for now, and click the second button on the Works opening screen to start Works. When you do this, you'll see the Works Startup window shown in Figure 1-8.

FIGURE 1-8.
The Works Startup window.

This type of window is often called a *dialog box*. A dialog box is the Works (and Windows) method of showing you options, displaying messages, or requesting information from you. This dialog box lets you choose the type of work you want to do.

In the Works Startup dialog box you can chose to create a new document or work with an old one. Here's what each of the buttons you see in Figure 1-8 does.

■ The *New & Recent Documents* button allows you to create a new document by clicking on one of the four module buttons (Word Processor, Spreadsheet, Database, or Communications). You need not click on New & Recent Documents to create a new document. Just click the module you want to begin with.

- *Open An Existing Document* reveals an Open dialog box that allows you to open any of the files you have already created with Works, as well as import files created with other types of applications, such as Word for Windows.

- *Use A Template* is a shortcut to the wonderful templates you'll learn about in Chapter 3, "Easy Does It: Works for You," page 57. Templates are predesigned forms that you modify to fit your needs.

- *Use A WorksWizard* leads you to the Wizards that are part of Works. These miniprograms are ready to design a stationery heading or a simple database, among other tasks. You just make the selection and Works asks you the pertinent questions. Then Works does the work and produces the document.

- *Instructions* provides you with step-by-step instructions on how to use the various options in the Startup dialog box.

- *Word Processor, Spreadsheet, Database,* and *Communications* open their respective modules and display a document window in which you can create a new file.

You'll also notice in Figure 1-8 that there is a place for a list of recently used files that can be started by double-clicking on the file name. Works automatically places the names of all the files you have used last in that list.

The Works Menus

The Works application window offers three menus in the menu bar: File, Tools, and Help.

The File and Tools menus contain commands you see within the Works modules as well, so a quick survey will be enough for now. As you'll see in Chapter 3, "Easy Does It: Works for You," page 57, the Help menu is similar to Windows Help.

The File Menu

Although you'll normally begin Works from the Startup dialog box, the File menu offers another way to start a Works module. You can also specify whether you want to work on a new file or one you've already created. To see the contents of the File menu as shown here, simply click on the File menu.

File	
Create **N**ew File...	
Open Existing File...	
Wor**k**sWizards...	
Templates...	
Close	
Save	Ctrl+S
Save **A**s...	
Save **W**orkspace	
E**x**it Works	

The first two items on the File menu let you choose to create a new file or open one that already exists. These commands are the equivalents of choosing the Word Processor, Spreadsheet, Database, Communications, and Open An Existing Document buttons in the Startup dialog box.

The Close, Save, and Save As commands, respectively, let you close an open file, save a file under an existing name, and save a file under a new name in a different directory or on a different disk. These three commands are currently dimmed (grayed out) to indicate that you cannot use them now—because you can't close or save a file when you haven't yet opened one.

The Save Workspace command tells Works to remember which documents you have open and how you've arranged them in the application window. This feature lets you preserve a given situation so that you can return to it at another time and pick up where you left off.

The final command on the File menu, Exit Works, is the command you use to quit Works and return to Windows. If you want, you can double-click on the Control-menu box to do the same thing.

The Tools Menu

When you haven't yet started a Works application, the Tools menu includes only one command, Options. You use this command to set up Works the way you want. To see the options, choose Options from the Tools menu. When you do this, you will see the dialog box shown here.

Dialog boxes vary in appearance according to their purpose. Some, such as the Startup and Options dialog boxes, present sets of options. Others, as you'll see when you begin using Works, offer lists of choices or ask you to type information, such as the name of a file.

Every dialog box contains at least one button, usually labeled OK, that you can click to signal "I'm done." Most contain more than one button. The Options dialog box, for example, has three buttons: OK, Cancel, and Help. Cancel cancels or closes a dialog box and, hence, the command or option presented. The Help button takes you directly to help on using the dialog box, a useful feature when you need more information.

Notice that some options in the dialog box are preceded by circles (such as Inches), and others by squares (such as Show Status Bar). The circles are *option buttons* you can click to select a particular item. The squares are *check boxes* you can click to turn an item on or off. Although they seem to serve the same purpose, option buttons and check boxes differ in these ways:

- A dark circle appears in the option button of a selected item. You can select only one option button. You cannot, for instance, select both Inches and Centimeters as units of measurement.

- An X appears in a check box to show that an option is turned on. When check boxes appear next to sets of related items, you can turn on more than one. For example, you can check both the Show Status Bar and Use 3-D Dialogs check boxes.

The settings as they appear in the Options dialog box show the configuration we used when writing this book and using Works 3.

The Help Menu

The Help menu might be your best friend if you don't know quite what the next step is in creating a worksheet or saving a database. Although Help in both Windows and Works is easy to use, there are many commands or options that allow you to do many different things. In the beginning, it may seem a bit confusing. But you can access or ask for help at anytime. All you need to do is use the help menu. You will learn much more about help in Chapter 3, "Easy Does It: Works for You," page 57.

Coming Next

That's the end of Chapter 1. You should be familiar with how Windows works and what the Works opening screen looks like. Now it's time to get off on the right foot with an overview of three of the Works modules—the Word Processor, the Spreadsheet, and the Database.

Getting to Works

You probably purchased Works because it's an integrated software package—a single program that contains a set of different parts you can use to work with and organize letters, memos, lists, charts, budgets, and more.

Works offers the services of a word processor, a spreadsheet, a database, and a communications module, four parts that you would otherwise have to purchase separately. You do save money by buying and using such an integrated package, but Works has one other major advantage. Because Works is an integrated package, the four different modules were designed to work together. You only need to learn one basic set of commands and one basic way of working with the program and then apply what you know to any of the four modules. In addition, because Works is integrated, information from one module can be used by another.

This chapter will give you a look at three Works modules to help you become acquainted with Works as a whole (the communications module is covered in Part 6, "Using Works Communications," page 440). Later on in this book you'll get an in-depth look at each of these parts of Works and what you can do with them. Don't worry about memorizing details for now; they'll come soon enough.

A Sample Session with the Word Processor

Although computers originated as elaborate calculating machines, they are most commonly used today for processing words, not numbers. Of all applications, the word processor is the most popular—so it is a good module to try out first. The Works word processor is remarkably adaptable in many ways, particularly in its ability to insert drawings, spreadsheet charts, and database records into a document. That's the useful integrated nature of Works. You can even create links to charts and other items so that changes in them are automatically reflected in the word-processed document to which they are linked.

To keep the screen simple, start the word processor by telling Works you want to open a new file. Here's how to do it.

1. Start Works if necessary.

2. Click on the Word Processor button on the Startup dialog box. In a moment, you'll see the opening word processor screen shown in Figure 2-1.

TIP: Cue Cards may be displayed when you first enter this screen. To remove the Cue Card from the word processor window, click Close. When the Cue Card changes, click Close again. The Cue Card vanishes from this screen. You can also press Shift+F3 to remove the Cue Card from the word processor window.

You now are in the word processor, where the screen is much more detailed. Notice that you have two windows open, the application window (titled Microsoft Works) and a smaller document window within it (titled Word1). Each window has its own border, title bar, and control buttons.

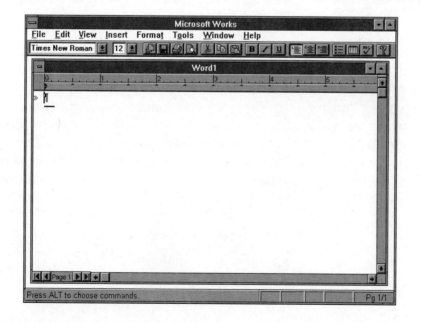

FIGURE 2-1.
The opening word processor screen.

In the document window, Works displays Word1 in the title bar. Word1 is the default name for your first new word processing document, be it a letter, memo, or a report. Until you name and save a new file, Works always gives it a generic name and number.

Regardless of the application within which you are working, Works automatically assigns an extension to a file name when it is saved for the first time. When you save a file, Works assigns the extension *.WPS* to a word processing document. In the spreadsheet, Works uses the extension *.WKS*; in the database, it uses *.WDB* as an extension. If you saved your first word processing document using the name *report*, Works would save it as *report.wps*.

TIP: Works always assigns its own extension to a document filename, so don't add one when you name any of your documents for the first time. Simply type up to eight characters—either letters, numbers, or any combination of letters and numbers—and then save the file. Works will add the file extension for you automatically. You cannot place any spaces in a filename.

As you can see in Figure 2-1, a fair amount of unused space surrounds the Word1 window, so maximize it to take advantage of your entire application window. The screen should look like the one in Figure 2-2, on the next page.

Notice that the two windows become much less distinct when the document window is maximized. Even though you still have two separate windows, they seem to have blended seamlessly into one. Because the document window no longer has a title bar of its own, the document name, Word1, is displayed in square brackets in the title bar of the application window.

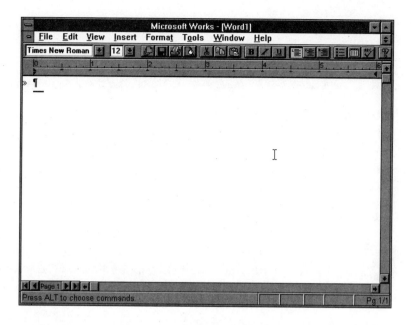

FIGURE 2-2.
Maximizing the
document window.

TIP: Notice there are still two Control-menu boxes available on your screen. The Control-menu box in the top left corner controls the application, or Works, window. Directly under this Control-menu box, on the menu bar and to the left of the File menu, is the Control-menu box for the document window. You can access either Control-menu box with your mouse.

The Application Window

Across the top of the application window is a more extensive set of menu names than the three you first saw when starting Works. To the right of the menu bar is a Restore button, which controls the document window. The Restore button above it controls the Works window.

Just below the menu bar is one of Works most useful on-screen features, the toolbar, shown here.

| Times New Roman | 12 | buttons... |

With the toolbar you can quickly and easily carry out common actions using the mouse. Instead of choosing commands from a menu, you simply click on a button on the toolbar to achieve the same result. Once you become accustomed to its speed and responsiveness, the toolbar quickly becomes indispensable.

NEW!

 TIP: If you cannot recognize what command is associated with a button on the toolbar, move your mouse on top of the button. A short description is displayed to tell you what the button will do. If these messages do not appear for you, open the Tools menu, choose the Customize toolbar command, and then select the Enable Tool Tips option. A sample of the Tool Tips is depicted in the illustration below.

If you think about it, there are often many ways to execute a command within Works. You might be able to complete a task by accessing a menu command, by using a keyboard shortcut, or by clicking on a button on the toolbar. You should use whichever method you like the best.

The toolbar you saw on the previous page is designed for use with the word processor. Each of Works' modules has its own toolbar. As we work through those modules later, you'll see how each differs and how each can greatly increase your Works effectiveness.

 See Also: For more information about toolbars, see Chapter 3, "Easy Does It: Works for You," page 57.

The Document Window

The document window, which was displayed within its own border before the windows were maximized, now begins at the top of the on-screen ruler, just below the toolbar.

Like the toolbar, the ruler is responsive to the mouse and lets you quickly carry out commands, such as setting margins and tab stops, you would otherwise choose from menus.

 See Also: For information about the ruler, see Chapter 5, "Formatting a Document," page 115.

At the top left corner of the document window's workspace is a blinking vertical line called the *insertion point*. This line marks the place where text will appear when you begin typing. Try typing some text. If you make a mistake, use Backspace or Arrow keys to move to the error and retype. Type in the following words:

```
This is the first document I've created with the Works
word processor.
```

As you type, the insertion point moves to the right, staying one space ahead of each new character.

The Changing Pointer

Somewhere else in the document window you should also see the mouse pointer. (If you don't see it, move the mouse around a little bit.) The mouse pointer changes shape in different parts of the screen depending upon its location. In the word processor, the mouse pointer can take three important shapes:

[I] A vertical line with short crossbars at the top and bottom. This is called an *I-beam cursor*.

[↖] The *arrow*, which you have already seen.

[⬍] A "cross" of sorts, with parallel lines as the horizontal bar and a double-headed arrow as the vertical bar. This is called a *split cursor* and on the screen it is labeled *adjust*.

Each of these shapes indicates the task the pointer can perform. Within the document workspace, the mouse pointer appears as an I-beam cursor. You can easily move the insertion point to the location where you want to insert text or select text for editing by moving the mouse cursor to the desired location, and clicking. Using the text you just entered, practice moving the insertion point and highlighting as follows.

1. Place the pointer just in front of the letter *d* in the word *document*.

2. Click on the left mouse button and watch as the insertion point jumps to that position.

3. Double-click the mouse. (The pointer should still be on the word *document*.) A dark highlight covers the entire word, indicating that it is selected as you see in Figure 2-3, on the next page.

 TIP: You can also highlight text by holding down the left mouse button and dragging the mouse cursor across the text to be selected.

In the scroll bars (used to move through a document), the menu bar, and the ruler, the mouse pointer takes on its usual form—the arrow. Let's demonstrate.

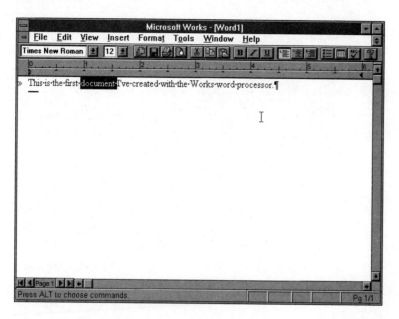

FIGURE 2-3.
Highlighting an individual word.

1. Move the pointer to the menu bar. Notice that the pointer changes to an arrow. Point to a menu and click to open it. The menu drops or opens for you.

2. Now move the pointer into the document workspace. Make sure you are not anywhere within the menu. Click to close the menu.

You've just used the mouse pointer for its usual point-and-click function. Because a menu was open and Works expected you to choose a command, the mouse pointer remained an arrow even though you moved it back into the document workspace. When you closed the menu, indicating you were finished with it, the mouse pointer returned to its I-beam shape. For a preview of the last shape (a cross), do the following.

1. Move the mouse pointer to the small rectangle (the split box) just above the up scroll arrow in the vertical scroll bar.

2. When you see the split cursor, hold down the left mouse button and drag down toward the middle of the screen.

3. Release the mouse button.

As you can see in Figure 2-4, the mouse pointer (labeled *adjust* on the screen) splits a window into two. When you split a window, you can scroll each window independently to view different parts of a long document. This is a great feature to use when you need to work in one part of a long document, yet see what's in another part of the same document.

FIGURE 2-4.
Splitting a window.

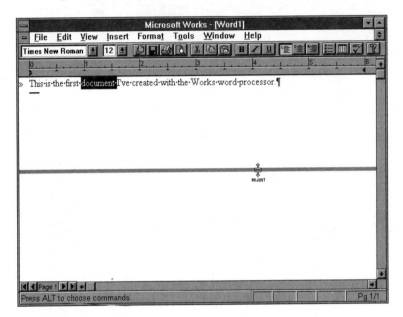

TIP: To remove the split and return to a single window, place the mouse pointer on the horizontal split bar separating the two windows. Double-click, or drag the split bar off the screen.

As you will see later, the mouse pointer assumes other shapes in the spreadsheet and database. When you explore these applications in detail, you'll see how the shape of the mouse pointer gives you visual clues to what it can do.

Managing Document Windows

Every time you open a document, whether it's a new or existing file, Works opens a document window. As in Windows, you can choose to cascade document windows, overlapping them on the screen, or you can choose to tile them, placing them side by side in the available space. You can maximize a document window to fill the application workspace, or you can minimize it and reduce it to an out-of-the-way icon.

To see how easily you can work with multiple documents, open a second window by following these steps. The Word1 document window should still be the active window.

1. Open the File menu, then choose Create New File.

2. In the Startup dialog box, click on the Word Processor button to create another word processing document.

3. When the second window opens, distinguish it from the first by typing in the following text:

   `This is my second document.`

4. Open the Window menu, then choose Tile to see both windows. Your Works screen should appear as shown in Figure 2-5.

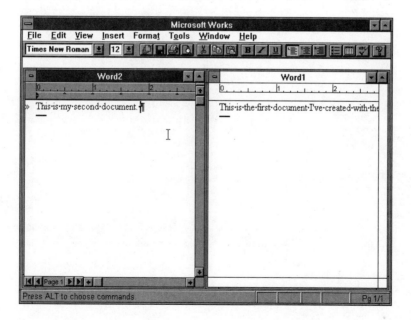

FIGURE 2-5.
Tiling more than one window.

Tiling windows makes it easier to work with two or more documents. The highlighted title bar tells you that Word2 is the active document window (because it is the one you worked with last). Each window is equipped with its own title bar, scroll bars, and control buttons, so you can manipulate each as you choose. To switch from one document to another, just click in the window you want.

Notice, however, that the text in the first document (Word1) is no longer completely visible. The window is too small to display the entire line. You could use the scroll bars to view the rest of the text, but that would become tedious if you were working with a long document. Works provides this easier way:

1. Click anywhere in the Word1 window to make it active.

2. Open the View menu, and then choose Wrap for Window.

When you do this, Works knows to "wrap" the text of your document and fit it into the window area so that all words are visible, as you see in Figure 2-6.

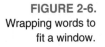

FIGURE 2-6.
Wrapping words to
fit a window.

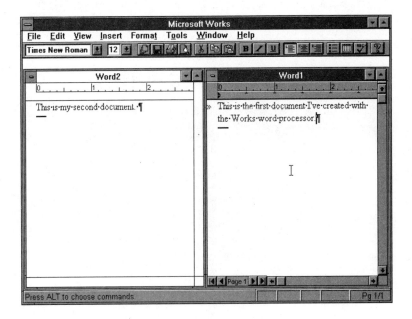

Now change the window's size by moving the right window border so that the window is about two inches wide.

Works rebreaks the lines to display all of your text. Such a narrow window is usually impractical, so drag the border back to return the window to its former size.

TIP: You can easily check to see if the Wrap for Window option is on or off. Simply click on the View menu, and look at the Wrap for Window selection. If a check mark appears to the left of the Wrap for Window, the option is on. Should a check mark not be there, the option is off. This purely a matter of preference, and how you want to work with your document windows.

Let's take the word processor on an extended test run. To clear the screen a bit, close the second document window without saving your sample text by following these steps.

1. Make the Word2 window active.

2. Double-click on its Control-menu box or the File menu, then choose Close. Works displays the Microsoft Works dialog box shown here.

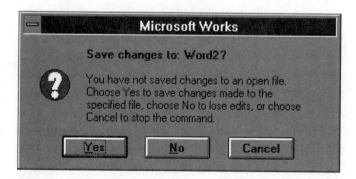

3. Choose No to discard this practice document.

These steps are the way to "toss out" an unnamed document you no longer want. You can eliminate the empty space left by the closed document. To do so, open the Windows menu, and then choose Tile. Finally, maximize the document window by clicking on the maximize button.

TIP: The dialog box on page 41 is extremely important. It is likely that you have made an error when it is displayed. You are only one step away from throwing out or discarding all of your work in the current document. Make sure this is what you really want to do. Works is trying to help you with this box, asking you if you want to save your work. In most cases, this is what you want to do. Of course, there are times you want to discard your work, and you can also use this dialog box to do so.

Shaping and Viewing Text

Let's try out the toolbar by following these steps.

1. Select the word *first* by placing the mouse pointer on it and double-clicking. The highlight expands to cover the entire word.

2. Make the word boldface, so it appears in dark type. You do this by pointing to the button labeled B (for Bold) on the toolbar and clicking. Notice that when you click on a toolbar button it changes color.

3. Place the mouse pointer in a blank part of the window and click to deselect the word *first*.

4. Click on the Print Preview button on the toolbar (the button right under the Tools menu that looks like a magnifying glass).

The screen changes to show a page with your small bit of text on it as you see in Figure 2-7.

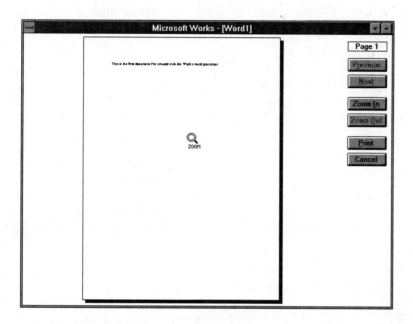

FIGURE 2-7.
The Print Preview screen.

The words are indecipherable, but you can change that. Here's how.

1. Click on the button labeled Zoom In or move the mouse pointer over the page until it changes shape to the name *Zoom* and looks like a magnifying glass, then click.

To make the words even larger, click on the Zoom In button again, or click on the page again. Each time you zoom in on the page, Works magnifies the words. The first time, it zooms in halfway; the second time, it zooms in all the way.

To reverse course and see the entire page again, click on the button labeled Zoom Out, or click once on the preview page. To leave the Preview feature, click on the Cancel button.

That's enough of the word processor for now. If you don't want to leave the Wrap for Window option turned on, open the View menu and click the option again.

The Works Spreadsheet

The Works spreadsheet lets you work with and manipulate numeric data, such as financial statements, budget projections, salary information, and the like. Because much of the work you do with numbers involves calculations, the spreadsheet enables you to build formulas to add, subtract, multiply, work out percentages, and so on.

For certain calculations, such as averages, loan payments, and return on investments, the spreadsheet also includes predesigned formulas called *functions* that you can use by simply plugging your numbers into the formulas and letting Works take care of the rest.

You can also experiment with different possibilities (the so-called "what if" scenarios) to see which of several alternatives works best for you. For example, you can calculate the difference in payments on a loan extending 5, 10, and 15 years. How do those payments fit into your current budget? Which payment comes closest to your projected future income? For that matter, what is your projected future income?

The spreadsheet can't decide any of these things for you, but it can help you see the figures more clearly, especially if you use it to transform those numbers into a graph or chart that illustrates what you see numerically.

You can start the spreadsheet while the word processor is running by following these steps.

1. Open the File menu, and then choose Create New File.

2. Click on the Spreadsheet button.

A new document window appears as in Figure 2-8, this one containing a blank document named Sheet1 and a rectangular grid of small boxes called cells.

A spreadsheet consists of rows and columns. Each place where a row and column intersect is called a *cell.* Each of the cells on your screen can contain a numeric value, an item of text, or a formula that performs a calculation. Notice the letters across the top of the window. Each letter refers to one vertical column of cells on the spreadsheet. Similarly, you can see numbers running down the left side of the window. Each of these numbers refers to one horizontal row of cells. Because each cell occupies a unique position in the spreadsheet, it has its own *address* that describes the column and row in which the cell appears. For example, the cell in the top left corner of the spreadsheet (currently outlined by a double-lined box) is cell A1 because it is in column A, row 1. You and Works use cell addresses whenever you want to refer to a specific cell or group of cells.

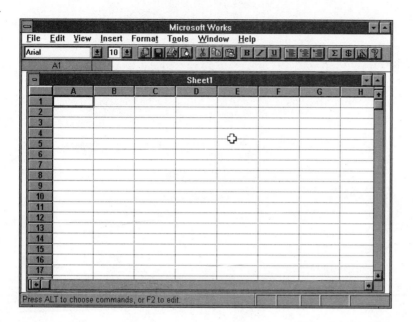

FIGURE 2-8.
The opening spreadsheet screen.

Recall that the mouse pointer looks like a slender I in a word processor document. In the spreadsheet, it looks like a chubby cross. But as with the word processor, the mouse pointer changes as it does its job. Move it around on the screen and you'll notice it changing shape, depending on the screen region it touches.

Entering and Calculating Numbers

You've probably noticed that the toolbar in the spreadsheet looks different from the toolbar in the word processor. Specifically, several buttons toward the right side of the toolbar have changed.

In the word processor, buttons control the use of bullets (such as •), the insertion of tables, and the use of the spelling checker. These buttons are not needed in the spreadsheet, so they are replaced by other buttons that let you automatically sum a column or row of numbers, format numbers as currency, and create charts with just a few clicks.

You can try out some of these buttons now. Follow these steps.

1. Verify that the highlight is in the top left corner of the grid (cell Al). If not, just move the mouse pointer there and click.

2. Type *123* in cell A1. Press the Down arrow key to enter the number and, at the same time, move the highlight down one cell.

3. Type *456* in cell A2. Press the Down arrow key again.

4. Type *789* in cell A3. Press the Down arrow key again.

The spreadsheet should appear as shown in Figure 2-9.

FIGURE 2-9.
Entering numbers in a spreadsheet.

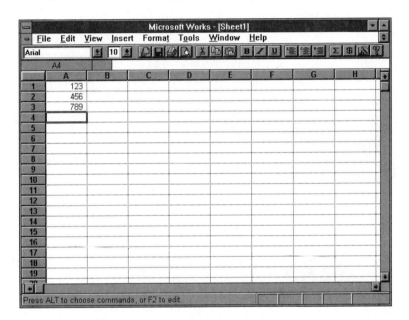

The numbers are rather plain at the moment. Let's have Works display the numbers as dollar values by using the toolbar.

1. Place the mouse pointer on cell Al. Press the left mouse button and drag the mouse pointer down until the highlight covers cells Al through A3.

2. Click on the Currency button (labeled with a $) on the toolbar. Works automatically formats the text you just typed as currency.

46

3. Click on the New Chart button (second from the right that looks like a bar chart) on the toolbar. You'll see the New Chart dialog box.

4. Click OK.

A new document window opens, displaying the chart shown in Figure 2-10.

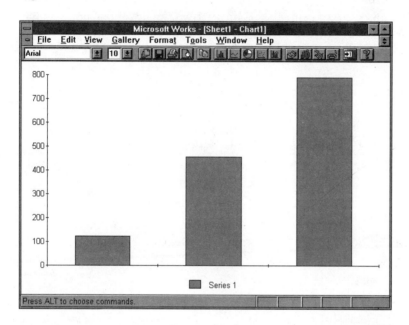

FIGURE 2-10.
The easiest way to create a chart!

You've now turned the numbers into a graphic display. If anything can demonstrate the ease with which Works can help you master data, creating a chart can. Return to the spreadsheet layout by opening the Window menu, and then choosing Sheet1.

You have worked enough for now with the spreadsheet, so let's close it up and move on to the database. Follow these steps to close the spreadsheet.

1. Open the File menu, then choose Close to close Chart1.

2. Open the File menu, then choose Close to close Sheet1.

3. Choose No when a dialog box appears and asks if you want to save the changes to Sheet1. Word1 should still be active.

The Works Database

With the word processor you can write anything from a letter of complaint to a bid proposal. With the spreadsheet you can track numbers ranging from pennies to your Fortune 500 stocks.

What's left? A place to organize information into lists and manipulate it as well. You can keep lists of any kind, for any purpose, but you will most likely keep lists of entries you want to sort in some way, from names and addresses to warehouse inventories, catalog items, or a lifetime list of bird species spotted in your backyard.

All of these lists can be turned over to the Works database, a far more organized and efficient list maker than most humans. A database is a set of records related to a particular topic. Each record forms a unit of information made up of one to several fields. Each field contains one piece of data about the record. For this chapter, you'll create a sample database with three fields—Last Name, First Name, and Dept—which form records for several people employed by Acme Widgets. Here's the information that will be placed in the database.

Last Name	First Name	Dept
Dillion	Mariane	Accounting
Tanaka	George	Accounting
Mayer	Oscar	Sales
Donatello	Raphael	Graphic Arts
Smith	Georgia	Sales

The spreadsheet helps you by manipulating numbers, calculating formulas, and creating charts. Similarly, the Works database sorts records for you, finds specific entries, and even examines records to find those that match qualifications you specify. If you want, the database can calculate averages, find the highest and lowest values in a given field, generate a report, and more.

To start the database follow these steps.

1. Open the File menu, and then choose Create New File.

2. Click on the Database button.

Once again the screen changes, as do the document name (Data1) and the toolbar. Works presents you with a blank slate, but unlike the word processor, the database opens on a blank form that includes an information dialog box, as shown in Figure 2-11.

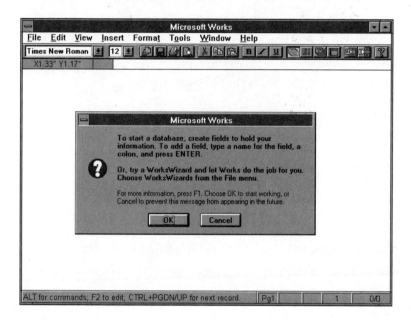

Figure 2-11.
The opening database screen.

You must choose OK to proceed to create a database. You create the fields that will hold the data for each of the records in your database on this form. You can arrange the fields in any way, much as you would when creating a paper-based form for employee information, test scores, insurance coverage, or any other set of records.

Unlike the other Works applications, the database has four views. In Figure 2-11, you see its *form view*. In form view you can create a form and enter information one record at a time. Several buttons in the toolbar let you quickly change views. *List view* displays groups of records in a spreadsheet-like format, *query view* lets you search for and display specific records, and *report view* generates a printable report listing the records and calculations you choose to include.

Entering Records and Viewing a Database

Let's create a form for the data shown earlier. The insertion point should be in the top left corner of the form view window. Don't worry about arranging the fields artistically at this point. Follow these steps.

1. Type *Last Name*: (don't forget the colon; it tells Works to create a field).

2. Press Enter. Works displays a dialog box like the one in Figure 2-12, asking how large you want the field to be:

FIGURE 2-12.
The Field Size
dialog box.

3. Press Enter to accept the suggested size. A dotted line will appear after the field name, and the insertion point drops to the next line.

4. Type *First Name*:, and press Enter twice to create the field and accept the suggested size.

5. Create a third field, *Dept*:, as you did the other two. The form, ready for data entry, should appear as shown in Figure 2-13.

   Now you're ready to enter some data. To do so, follow these steps.

1. Click on the field (not the word) named Last Name: (or press the Up arrow key and Right arrow key). A large highlight appears on the dotted line after Last Name:.

2. Type *Dillion* and press Tab.

3. When the highlight moves to the next field, First Name:, type Mariane. Press Tab.

4. Type *Accounting* in the Dept: field.

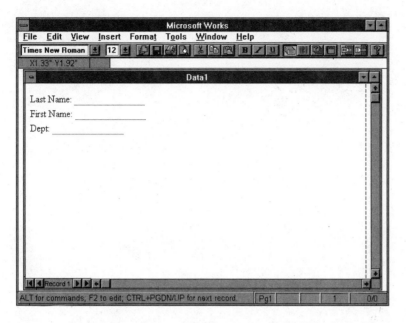

FIGURE 2-13.
A database form,
ready for data entry.

5. Press Tab to start a new record. Create records for the following entries. Press Enter when you complete the last record.

Last	First	Dept
Dillion	Mariane	Accounting
Tanaka	George	Accounting
Mayer	Oscar	Sales
Donatello	Raphael	Graphic Arts
Smith	Georgia	Sales

To see what your database looks like, click on the List View button, the sixth button from the right in the toolbar.

The screen changes to the list of records shown in Figure 2-14.

FIGURE 2-14.
The list view of a
database.

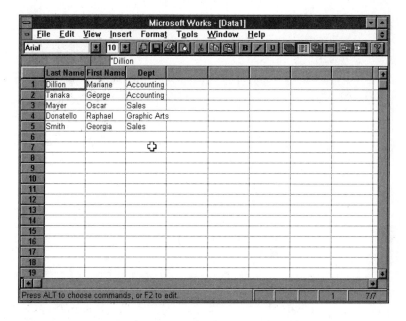

Let's look at the query feature of the database, where you can specify the records to search for. Here's how to perform a simple query.

1. Click on the Query View button in the toolbar. It's the fifth button from the right with the question mark in a square. You'll see a New Query dialog box, as shown in Figure 2-15, on the next page.

2. Select the field you want to compare, in this case Dept.

3. Type *Accounting* in the Value to compare the field to box.

4. Click on the Apply Now button. Works will go through the database and select only those records that meet the criterion of having the word Accounting in the Dept field.

You see only selected records: those for Mariane Dillion and George Tanaka, the only employees in the database who work in Accounting.

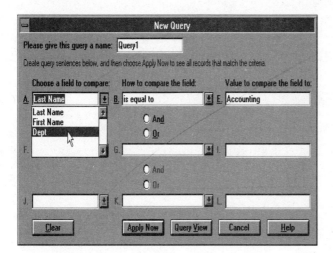

FIGURE 2-15.
The New Query
dialog box.

Combining Data from Applications

As a final exercise, try moving a few records from your database into the word-processed "document" you created earlier.

In the past, transferring data between documents created by different applications was one of the most difficult and frustrating activities in personal computing. With Works, it's a breeze, thanks to Windows and a special Windows feature called the Clipboard.

About the Clipboard

Chapter 1 explained that Windows and Works form a partnership to help you get things done. Although you can't see the Clipboard, it is an important part of Windows.

The Clipboard is a portion of your computer's memory that Windows sets aside specifically for holding data that you want to move from one part of the document to another part of that same document, or from one document to another. After you place information on the Clipboard, whether it's text or a graphic, one paragraph or several pages, that information remains in your computer's memory and is available to programs that can accept it until you place new data on the Clipboard.

To move data from document to document, you use a process called *cut and paste*. Cut and paste is the electronic equivalent of scissors and tape. You've no doubt snipped apart a letter, report, or proposal and reorganized it or inserted parts of a different document by putting the pieces together in a new order. You use cut and paste in Windows applications such as Works in much the same way, but without the mess. Windows, in fact, is better than real-life cut and paste, because it lets you copy and paste as well.

You can rearrange or duplicate information across documents with only three basic commands in the Edit menu: Cut, Copy, and Paste. Cut, as its name implies, removes information and places it on the Clipboard. Copy duplicates information, placing a copy on the Clipboard but leaving the original where it belongs. Paste inserts the contents of the Clipboard into an open document.

Using the Clipboard

You've already built a small set of records in the Works database, and you've got an open "letter" in the word processor. Your screen should be showing the list view in the database, with two selected records on it: the names of the employees in the Accounting department of Acme Widgets. To insert those records into the open document in the word processor, follow these steps.

1. Drag the mouse pointer to extend the highlight to cover the six cells containing the names and departments of the two employees.

2. Open the Edit menu, and then choose Copy.

3. Return to the word processor by choosing Word1 from the Window menu.

4. Place the insertion point on a new line.

5. Open the Edit menu, and then choose Paste.

The two records appear in your word-processed document as you see in Figure 2-16, neatly laid out on separate lines. That's all there is to it.

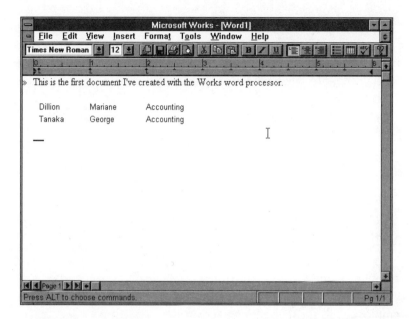

FIGURE 2-16.
Pasting database information into a document created with the word processor.

Now let's clean up the screen so we can move on to Chapter 3 and some terrific Works helpers.

1. Double-click on the Works window's Control-menu box.

2. Choose No when Works asks if you want to save the changes to Word1 and Data1.

You're back to Windows and ready to move on.

Coming Next

We hope this chapter gave you a taste of what Works is all about and what it can do. Before we start a detailed discussion of how to use the word processor, spreadsheet, and database, let's first turn to a set of powerful helpers, including Works Help, templates, toolbars, and Cue Cards, that comes with Works.

3

Easy Does It: Works for You

Using Document Templates

Ever find yourself using parts of the same document over and over again? You can create a template that allows you to save text, format, and graphics in a form that can be reused.

About AutoStart Templates

Even better than designing your own templates are Works AutoStart templates, where you can select a predesigned template with a few clicks of the mouse. Now that's easy.

Chapters 1 and 2 introduced you to Windows, the Works environment, and the various Works modules. In this chapter, you'll see how to be instantly productive with the help of a variety of miniprograms and tools.

We begin with the old standby, Works Help. You may be familiar with Windows Help; Works Help does not differ considerably. We'll review how to use it here.

WorksWizards are predesigned sets of instructions that walk you through the process of creating a general database form, a file organizer, a footnote, a form letter, and a letterhead. WorksWizards are easy to use; to convince you, we'll go through the creation of a letterhead step by step. That should be enough for you to take on the creation of any other WorksWizard.

Did you know that you can customize toolbars so that they contain the specific tools you want? If you don't want the print button on the word processor toolbar, so be it. Replace it with a button that sets specific margins or starts a particular font.

We'll also introduce you to Cue Cards, Works' coachlike tool that walks you through the steps of almost any Works feature. Just follow the instructions and you'll be able to complete the operation.

Finally, version 3 of Works comes with more than 40 AutoStart templates, predesigned forms ranging from stationery to fax cover sheets to book collection forms, that are ready for you to use.

All About Help

If Help is what you need, you've come to the right place. Works Help is context-sensitive, which means that Works knows what you are doing when you are doing it. All you need to do is ask for help; Works will provide help on whatever you are currently doing. Works offers a very extensive Help system, so the more you know about using Help, the more you know about using Works.

Fast and Easy Help

Let's look at the easiest way to get Works Help and at the same time illustrate Works' context-sensitive feature.

Here's an example of getting Help on printing a file in the word processing module. To use context-sensitive Help, follow these steps.

1. Select a menu item on which you need help. For this example, open the File menu, then choose Print. When you do this you'll see the Print dialog box.

2. Press the F1 key. Works will immediately take you to the Help screen about printing, as shown in Figure 3-1. You can get help on any menu command or any dialog box using this method.

FIGURE 3-1.
Using context-sensitive Help.

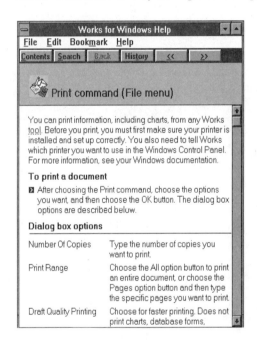

TIP: Context-sensitive Help is the fastest way to get Works Help.

Using Works Help

You don't have to use context-sensitive Help. To get help on any topic using the Help menu, follow these steps. Let's say you need help on changing the appearance of a document.

1. Open the Help menu, then choose Contents. You'll see Step-by-Step Help.

2. Click on the general topic for which you want help. For example, if you want help with word processing, click on the icon or the title *Word Processor*. When you move the mouse pointer to the icon title, you'll see that the shape of the mouse pointer changes from an arrow to a pointing hand.

    When you click on a general index entry, you'll get a listing of available topics, such as those shown in Figure 3-2, on the next page.

3. Now click on a particular topic for additional information. For example, in Figure 3-2, you would click on the topic *Changing the appearance of your Word Processor document*. When you do that, you are taken to a Help screen full of information on how to change the appearance of a document you created with the word processor.

TIP: If you want to print out the contents of the Help window, open the File menu in the Help window, then choose Print Topic. The complete contents will be printed for you to read at your leisure.

When you are done reading about that topic, you can exit Help by double-clicking on the Control-menu box in the upper-left corner or by opening the File menu, and then choosing Exit to return to Works.

FIGURE 3-2.
Selecting a topic
for help.

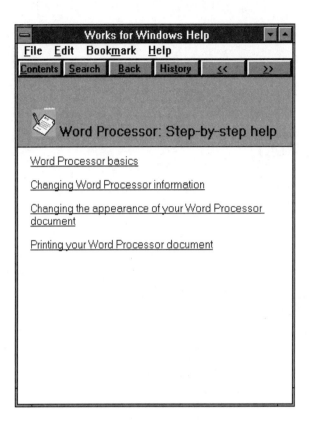

That's the general method for using Works Help—simply click your way through windows until you reach the information you need.

Using the Help Window Buttons

In most Works Help windows there are six buttons that can be used to quickly access other topics.

The Contents button will return you directly to Works for Windows Help Contents, a list of all the major Works Help categories.

The Search button allows you to search for a topic using certain key words. The Search button opens up the window shown in Figure 3-3. Here you can enter a description of what you need help with or scroll down the list of all the possible Help topics until you find what you need. If you enter a word and then click on the Show Topics command button, you'll see a list of topics for which Help is available. You can then access Help on a listed topic by selecting the topic in the lower part of the window and clicking Go To.

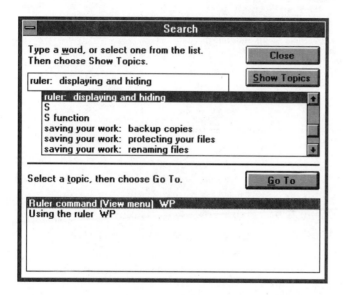

FIGURE 3-3.
Using the Search button to find information on using the ruler.

If you have moved to another topic, but still need help on a topic that you already read about, the Back button will move you through the Help topics you previously selected.

The History button opens a list of all the Help topics you've reviewed since opening Help, as shown in Figure 3-4, on the next page. It shows a trail of where you've been. Best of all, you can double-click on any of the topics listed in Windows Help History and get right back to that topic.

This is a great way to return to a topic you missed or didn't have time to explore. Each time you close Help, the most recent history or record disappears. You can see the Windows Help History screen that results from the Help topics you have accessed thus far in this chapter in Figure 3-4.

FIGURE 3-4.
A sample
Windows Help
History screen.

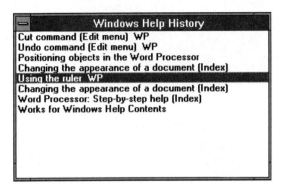

The >> Browse Forward button will move you forward through the Help index, stopping on related topics. For example, if you selected Using the ruler WP and then clicked the >> button, you would see a Help screen titled Creating columns in a Word Processor document.

If you clicked >> again, you would go to the next Help screen in the sequence, which is Hyphenating words automatically. The << Browse Backward button also moves you through related topics, only in the backward direction.

TIP: When a button appears dimmed or gray, that button is not functional. For example, you can't use the << button from the first Help screen (there's no place to go backward.)

About Underlined Words

Help can do even more than you have seen so far.

In many Help screens, words are underlined with dots (such as the word *dragging* in Figure 3-5). When you click on them, you get a definition for that word, as you see in Figure 3-5.

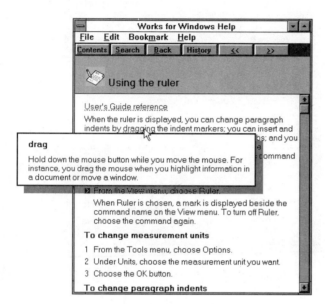

FIGURE 3-5.
An example of a dotted underlined word and its defintion.

TIP: Words and phases underlined with a solid line (not dots) can be used to jump from topic to topic. For example, if you click on a word or phrase that has a solid underline, Works Help will take you to a related topic. Such words and phrases are usually located at the end of a Help topic.

Now let's move on to those wonderful WorksWizards.

Starting a WorksWizard

You can call for a WorksWizard with the click of a button. After starting a Works session, choose WorksWizards from the Startup dialog box (Figure 1-8, page 23), and you'll see the list of WorksWizards shown in Figure 3-6.

FIGURE 3-6.
The list of Wizards
from which
you can select.

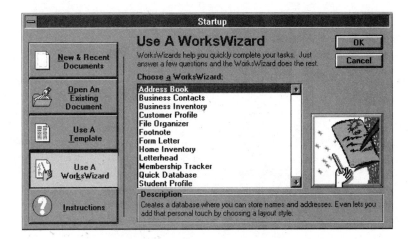

Even at this early point in the creation of a WorksWizard, Works tells you what the Wizard does and even shows you a preview of what the Wizard looks like.

 TIP: If you decide you need to create a WorksWizard later in a Works session, open the File menu, and then choose WorksWizards. You'll see the Startup window for Works-Wizards.

A Sample WorksWizard Session

In this chapter you'll see how the Letterhead WorksWizard is created and how it can be used. You can use any WorksWizard by following a few simple steps.

Creating a WorksWizard

Here's how to start and complete the Letterhead WorksWizard.

1. Click on the Use A WorksWizard button in the Startup dialog box, or open the File menu, and then choose WorksWizards. Works will display the 12 WorksWizards from which you can select, as shown in Figure 3-6.

2. Select Letterhead and click OK. Now Works goes to work, creating a custom letterhead for you; the first step is the Letterhead WorksWizard opening screen, shown in Figure 3-7.

    As you work through the various screens of any WorksWizard, you need to tell the Wizard when to move ahead. You can do this by pressing the Enter key or by clicking on the Next button.

3. Click on the Next button to move to the next Letterhead screen.

4. Select Yes to personalize the letterhead, and click on the Next button to move on.

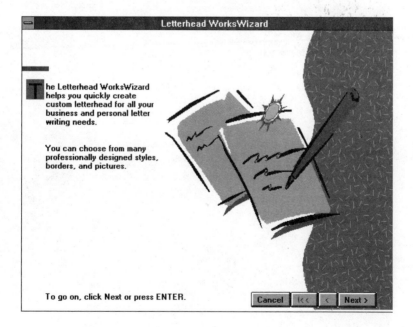

FIGURE 3-7.
The Letterhead WorksWizard opening screen.

5. Click My Name to emphasize that part of the letterhead. You can also emphasize a business name or your initials, but only one of the three.

6. Click the Next button to move on to the next Letterhead screen.

7. Now it's time to enter the information you want to appear in the letterhead, as shown in Figure 3-8. Use the Tab key to move from field to field. When you're done, click the Next button to move on to the next Letterhead screen.

8. Now it's time to get fancy. Works will give you the option of selecting from six different letterhead styles. As you make a selection, you'll be able to see what the actual letterhead will look like in that style in the preview area. There's no need to print something before you see what it will look like. Select the style you want and click the Next button to move on to the next Letterhead screen.

FIGURE 3-8.
Entering information to be used in the letterhead created with Letterhead WorksWizard.

Letterhead WorksWizard

Now type only the information you want to appear in your letterhead.

Your name:
Neil J. Salkind

Address:
POB 1465

City, State, ZIP Code, Country:
Lawrence, KS 66044, USA

Telephone:

Business name:
Delphi Associates

Second address line:

Your job title:
President and CEO

Fax:

Cancel | I<< | < | Next >

9. The Letterhead WorksWizard asks if you want to add a line to the heading, as shown in Figure 3-9.

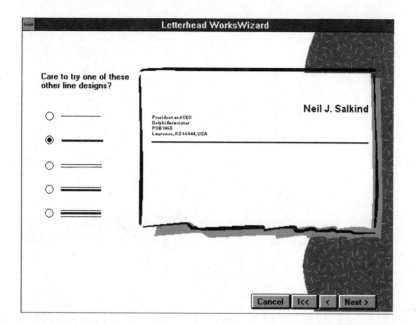

FIGURE 3-9.
Adding a line
to a letterhead.

In this example, we added a solid line and then we clicked the Next button to move on to the next Letterhead WorksWizard screen.

10. Finally you can add a border or a picture (or neither) to the letterhead. We opted for neither and then clicked the Next button to move on to the next WorksWizard screen.

11. Ta Da! Now click on the Create button and sit back while Works creates the letterhead just as you defined it through these very simple steps. When it's all done, click OK. You can see the finished product in Figure 3-10 on the next page.

FIGURE 3-10.
A finished letterhead
created with a
WorksWizard.

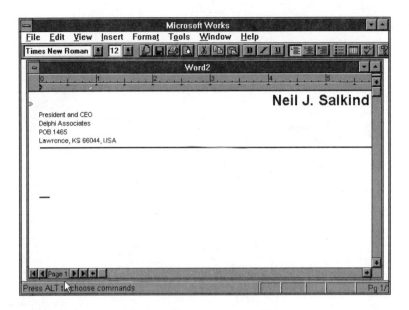

Of course, you could have created a letterhead like this one from scratch (if you knew how to use the word processor). The ease with which WorksWizards allow you to create useful forms is unbeatable. Once a WorksWizard creates something for you, you can modify it by changing the font, the spacing, or even by entering more text.

TIP: Once a WorksWizard creates a document, it must be saved—like any other Works document—if it is to be used again. In Figure 3-10, you can see that the letterhead is titled Word2, indicating a temporary document. Remember to save the product of a WorksWizard as a file once it is finished.

Customizing the Toolbars

You learned something about the toolbars in the last chapter and saw how useful they can be in your everyday Works activities. Each of the four main modules of Works—the Word Processor, Spreadsheet, Database, and Communications—has its own toolbar. Other parts of Works have more specialized toolbars.

Each toolbar comes with a specific set of buttons. For example, on the Word Processor toolbar, the first four buttons take you to the Startup dialog box (Startup Dialog), save the active document (Save), print the active document (Print), and display full pages as they will be printed (Print Preview).

A specific toolbar might not have all of the buttons you want. Instead buttons that you never use might be there. For example, you might never have any use for the Bullets button; but you would like a button that double-spaces text. In other words, you want to customize the toolbar to fit the way you work. To make room on the toolbar, first you have to remove the buttons you don't want; then you can add the new ones. In this example, we'll remove the Bullets button and add one that double-spaces text.

Here's how you do it.

1. Open the Tools menu and choose Customize Toolbar, or double-click on any blank space on the toolbar. When you do this, you will see the Customize Works Toolbar dialog box shown in Figure 3-11. Unless this dialog box is active, you can't remove or add buttons.

2. Position the pointer on the Customize Works Toolbar title bar and drag the dialog box downward so that you can see the toolbar you want to change.

3. To remove any button, simply drag it off the toolbar. In this example, drag the Bullets (fourth from the right) button off the toolbar.

4. Select the category of the button you want to add from the list in the Categories box. In Figure 3-11 we selected Format.

FIGURE 3-11.
The Customize
Works Toolbar
dialog box.

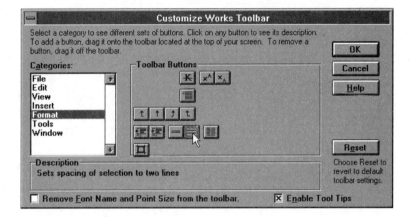

When you select a category, you see the buttons that are available in that category to add to the toolbar.

 TIP: To find out what a button does, place the mouse pointer on the button, and then press and hold down the mouse button. In the Description box you'll see a description of the button's function.

4. Drag the button you want to add—in this example, the button for double-spacing—to its new location on the toolbar. You can add as many buttons as you make space for.

5. Click OK in the Customize Works Toolbar dialog box and you've added a button!

You can easily customize or change the toolbar to make Works easy for you to use. Because we all use our computers differently and for different reasons, by customizing the toolbar you can place the buttons or commands you use the most on your computer. For example, if you find yourself always creating documents that you want to double-space, you should add the double-space button to your toolbar.

A Works toolbar cannot be moved to a new location in a window, nor can you create a totally new toolbar. If you find that you want to return to the button arangement on the original toolbar, just click Reset in the Customize Works Toolbar dialog box.

Using Works Cue Cards

So far you've gotten quite a bit of information on how to complete tasks with Works Help and the WorksWizards, and how to customize toolbars. But think how great it would be if you had someone by your side, walking you through Works tasks. Even if Microsoft can't go that far, it has designed Works Cue Cards.

Using Cue Cards

To use Cue Cards, open the Help menu, and choose Cue Cards.

Or, you can set Works to display Cue Cards by accessing Cue Cards in the Learning Works dialog box. To do this, click on the Learning Works button on the toolbar (it resembles a question mark). The dialog box shown in Figure 3-12 will appear.

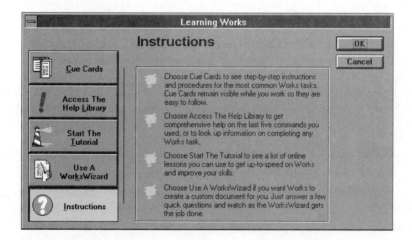

FIGURE 3-12.
The Learning Works dialog box.

73

When the Learning Works dialog box appears, click on Cue Cards. Your screen will resemble Figure 3-13.

FIGURE 3-13.
The Cue Cards opening Window.

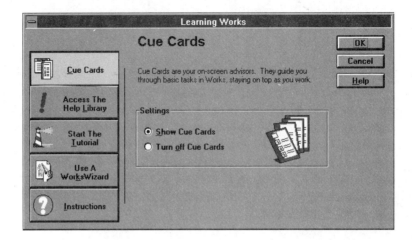

Here you can see the two options available to you. You can

- Click on the button that tells Works you want to see and work with Cue Cards (Show Cue Cards)

- Click the button that tells Works you want to work on your own (Turn off Cue Cards)

TIP: What happens if you turn off Cue Cards but find yourself lost and needing help? You can get help in one of the ways we described earlier in this chapter, or you can choose Cue Cards from the Help menu. Then you'll be back to Cue Cards in a flash.

If you select Show Cue Cards and click OK, you'll see a Cue Card with instructions about using Cue Cards. If you click the button confirming that you want help from Cue Cards, you'll see another Cue Card with a list of tasks relevant to the module you are using.

In Figure 3-14 you can see the Cue Card for working with the word processor menu—almost every conceivable word processing task is listed, either specifically or as a more general category.

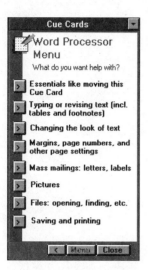

FIGURE 3-14.
The Word Processor Menu Cue Card.

If you choose Changing how text looks, the next Cue Card asks "What do you want to do?" and provides a list of options. If you choose Change font or font size, you will see a How? button. Once clicked, it lists the exact steps to take in performing a particular operation, complete with graphics. For example, in Figure 3-15 on the next page you can see the result of clicking the How? button on Highlight the text you want to change.

Cue Cards are very much like Help, only more closely focused. You don't have to determine what you need help on, as you do with Help.

TIP: In Cue Cards, you can always return to the main menu or the first Cue Card by clicking on Menu at the bottom of any Cue Card. You can also go back through the sequence of Cue Cards by clicking on the < button at the bottom of the Cue Card.

FIGURE 3-15.
The Highlighting
text Cue Card.

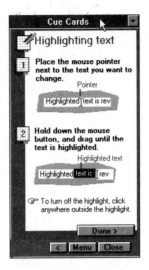

Canceling Cue Cards

Admittedly, Cue Cards are great when you are beginning to learn Works or when you need assistance on a very specific task. But their constant presence can get a bit tiring.

If you find that you no longer want Cue Cards to appear, open the Help menu and click on Cue Cards so the check mark disappears. The screen will be a little less cluttered.

Using Document Templates

After you've spent a long time formatting a document and making it look exactly the way you want it to, you might want to use the same layout and formatting for other documents. Business letters, bid proposals, reports, and many other types of documents tend to take on the same appearance and, often, the same structure. The content might change, but the overall appearance remains the same.

With Works you can create your own (Custom) templates or take advantage of predesigned (AutoStart) templates. This section covers templates generally; "About AutoStart Templates" begins on page 81.

A document template can be based upon a word-processed document, a spreadsheet, or a database file. Anything you create, you can save for later use.

The following example shows a template for a business letter:

For the Kid in All of Us

Go
Fly
a Kite

Single-spaced paragraphs
for recipient's name and
address

Dear [name]

Type body of letter here; press Enter to create new paragraphs.

Sincerely,

Mark S. Donoghue, owner
Go Fly a Kite

cc:

- The salutation (For the Kid in All of Us) is formatted as a single-spaced paragraph with two lines before it.

- A Go Fly A Kite graphic was created using Draw (see Chapter 13, "Getting Started with Microsoft Draw," page 397).

- The body paragraph is double-spaced with one line after it.

- The closing is a plain double-spaced paragraph.

- The signature line is a single-spaced paragraph with three lines before it to allow for the person's signature. An end-of-line character after the word *owner* breaks the paragraph to a new line for the name of the company.

- The cc: line is single spaced with two lines before it and is left-aligned.

Here are the general steps for creating any type of custom template.

Creating a Custom Template

To create a template, follow these steps.

1. From the File menu, choose Create New File.

2. From the New and Recent Documents Window, choose the type of document (word processor, spreadsheet, database) you want to create.

3. Set up the document exactly as you want it to appear, including graphics, text, and so on.

4. From the File menu, choose Save As.

5. Click on the Template button. When you do this, you will see the Save As Template dialog box, shown in Figure 3-16.

FIGURE 3-16.
The Save As
Template dialog box.

Save As Template
Template **N**ame: [   ]
OK
Cancel
Help

6. Enter a name for the template.

7. Click OK.

The format is now saved as a template.

How To Use a Template

Once you create a template, it can be used over and over again.

To use this saved format, follow these steps.

1. From the File menu, choose Templates. When you do this, you will see the Startup dialog box shown in Figure 3-17 listing template groups, categories, and specific templates. The one that was created for this example is called Acme Stationery and is in the Custom group.

2. Select the template you want to use.

3. Click OK.

Whatever was saved as the template will appear in a window, ready to modify as you see fit.

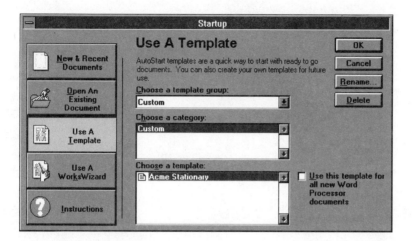

FIGURE 3-17.
The Startup dialog box where you select a template.

 TIP: All of the templates based on documents you've created will be custom templates. When they are saved, they are placed in the Custom group. As you will see later in this chapter, Works comes with over 50 AutoStart templates, predesigned forms you can customize.

Modifying a Template

Once a template is created, it is not unalterable. For example, what if you spent hours creating an attractive brochure template and your business phone number changes? Works makes it easy to alter templates.

Modifying a template is relatively simple, as long as you remember that you need to use exactly the same name for the template after any changes are made. Here's how you do it.

1. From the File menu, select Templates.

2. Double click on the name of the template you want to modify.

3. Make the changes in the template you want to make. They can be limited or extensive. Just remember that once you change and then save a template, the changes are now a part of that template.

4. From the File menu, select Save As.

5. Click Template.

6. The Save As Template dialog box appears. If you want this modified template to replace the earlier template with the same name, press OK. (If you want to continue to use both versions of the template, you must use another name.)

7. Click OK. When Works asks you to confirm the replacement, click Yes and you're on your way!

Renaming a Template

If you do want to rename a template (maybe the business name changed or you have a new use for the template), follow these steps.

1. From the File menu, choose Templates.

2. From the Choose a template group box, choose Custom.

3. Choose the template you want to rename.

4. Click on the Rename button.

5. In the Name Template dialog box, enter a new name.

6. Click on the Rename button. You've just changed the name of a template.

Deleting a Template

Finally, there's the case where you no longer have any use for a template. You may have created a new one to take its place, need some room on your hard drive, or just don't like the way it looks.

To delete a template, follow these steps:

1. From the File menu, choose Templates.

2. From the Choose a template group box, select Custom.

3. Highlight the name of the template you want to delete.

4. Click Delete.

5. Confirm that you want to delete the template by choosing Yes.

The template deletion cannot be undone. If you want to use this template again, it will have to be re-created.

About AutoStart Templates

Works AutoStart templates are predesigned templates, in a variety of different categories, that are readily accessible and easy to use.

Before we show you how to use them, let's look at the different categories of AutoStart templates and what they have to offer. They are displayed in the following table.

Template Group	Template Category	Template Name
AutoStart Business	Billing	Accounts Receivable
		Sales Invoice
		Past Due Statement
		Service Invoice
		Account Statement
	Business Planning	Business Budget
		Breakeven Analysis
		Cash Flow Statement
		Personal Financial Statement
		Income Statement
	Documents	Fax Cover Sheet
		Three Column Newsletter
	Expenses	Mortgage and Loan Analysis
		Purchase Order
	Inventory	Product Inventory
		Vendors

(continued)

Template Group	Template Category	Template Name
	Management	Credit Cards
		Check Register
		Customers
		Employees
		Key Contacts
		Weekly Time Sheet
	Sales	Job Estimate
		Order Form
		Price List
		Monthly Sales Goals
AutoStart Personal	Addresses	
	Documents	
	Household Management	Book Collection
	Personal Finances	Mortgage and Loan Analysis
AutoStart Education	Classroom Management	Book Collection
		CD/Tape Collection
		Student Records
		Video Collection
	Productivity	Grade Book
		Three Column Newsletter
		Personal Directory
		Résumé
		Class Schedule
	Testing	Essay Test
		Multiple Choice Test
		True-False Test

For the most part, the titles of the templates are self-explanatory (and some are placed in more than one category). The best way to see what they can do for you is to spend some time opening up those you might be interested in using and printing out a copy. That way, you'll be able to see the complete template and what it has to offer. Then you can decide if you want to use it.

Using an AutoStart Template

To open an AutoStart template, follow much the same steps as you did to select a custom document template.

1. From the File menu, choose Templates.

2. From the Choose a template group box, choose the group that contains the template you want to open.

3. In the Choose a category box, choose the category that contains the template you want to open.

4. In the Choose a template box, choose the template you want to open. For example, in Figure 3-18 we are about to open the template named Mortgage and Loan Analysis.

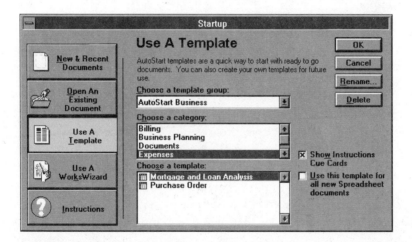

FIGURE 3-18.
Opening a template.

5. If you want Cue Cards along with your template, check the Show Instructions Cue Cards box.

6. Click OK and the template you want to use will appear as shown in Figure 3-19 on the next page.

FIGURE 3-19.
An AutoStart
template.

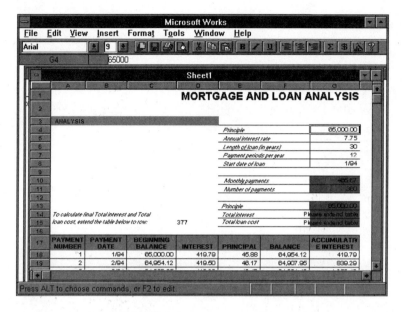

As you can see, Works has done all the work! We entered the principle ($65,000), the annual interest rate (7.75%), the length of the loan in years (30), payment periods per year (12), and when the loan starts (1/94). Works takes it from there and produces a completed payment schedule, the beginning of which you see at the bottom of Figure 3-19. If you explored this template further, you'd find it to be the creative kind of spreadsheet that anyone can design with some time and basic understanding of formulas. Open this template and place the cell pointer in different locations. Examine the variety of formulas that were used and see if you can figure out what they do. Also, any AutoStart template can be modified and then saved under another name for further use.

For example, let's say you need a three-column newsletter. Take a look at the print preview of the Three Column Newsletter template, shown in Figure 3-20. (You'll find this template under AutoStart Business, Documents.)

You can plainly see the word NEWSLETTER, but it may be more difficult to see that the actual text is just gibberish. If you use this template, you enter the text you want (such as your company's name), and then save the template under a name such as *news.j93* for the July, 1993 newsletter.

FIGURE 3-20.
The Three Column Newsletter template.

Coming Next

We hope that all the help you need can be found in Help, WorksWizards, the toolbar, and Cue Cards. Although you may not want to become dependent upon these aids, it's perfectly fine to use them when you are learning Works. Eventually, you'll find Works to be so intuitive that you will no longer need to use a Cue Card or Help to get where you're going. So, end Part 1 of Running Works. Now let's turn our attention to the first of the modules we'll discuss in detail, the Works word processor.

Using the
Word Processor

4

Getting Started with the Word Processor

Entering Text

Characters, words, lines, paragraphs, and pages. They're all part of your document and entering them is as easy as using a typewriter. Works goes beyond that standard and allows you to work with special features.

Revising Text

Now that you've entered some text, it's time to get on with revising and editing. Everyone edits their work, so stick with us to learn Works techniques for the best editor in the world—you!

One of the pleasures of using a word processor is the ability it gives you to concentrate on what you want to say, without giving a thought to how those words appear on your screen. Just close your eyes and start typing. Microsoft Works 3 for Windows will faithfully remember every key you press, without ever breaking into your thoughts by stopping at the end of a line with that nasty typewriter bell or blindly running your words off the paper and onto the platen when you reach the end of a page!

This chapter introduces you to the basic skills involved in word processing, including the creation and revision of a document. A word processor can't help you think, nor can it make the words flow when the creative pipeline is clogged. You have to do that yourself. But a good word processor can automate the mechanical tasks required to produce well-organized and thoughtful text.

WYSIWYG

You're seeing correctly. WYSIWYG (pronounced "wizzywig") stands for *What You See Is What You Get*. It also describes an important and attractive feature of the Works word processor. Unlike some non-Windows programs, Works shows on the screen what your document will look like when printed—what you see is what you get. If you set narrow margins, for example, that's how your document will appear on-screen and when it is printed.

WYSIWYG might not seem like a big deal right now, but you will find that, in addition to making your screen a friendlier place to work, it helps you envision what your documents will look like when you print them. Thanks to WYSIWYG, you can see what a heading in large, **bold**, <u>underlined</u> type will look like *before you print* your document. You can also see what will happen if you combine different styles of type. Although Works can't help your sense of style and proportion, its WYSIWYG capability will, at the least, help you see what you're doing and avoid wasting paper on unsuccessful print-outs.

Getting Started

In this chapter and throughout the remaining chapters in this book, we'll provide you with examples to try on your own computer system. Occasionally, you'll be told to save a sample document. To keep your hard disk tidy, take the time now to create a directory where you can keep these examples. Later on, you'll be able to delete the samples easily, without worrying about deleting valuable files or leaving a stray example on the disk.

Here's how to create a directory using Windows File Manager:

1. Open File Manager. (Double-click on the File Manager icon, located in the Main Program Group.)

2. Select the directory where you want to create the new directory. (You can do so by clicking your mouse on any directory already displayed in the File Manager directory tree window pane.) The directory you create becomes a subdirectory of the currently selected directory.

3. Open the File menu and choose Create Directory. (You can do so with your mouse or by pressing Alt, F, E.) The Create Directory dialog box appears.

4. Type the name of the new directory (up to eight characters long).

5. Click OK (or press Enter).

 TIP: Remember that at any time you can press F1 or choose the Help button to get additional information from the File Manager Help screens.

Now, following these instructions, create a directory called WKSBOOK. This will be located on the root of the C drive.

1. Open File Manager.

2. Go to the root of the C drive. (This means click on the C:\ icon on the top of the directory tree.)

TIP: If you have a directory folder selected, press the Backslash key (\) to go instantly to the root directory.

3. Open the File menu by clicking on the menu name.

4. Choose the Create Directory command.

5. Type *WKSBOOK*.

6. Click OK.

Your directory, WKSBOOK, is now created.

You can also create the directory from the MS-DOS prompt. To do so, follow these steps:

1. If Windows is running, click on the MS-DOS prompt in the Main program group. If you're already at the MS-DOS prompt, skip this step.

2. When the MS-DOS prompt (C:\WINDOWS>) appears, type the following command:

md\wksbook

Be sure to include the backslash.

You have just created a directory named *wksbook* to store your creations.

3. Press Enter to complete the command. If you started from Windows, type *exit* to return. If you started from MS-DOS, start Windows by typing *win.*

Now start Works. Start the word processor with a blank workspace, as shown in Figure 4-1.

FIGURE 4-1.
A blank
word processor
workspace.

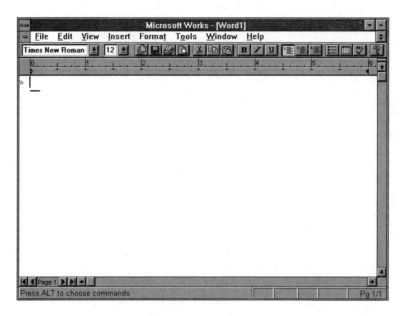

You may want to maximize both the application and document windows to give yourself plenty of room. (The *application window* is the window containing Works. The *document window* is the Works word processing window.)

Saving Works for Later

There's a good chance that you will not always have the time to complete each chapter or example in a single session, so here's how to save your work and return to the same place later on.

1. Open the Tools menu, and then choose Options.

2. When you see the Options dialog box shown here, verify that the Use saved workspace option is checked.

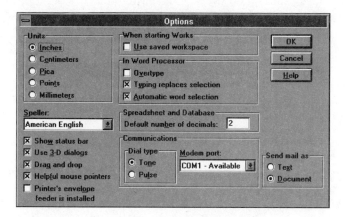

3. If the setting is not checked, click on it, and then click on OK to close the dialog box and save the settings.

4. When you want to quit, open the File menu, and then choose Save Workspace.

5. To quit Works, double-click the Control-menu box in the top left corner of the Works window. If you have any unsaved work, Works will display a dialog box asking if you want to save your changes. If you do, select Yes. Type a file name and click on OK in the Save As dialog box.

The next time you start Works, it will restore your screen, example and all, exactly as you left it.

Entering Text

In Chapter 3 (page 57) you saw how WorksWizards can help you create certain types of documents quickly and easily. The Wizards, however, aren't for all occasions. Most of the time, you'll need to create a document for which no Wizard is available.

Starting with a blank word processing window, type the following paragraphs. Press Enter only where you see [Enter] in the text. Don't worry about your lines running off the screen as you type, and don't be concerned about typos. You'll learn how to correct and change the appearance of the text later.

```
To all our friends:[Enter]
```

```
You're invited to help us celebrate our 10th anniversary
as a business here in beautiful, rainy western Wash-
ington.[Enter]
```

```
We're having the biggest, best blowout sale of our
history--a real sales extravaganza. Stock up on all
your rain gear needs: umbrellas, slickers, ponchos,
waterproof boots, hats, and more. At prices you won't
believe. Fifty percent off regular prices, fifty percent
more off the last marked sticker price on all sale
items. Come see us now and save![Enter]
```

```
It's summer now, but remember: Fall is right around the
corner.[Enter]
```

Your screen should look something like this.

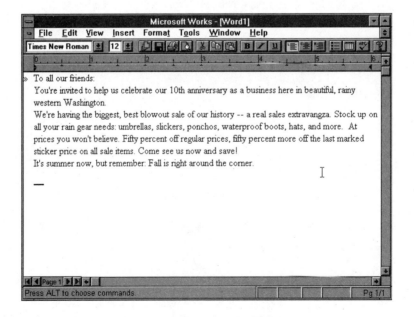

If some of your characters look different, or if your on-screen lines break in different places, you haven't done anything wrong. Works tailors itself to the capabilities of your computer and printer. The examples in this book show Works running on a computer connected to a Hewlett-Packard LaserJet printer equipped with the Times New Roman and Arial typefaces (which determine the look of the characters on the screen). If you have a different printer, your lines may be shorter or longer on the screen. As you work through the examples, remember that they are merely examples. Use them as guides, but feel free to experiment with settings or choices that produce comparable or better results on your equipment. After all, your goal is to see what Works can do for you.

Word Wrap

As you typed, you probably noticed how Works moved the insertion point to a new line whenever your words came close to the right edge of the screen. This Works feature, typical of word processors, is known as *word wrap*. One of the first differences you notice between using a typewriter and using a word processor is that word wrap eliminates the need to press the carriage return to keep lines from extending into the margin. To prevent strange formats from being created in your Works documents, do not press Enter after typing each line of a paragraph. Press Enter only at the *end* of each paragraph.

Seeing Special Characters

You now have several paragraphs on the screen. Works is using its default format for paragraphs: single-spaced, with no extra spacing above or below, and with no indent for the first line. It might be difficult to tell where one paragraph ends and the second begins. Even if you opt for a format like this, you can tell exactly where your paragraphs begin and end by opening the View menu, and then choosing All Characters.

Now your display looks like the next illustration.

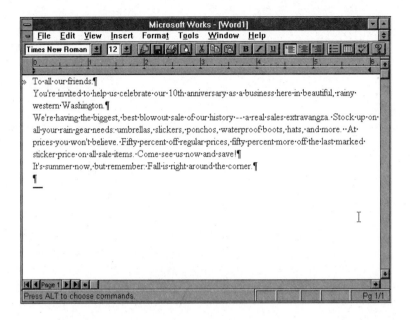

The word processor can display four special characters: tabs, end-of-line marks, paragraph marks, and spaces. You can see two of the characters in your display. The small dot between words is the Works symbol for a blank space, the character entered whenever you press the Spacebar. At the end of each paragraph, you can see a paragraph mark (¶), which appears wherever you pressed the Enter key while typing.

TIP: One good reason to work with the special characters visible: When you select text, you can easily see where to select the spaces surrounding characters and words.

Works doesn't print these characters (or other special characters you'll encounter later), but displaying them while you're writing helps you see exactly what you're doing. With some fonts and some styles (such as italic), it may be difficult to locate the spacing between words. After you're comfortable with the word processor, you might want to turn off the display (by choosing All Characters again) to simplify the screen's appearance.

Creating Paragraphs

Paragraphs are the building blocks of any document. You're probably accustomed to thinking of a paragraph in the traditional sense: a unified block of text that presents a single idea or part of a topic. As a computer user, however, you have to extend this definition. Think of a paragraph as any amount of text you want to present in a particular way on a page, with special indents, for example, or with extra spacing above and below it. A paragraph is any text—such as a character, a word, several words, a sentence, or many sentences—that ends with a paragraph mark, which is added to your document each time you press Enter.

As you type, Works used the same single-spaced format for each paragraph. Whenever you press Enter, Works "clones" a new paragraph, giving it the same spacing and indentation as the previous paragraph. If you had started out with a double-spaced paragraph, Works would have double-spaced them all.

Revising Text

It takes lots of work to turn a first draft into a final draft. Most writing, in fact, boils down to the tedium of revising and rewriting—processes that include lots of inserting and deleting. Works can't help with the actual rewriting, but it can make the revision process easier and cleaner than it is with a pen, pencil, or typewriter.

Moving the Insertion Point

As you revise a document, you'll often need to move the insertion point, select text, or do both to produce the effect you want. To move the insertion point with a mouse, all you do is point to the new location and click.

You might want to use the keyboard for these insertion point tasks too, especially if you're really comfortable with a keyboard and decide to fix a typographical error or change a sentence or paragraph as you're writing. The next page shows some quick ways to move around in a document with the keyboard.

To Move	Press
Left or right one character	Left arrow (←) or Right arrow (→)
Up or down one line	Up arrow (↑) or Down arrow (↓)
Left or right one word	Ctrl + Left arrow (Ctrl+ ←) or Ctrl + Right arrow (Ctrl + →)
Up or down one paragraph	Ctrl + Up arrow (Ctrl + ↑) or Ctrl + Down arrow (Ctrl + ↓)
Beginning of line	Home
End of line	End
Start of document	Ctrl+Home
End of document	Ctrl+End
Top of document window	Ctrl+Page Up
Bottom of document window	Ctrl+Page Down
Up one window	Page Up
Down one window	Page Down

Using the Navigation Buttons

There's another way to move around a Works word processor window—using the Navigation buttons you see here, located in the lower left corner of the document window.

These buttons require only a click to take you in the direction you want to go, page by page. As you can see in the window shown here, you can use the Navigation buttons in this way:

Click [◄◄] to move to the first page of the document.

Click [◄] to move to the previous page.

Click [►►] to move to the last page of the document.

Click [►] to move to the next page.

You'll also find the current page number shown between the Navigation buttons.

Selecting Text

For many revisions, you'll both move the insertion point and select text. The following list shows you how to use the mouse and the keyboard to select various amounts of text:

Mouse Selection Actions:

To Select	Use the mouse to
A word	Double-click the word.
A line	Click in the left window margin, beside the line.
A sentence	Drag over the sentence (or press Ctrl and click the sentence).
Several lines	Drag the pointer up or down in the left margin.
A paragraph	Double-click in the left margin, beside the paragraph.
Entire document	Press and hold Ctrl, then click in the left margin.

Keystroke Commands:

To	Press
Extend a selection	F8+Arrow *
Quit extending	Esc
Collapse a selection	Shift+F8

To Highlight	Press
A word	F8 twice *
A sentence	F8 three times *
A paragraph	F8 four times *
A document	F8 five times *
The previous character	Shift+Left arrow (←)
The next character	Shift+Right arrow (→)
The previous word	Ctrl+Shift+Left arrow (←)
The next word	Ctrl+Shift+Right arrow (→)
To the beginning of line	Shift+Home
To the end of line	Shift+End
To the beginning of document	Ctrl+Shift+Home
To the end of document	Ctrl+Shift+End

* To remove the highlight applied by pressing F8, press the Esc key.

To deselect text you highlighted with the mouse, click elsewhere in the document or press an arrow key. To deselect text you highlighted with the keyboard, press Esc and an arrow key.

Before you go on, practice moving the insertion point and selecting various amounts of text in the same document. When selecting text becomes almost instinctive, you'll begin to feel at home with word processing.

Working with Paragraphs

After you've typed a document, you're not stuck with the paragraphs you created. You can break one paragraph into two, combine two into one, and add new paragraphs wherever you want. Try this with your sample document:

1. Place the insertion point before the word *umbrellas*.

2. Press Enter to create a new paragraph.

3. Do the same with *slickers, ponchos, waterproof boots, and hats*, and in front of the words *At prices*. Don't worry about trailing punctuation in your list; you'll take care of it later.

Your first two paragraphs are pretty short now, so combine them by following these steps.

- Place the insertion point before the paragraph mark after the period at the end of the first sentence.

- Press Delete and the Spacebar.

 TIP: Remove a paragraph mark to join paragraphs. When you press the Spacebar, a space will be added after the period and before the next sentence.

That's better. Your document should now appear as shown here.

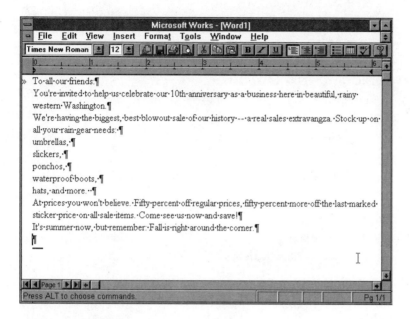

Adding Text

Adding new text is the easiest type of revision you can make with Works. Suppose, for example, you want to add a new sentence to your practice document. Do the following:

1. Use the mouse or the keyboard to place the insertion point at the beginning of the sentence *Come see us now and save!*

2. Type *Sizes for children and adults.* Press the Spacebar to add space after the new sentence.

    When you insert new characters, Works normally moves the existing text to the right to make room for the new text, so adding text to a document does not write over the existing text. Works does not automatically overtype or destroy any text when you are adding or inserting additional words.

Replacing Existing Text

You may want to replace, rather than add, text. You can do this in two ways. Choose Options from the Tools menu, then select the Overtype option or the Typing replaces selection option.

The Replacing Text Option

If you select the Typing replaces selection option, Works deletes selected text as soon as you begin typing new text to replace it. Because Works adjusts the spacing to fit, it doesn't matter whether the deleted text is longer or shorter than the new text. For example:

1. Select Typing replaces selection in the Options dialog box if you don't see a check mark next to this item. Be sure that the Overtype option is not checked.

2. Select the words *regular prices, fifty percent more off the last marked sticker price on all sale items*.

3. Replace this wordy mess by typing *everything in the store*.

The old text disappears and is replaced by the new text. Now your document looks like this.

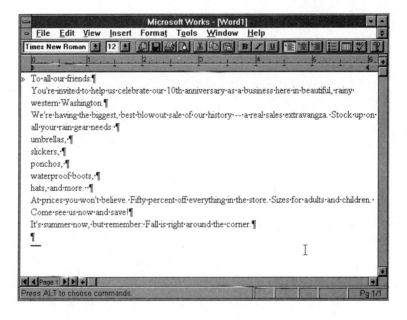

The Overtype Option

In contrast, if you select the Overtype option Works replaces existing characters with new ones as you type. To try it, follow these steps.

1. Click Typing replaces selection in the Options dialog box to turn replacement off, and then click OK.

2. Move the insertion point to the space before *won't* in *prices you won't believe.*

3. Turn on Overtype either by pressing the Insert key or by selecting Overtype from the Options dialog box. Notice that the letters OVR appear in the status bar to show that Overtype is turned on.

4. Type *ca* in place of *wo* in the word *won't.*

   The word *won't* turns into the word *can't* with a few keystrokes.

When you turn on the Overtype option, you must remember that length matters. Works deletes one character of existing text for each new character you type. Suppose, for example, you wanted to change the sentence *The canary ate the cat.* Turning on Overtype and replacing *canary* with *parrot* would produce *The parrot ate the cat.* But replacing *parrot* with *duck* would produce *The duckot ate the cat.* When you toggle Works to Overtype, remember that you've done so. If you're a touch typist accustomed to working from drafts on paper, it can be extremely frustrating to glance at the screen and find you've overtyped an entire sentence or paragraph when you meant to insert text.

- Turn off Overtype by opening the Tools menu, choosing the Options command, and selecting Overtype, or by pressing Insert again to avoid possible confusion in later examples.

TIP: You can always see if you are in Overtype mode by looking at the Status Bar.

Deleting Text

Professional writers have professional editors who find and delete unnecessary words, sentences, and even whole sections of an article or book. If you're working with Works on your own, you'll probably have to be your own editor, a thankless task when you've struggled with a document. Often, however, careful editing pays off in clearer, more understandable text.

For example, your practice document doesn't really need the words *a real sales extravaganza*, so delete them. To delete text, follow these instructions.

1. Select the text.

2. Press the Delete key or open the Edit menu, and then choose Clear. (You can also choose the Cut command, which will place the deleted text on the Windows clipboard).

TIP: You can also press Backspace to delete highlighted text.

Using Undo Editing

Oops! Want that text you just deleted? Although deleting your words seems final, it doesn't have to be. You can undelete text if you change your mind, as long as you haven't made any other changes to your document in the meantime. Suppose you decide you liked the upbeat sound of *a real sales extravaganza*.

- Restore the text by opening the Edit menu, and then choosing Undo Editing, or, for a quicker method, press Ctrl+Z. (The Alt+Backspace key combination works as well.) The words return to the sample document, exactly where they were before you deleted them.

As you'll see in other examples, the Undo Editing command reverses more than just deletions. Essentially, Undo Editing reverses the effect of any editing operation that alters the appearance or content of a document. Use Undo Editing when your fingers outpace your thoughts, you've changed fonts and styles, and you want to undo the change. Remember, though, that you can't undo selectively. You can reverse only your last change.

TIP: This is serious stuff. Undo Editing will only undo your last action. If you make an error, don't try anything else. Select Undo Editing immediately! Undo Editing undoes editing; it can't retrieve lost files or retrieve earlier versions of a file.

Before you continue, delete the punctuation at the ends of the lines reading *umbrellas, slickers, ponchos, waterproof boots,* and *hats, and more.*

TIP: Don't get confused about Cut, Copy, Paste, Clear, and Undo Editing. Cut, Copy, and Paste allow you to delete, copy, and retrieve in any Windows application. Clear and Undo Editing are only used in Works. What is deleted is not placed on the Windows Clipboard. It can only be retrieved immediately with the Undo Editing.

Moving Text with the Clipboard

You learned in Chapter 2 about the Windows Clipboard and the concept of cutting and pasting. In the next exercise, you'll use Cut and Paste to reorganize text. You'll remove text by cutting it from the document and then pasting it in somewhere else.

See Also: For more information, see "About the Clipboard," page 53.

Before you start, open the Edit menu. Note that Cut and Copy are displayed in dimmed letters. When a command is dimmed, it is not available for use. Since nothing is selected, no text could be cut or copied. Paste would be dimmed if you have not cut or copied any text yet. If the Clipboard is empty, Works has nothing to paste into your document. You'll now paste text. Do the following.

1. Select the sentence *Come see us now and save!* (Include the space before the sentence in your selection.)

2. Open the Edit menu, and then choose Cut, or, as a shortcut, use the Ctrl+X key combination.

   The text disappears as if it were deleted. The cut text is in the Windows Clipboard. From the Clipboard you can paste text back into any area of a document.

3. Move the insertion point to the end of the document, after *Fall is right around the corner.*

4. Open the Edit menu, then choose Paste, or press the Ctrl+V key combination.

   Now the end of your document appears as you see here.

At·prices·you·won't·believe.·Fifty·percent·off·regular·prices,·fifty·percent·more·off·the·marked·
sticker·price·on·all·sale·items.·Sizes·for·children·and·adults¶
It's·summer·now,·but·remember:·Fall·is·right·around·the·corner.··Come·see·us·now·and·save!¶

Cut and paste is that simple. Bear in mind, however, that the Clipboard holds only one item at a time. Thus, if you cut text and then go on to cut (or copy) another selection of text, the second block of text replaces the first on the Clipboard. The first block of text is gone and cannot be retrieved.

 TIP: You can cut, copy, and paste from Works document to any other Works document, or any other Windows application.

Moving Text with Drag And Drop

The title of this section might sound like the name of a new dance, but it's really the name of a terrific new feature of this latest version of Works. With Drag And Drop, you simply drag the selected text wherever you want it to appear. Here are the exact steps.

1. Select the text you want to move.

2. When you place the mouse pointer on top of the selected text, it changes to a Drag, as you see here:

3. Drag the selected text to where you want it to appear. When you move the mouse, the pointer changes from Drag to Move, as you see here:

As you drag the mouse, the insertion point moves with it, allowing you to place the text precisely. When you release the mouse button, the text will disappear from its original location and will appear in the new location. Keep in mind that this procedure is not cutting or copying text since the moved text is not stored temporarily in the Clipboard.

Not only can you use the mouse to move text within your Works word processing document, but you can copy text or other information by dragging to a new location. You can Drag And Drop information within the same word processing document, between different Works documents, or (sometimes) between a Works document and a document created in another Windows-based application.

To copy or move information from or within Works using the mouse, open the documents you want to change. Tile the document windows. Always make sure the location where you want to drop the text is visible in the destination document. Use the scroll bars if necessary.

After highlighting or selecting the text you want to copy or move, follow these instructions:

To	Destination	Do This
Move	To another Works document or to a document created in another Windows-based application	Highlight the text, click within the selection, and then hold Shift as you drag.
Copy	Within a single Works document, or to another Works document or a document created in another Windows-based application	Highlight the text, click within the selection, and then hold Ctrl as you drag.

TIP: When you click within any selection to drag, Works adds a drag, move, or copy label to the mouse pointer to indicate that you are transferring information from within your document window.

You might see a message or a cursor indicating the text cannot be dropped. If this occurs, it means the application you are dragging the selected text to does not support the Drag And Drop editing.

Works always inserts the information at the location of the mouse pointer. If you make an error, simply undo the Drag And Drop action by opening the Edit menu, and then choosing Undo. If you want to cancel a drag and drop operation in progress, simply press Esc.

The ability to perform Drag And Drop editing can be turned on or off from the Tools menu. Choose Options, and then select or clear the Drag and drop check box.

Copying Text

Information gets onto the Clipboard in one of two ways: You cut it with the Cut command on the Edit menu or copy it with the Copy command on the Edit menu. When you cut information, you remove it from the document. When you copy information, you duplicate that information, keeping the text in its original location. In other respects, Cut and Copy are the same.

Suppose you have some ideas about revising the first paragraph of your document, but you'd like to keep the original to compare the two versions. You can copy the paragraph to the Clipboard, paste it back into the document, and make revisions to one copy while leaving the other intact. Let's try that now by following these steps.

1. Select the paragraph beginning with *You're invited.*

2. Open the Edit menu, and then choose Copy; or use the key combination Ctrl+C.

3. Place the insertion point in front of *umbrellas*, open the Edit menu, and then choose Paste (or use the key combination Ctrl+V).

TIP: You can continue to paste the same text in more than one location in the same document or even into another document or another Works application. It's a great way to enter text you want to repeat. Simply use the Paste command or the Ctrl+V key combination.

The paragraph you copied is pasted into the document below the original. If you find it difficult to distinguish one paragraph from the other, be sure the insertion point is in front of *umbrellas* and press Enter to add a blank paragraph. That's what we did to make the paragraphs a bit more distinct. The finished project appears at the top of the next page.

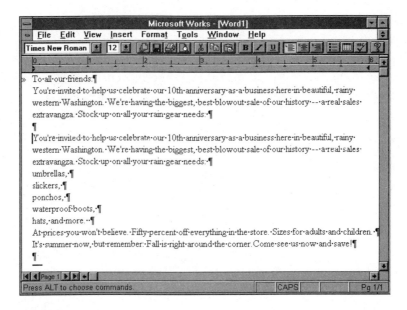

Saving a File

You'll try other examples shortly, so save your sample document for now.

1. Open the File menu, and then choose Save. Type (one word) *raingear* in the File Name box.

2. Under Directories, you probably see c:\msworks. You want to save the example in the directory you created named WKSBOOK. Double-click on the folder for drive C (c:\). The directories on drive C will appear.

3. Scroll down if necessary until you see WKSBOOK.

4. Double-click to make it the current directory (the one in which Works will save your file).

5. Click OK to save the file.

Works saves your file and tells you so by changing the filename in the document window's title bar from Word1 to RAINGEAR.WPS. Works always attaches the .WPS extension to any word processing document file it saves.

Automatic Backups

Works knows how busy you are. And when you're busy, it's sometimes easy to make a mistake. To protect your work, Works will automatically make a backup copy of a document. This takes place if you check the Make backup copy of old file check box in the Save As dialog box. Works will then make an extra copy of the document each time you save your file and the copy will be placed in the same location as the original is saved. The only difference is that Works will use a different extension attached to the file. You learned in Chapter 2, see page 29, that Works assigns the .WPS extension to all word processed documents. When you save a word processed document and have a backup created, it will be saved as *filename.bps*, or, in our example, *raingear.bps*. Here's a small chart showing you what the extensions are when backups are made.

Module	Backup Extension
Word Processor	.BPS
Spreadsheet	.BKS
Database	.BDB
Communications	.BCM

As you can see, when Works creates a backup file, the backup copy has the same filename, except its filename extension begins with *B* instead of *W*.

TIP: Always make backup files. If something happens to the original file, you can open the backup file and recover a recent copy of your document.

Works saves the new version of your document and also saves a copy as it was before you made any changes. Works always places the backup copy in the same directory as the document you are working on. If the backup option is on, Works automatically updates the backup copy each time you save your file.

The Two New Views of Works

Here's one more Works word processing feature before we move on to learning how to format a document.

In addition to the Normal view, which you've been working in up to now, the Works word processor comes with two new viewing options, each available on the View menu. The first, Page Layout, displays each page of a document as it will look when it is printed. Objects, pictures, headers and footers, columns, and footnotes all appear as they will when you print. This is WYSIWYG, which we discussed on page 91.

An advantage of using this option is that you can actually edit a header or a footer—or any other document element—in Page Layout view. You can also move objects in Page Layout by dragging them to a new location. To use this option, simply open the View menu, and then choose Page Layout.

The other view, Draft View, shows you all the text in a document but only in a single font and a single font size, with none of the Works goodies such as columns and footnotes. The Draft View might be less convenient to use, but it is faster because Works has to use less memory to get the job done. Especially with a large document, the Draft View lets you scroll more quickly through the document. To use this option, simply open the View menu, and then choose Draft View.

TIP: Create your documents in Draft View and then when you are ready to print, switch to the Page Layout view. That way you can save time in the creation process and still get to see how your document will look.

Coming Next

Even though the word processing skills you learned in this chapter are the most basic, they may well be the most important. You need a good foundation to build upon to tackle the more advanced and complex word processing features that make Works so powerful. Let's move on to some of those now and focus on formatting a document.

Formatting
a Document

No matter how well it is written, the appearance of your document can make the difference between a bunch of sentences and an effective presentation. That's why Works has so many different options available for formatting words, paragraphs, and pages. And, most of these changes are as close as a few clicks away. We'll begin exploring them with a general overview of how to format a document with lots of hints about using the toolbar and Ruler.

Formatting a Document

What a document says is always important, but the way it looks can increase the impact of what you say and ensure that you effectively communicate your message. Good formatting can mean the difference between a document that is read carefully and one that is tossed aside. This chapter is all about how to format your text.

Using the Toolbar

The toolbar is your shortcut to the most common commands the word processor offers. You'll use the toolbar a great deal when you format, revise, and print documents. Now is a good time to become familiar with the various boxes and buttons on the toolbar you see here and what they do.

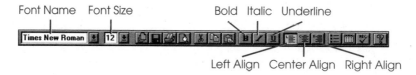

The following sections describe the toolbar buttons that relate to formatting and the menu commands they represent.

You'll probably want to take the toolbar for a test run, so open a new word processor document using the Create New File command on the File menu, and then click the icon representing the Word Processor.

Selecting Fonts and Font Sizes

At the left end of the toolbar is a box for font names and a box for font sizes. Each font is a different design of type; each has a name, such as Courier, Helvetica, Script, or Times Roman; each creates characters with a particular look and style. Your printer's capabilities determine which fonts are available. Your Works screen might not look exactly like the illustrations in this chapter, but don't worry. All the basic how-to's are the same.

The Font Name box on the toolbar displays the name of the font you're currently using. Try out your fonts by following these steps.

1.   Click the button to the right of the Font Name box to see a list of available fonts, as shown here.

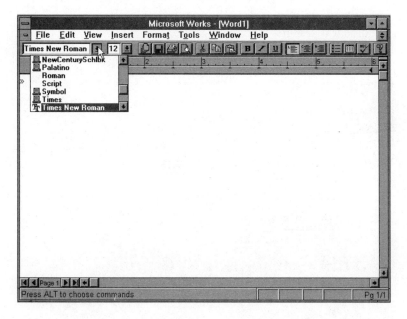

2.   Click on a font name other than the one that is highlighted.

3. Type its name and press Enter.

4. Do the same for the rest of the fonts.

Or you can change the font after text is entered by highlighting the text and then selecting the font you want to use.

Selecting a Font Size

Font sizes are measured in units called points. There are approximately 72 points to an inch. Standard documents are printed in either 10-point or 12-point type, the latter being larger and easier to read.

The Font Size box to the right of the Font Name box displays the current font size. You can change font size by following these steps.

1. Click the button to the right of the Font Size box to see what other sizes are available.

2. Click the size you want.

TIP: If a size is not listed, you can type a size you want in the Font Size box.

Here's a sample of different-size fonts.

This is Bookman 8 point

This is Bookman 12 point

This is Bookman 16 point

This is Bookman 20 point

This is Bookman 24 point

Selecting a Character Style

The main part of the toolbar that deals with formatting consists of six buttons grouped by function. The first three buttons, labeled B (for **bold**), I (for *italic*), and U (for <u>underline</u>), assign a special appearance to selected characters. Try these out by doing the following.

1. Enter a few lines of text.

2. Using the mouse, select one word by double-clicking.

3. Click on the B button on the toolbar. The text's style or appearance will change to **bold**.

4. Using the mouse, select another word by double-clicking.

5. Click on the I button on the toolbar. The text's style or appearance will change to *italic*.

6. Using the mouse, select a third word by double-clicking.

7. Click on the U button on the toolbar. The text will be <u>underlined</u>.

TIP: You can also bold, italicize, or underline by first selecting text and then using the Ctrl+B, Ctrl+I, or Ctrl+U key combinations.

Another Way to Work with Fonts and Styles

Fonts, font sizes, and character styles are also accessible through the Font and Style command on the Format menu. When you select the Font and Style command, you will see the dialog box shown in Figure 5-1.

Using this dialog box, you can select the font, size, and style; you can also see what the font will look like before you make the actual selection. In Figure 5-1, on the next page, you can see how 14-point Times Roman will appear.

You can also use the options in this dialog box to create subscript and superscript characters, such as $a^2 = b^2 + c^2$ and $R_{profit \bullet fun}$. Click on the Cancel button to get out of the Font and Style dialog box.

FIGURE 5-1.
The Font and Style
dialog box.

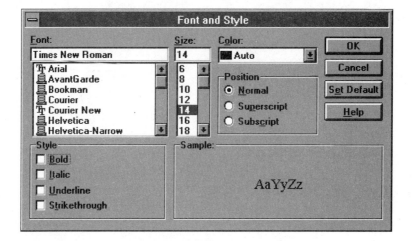

Font Junk

You can mix and match fonts, sizes, and styles. As long as the selected text remains selected, you can underline it, make it bold, and italicize it as well. But, as you can see here, you can also end up with **font junk <u>*where the message* becomes *the medium*</u>** (instead of the other way around). What you want to say is obscured by the way it looks. Be careful. Often the simplest combination of fonts, sizes, and styles is the best.

Here are some guidelines for how to use styles. <u>Underline</u> and **bold** are both used for emphasis, to make certain words or phrases stand out. You can use both interchangeably, but keep the following points in mind.

First, if you use either underline or boldface too much, they will lose their power to make the reader notice what you want to emphasize. In other words, don't underline every other word!

Second, underlining can have a special meaning. When documents are professionally printed, the underlined words are usually printed in italics. If you want your words printed in italics, underline them in the draft copy.

Finally, the bold feature is usually used to highlight a section heading, as in an outline. The underlining feature is more often used for emphasizing text.

Text Alignment

The three buttons on the toolbar labeled with lines of "text" and the letters L, C, and R affect the way selected text (be it a paragraph, a word, or a single character) is aligned (or *justified*) on the page. Figure 5-2 illustrates the three styles.

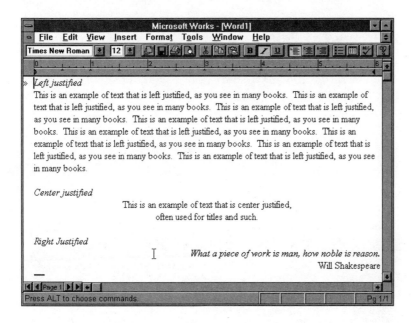

FIGURE 5-2.
The three text alignment styles.

To use any of these styles, follow these steps.

1. Place the insertion point anywhere in the text you want to align.

2. Click on the L, C, or R button.

L produces left-aligned text, much like you see in this book. The C button centers text between the left and right margins of the page.

R, the opposite of L, produces right-aligned text, in which the left edges are ragged but the right edges form a straight line down the page. Right justification is often used for quote attributions or for separating information on one line such as

Volume 1, Number 1   October 1993

TIP: Full justification, where the lines of text align on both the left and right sides, is available by opening the Format menu, choosing Paragraph, and selecting Justified from the Indents and Alignment tab.

Working with Paragraph

The toolbar is the fastest way to carry out many commands, but it is not the only way. With the toolbar's handy Font Name and Font Size boxes, and the six formatting buttons, you can do a lot quickly. But the toolbar's options for changing the appearance of a document are not the only ones available. Here we'll explore some of the other possibilities, available under the Paragraph option on the Format menu.

Once you choose this option, you see the Paragraph dialog box shown in Figure 5-3. This special dialog box includes three tabs. You click on the tab of the box you want to use.

FIGURE 5-3.
The Paragraph
dialog box.

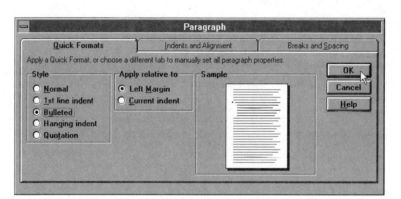

Quick Formats

The Quick Formats tab you see in Figure 5-3 contains option buttons that you can use to specify a format that can be quickly applied to paragraphs. You can specify a particular paragraph style and alignment. To use this tab, follow these steps.

1. Enter the paragraph of text you want to format, or place the insertion point in an already created paragraph.

2. Open the Format menu, and then choose Paragraph.

3. Click on Quick Formats.

4. Set the attributes you want by clicking on the appropriate option buttons.

5. Click OK.

You can even see a preview of what it will look like in the Sample area in Figure 5-4. The formatted paragraph that follows uses the Bulleted option:

■ This is an example of using the Bulleted option on the Quick Formats tab in the Paragraph dialog box. Bullets are great for setting off text.

Indents and Alignment

You can also change the appearance of paragraphs with the Indents and Alignment options by clicking that tab in the Paragraph dialog box, as shown in Figure 5-4.

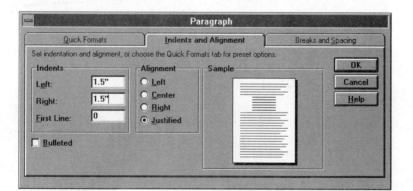

FIGURE 5-4.
The Indents and Alignment tab.

The Indents and Alignment options allow you to set the size of the indent, whether it should have a bullet preceding it, and how the indented text is aligned.

To use the Indents and Alignment tab, follow these steps.

1. Enter the paragraph of text you want to format, or place the insertion point in an already created paragraph.

2. Open the Format menu, and then choose Paragraph.

3. Click on Indents and Alignment.

4. Set the attributes you want by clicking on the appropriate option buttons.

5. Click OK.

In Figure 5-4, in the Sample area, you can see how a paragraph with left and right margins of 1.5 inches, and justified text, appears.

TIP: You can also add bullets to paragraphs through the Indents and Alignment tab by clicking on the Bulleted check box.

Breaks and Spacing

The last tab in the Paragraph dialog box is Breaks and Spacing, as shown in Figure 5-5.

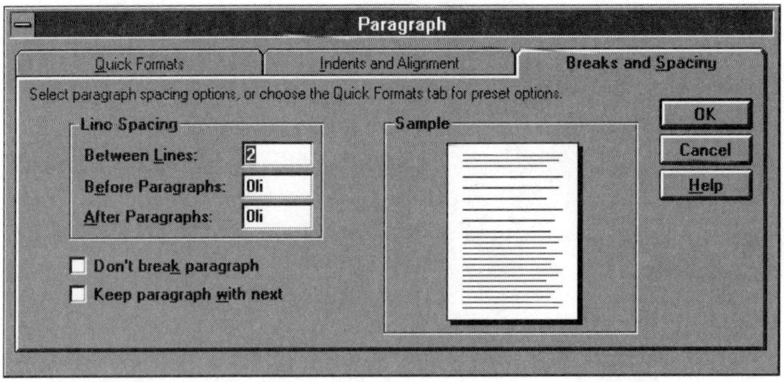

FIGURE 5-5.
The Breaks and
Spacing tab.

Using the Breaks and Spacing options, you can set spacing between lines, before paragraphs, and after paragraphs. As you can see in Figure 5-5, the spacing, set at 2 lines, is illustrated in the Sample area.

There is an interesting relationship between the Breaks and Spacing, Indents and Alignment, and Quick Formats tabs in the Paragraph dialog box. You can switch back and forth from one to the other, and the current sample area will reflect all previous settings. For example, if you select certain options in Indents and Alignment, those settings will be in force when you switch to Breaks and Spacing. It is quick, easy, and efficient to set line spacing, alignment, and other options in these two tabs and then use the Quick Formats tool to make it so in any paragraph.

The Ruler

Just below the toolbar, at the top of the document window, you can see an on-screen ruler.

First line indent marker

Left indent marker   Right indent marker

Your ruler, like the one illustrated, probably shows measurements in inches. If you want, you can use the Options command on the Tools menu to change the measurement unit to centimeters, picas (sixths of an inch), points, or millimeters.

Three black triangles on the ruler show where your lines of text will start and end, relative to the left and right edges of the page. Two small black triangles should appear directly under the 0 on the ruler to mark the left edge of your document. A second, larger triangle should appear under the 6-inch mark, showing that Works will make each line 6 inches long (standard on a page 8 inches wide).

Like most features in Works, the ruler responds immediately to changes. Like the toolbar, it gives you fast access to menu commands, in particular the Paragraph and Tabs commands on the Format menu.

First-Line Indents

A first-line indent is the amount, typically 0.5 inch, that the first line of a paragraph is indented, relative to the other lines. To indent the first line of one or more selected paragraphs, you can use either the ruler or the Indents and Spacing tab in the Paragraph dialog box.

With the ruler, you use the first-line indent marker (the top triangle at the left edge of the ruler).

To indent the first line in a paragraph, follow these steps.

1. Place the insertion point anywhere within the paragraph.

2. Drag the first-line indent marker to the right, letting it go at the 0.5-inch mark on the ruler. It might take some practice to position the marker precisely on the 0.5-inch mark.

Paragraph Indents

Left and right paragraph indents determine how far an entire paragraph is indented, relative to the margins of the page. When you use left and right indents, you are adding to the amount of white space at the edges of the page. With the ruler, you drag the left indent marker (the lower triangle at the left edge of the ruler) and the right indent markers to set the left and right indents. You can also use the Indents and Spacing tab in the Paragraph dialog box.

For example, you can see in the next illustraton how the left and the right indent markers have been set at 1 inch and the first-line indent marker has been dragged to 1.5 inches.

TIP: To give paragraphs a left indent of 0.5 inch, select them and press Ctrl+N. To indent further, in 0.5-inch increments, press Ctrl+N as many times as necessary. To undo one or more indents, press Ctrl+G.

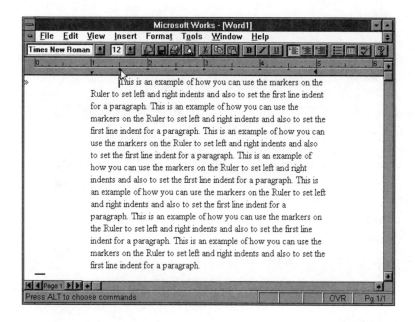

Practice Time

There's nothing like the real thing. Enter the following text so you can practice some of the things you have just learned.

Memo

Dear good friends of ACME Widgets:

Fun for you! The Bored of Directors theater group will be producing their annual review on November 14 at 1993 at 8:30 PM. If you remember last year we had tons of fun, lots of laughs, junk food galore, and a good time by all.

Tickets usually go fast for this event so get yours as soon as possible. See you there!

Jackson H. Jordan

VP for Fun & Games

Save this file as *memo.wps* since we'll be using it again later in this book.

In Figure 5-6, you can see what the memo looks like once we have finished with some simple, but impressive, formatting changes.

FIGURE 5-6.
A formatted
memo.

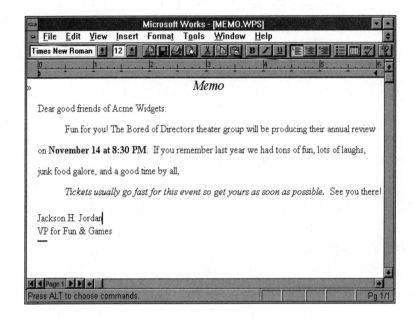

Here's what we did.

1. Selected the entire document by pressing Ctrl and clicking in the left margin.

2. Selected the Bookman font if it is available on your system. If not, select a different font.

3. Selected 12 for the font size.

4. Selected the word Memo and clicked the Center Align toolbar button.

5. Selected the word Memo and clicked 14 point for the font size.

6. Selected the word Memo and clicked the Italic toolbar button.

7. Selected the word Memo and clicked the Bold toolbar button.

8. Placed the insertion point in the first paragraph in front of the word *fun.*

9. Chose Paragraph from the Format menu.

10. Clicked on the Indents and Alignment tab.

11. Indented the first line 0.5 inch. (You could also drag the indent marker on the Ruler to accomplish the same change.)

12. Clicked on Alignment Left.

13. Repeated steps 10 and 11 for the second paragraph.

14. Highlighted the words *November 14 at 8:30 PM.*

15. Clicked B (the Bold button) on the toolbar.

16. Highlighted the words *Tickets usually go fast for this event so get yours as soon as possible.*

17. Clicked I (the Italic button) on the toolbar.

Now, that wasn't so bad, was it? In fact, it was pretty easy and it certainly made the document more attractive. Let's move on to other types of formatting tools that Works offers.

Working with Tabs and the Ruler

Tabs are used to align items in columns; they often make it easier to set up special alignments, such as lists like this.

These are the steps as I see them:

1. Get an enrollment form.
2. Contact your advisor.
3. Determine what course you want to take.
4. Enroll.
5. Pay fees.

Works lets you set several types of tabs: left-aligned, centered, right-aligned, and aligned on a decimal point. You can see what they look like in Figure 5-7.

FIGURE 5-7.
The different kinds
of Works tabs.

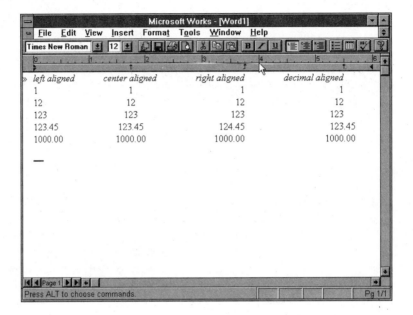

When a left tab is set, the text that is entered moves one character at a time to the right of the left tab setting. As you can see in Figure 5-7, the text is to the right of the tab stop. Works places a [↑] on the ruler for a left tab.

When a center tab is set, the text is centered under the location of the tab setting. As you can see in Figure 5-7, the text is centered directly to the left and right of the tab stop. Works places a [↑] on the ruler for a center tab.

When a right tab is set, the text that is entered moves one character at a time to the left of the right tab setting. As you can see in Figure 5-7, the text is to the left of the tab stop. Works places a [↑] on the ruler for a right tab.

Finally, when a decimal tab is set, the text appears to the left of the tab setting (represented by the decimal), until you press the decimal point. Then the text appears to the right. This is the ideal type of tab stop to use when you enter numbers that contain decimals. Works places a [↑] on the ruler for a decimal tab.

If you don't set any tabs, Works sets them for you. The default tabs are left-aligned at 0.5 inch intervals.

In the following examples, you'll use both the ruler and the Tab command on the Format menu to set tabs in your sample document. First, enter the following list:

hammer

nails

shingles

tape

cement

1. Now move the mouse pointer to the ruler, just below the 1.25-inch mark, and click.

   Works inserts a left-aligned tab stop (the only kind you can set with the ruler) at that location.

2. Place the insertion point in front of *hammer*. Type a lowercase *o* and press Tab.

3. Do the same for the other items in the list.

The list should look like this. We also turned on All Characters (on the View menu) so you could see how tab marks appear.

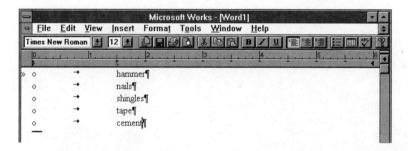

The bullets (the o characters) you just created work fine for single-line lists. For bulleted lists in which some or all entries are two or more lines long, combine a tab stop with indents to create the look you want. Drag the left indent marker to the location you want the text to begin, and then drag the first-line indent marker to the left, to where you want the bullet character to appear.

Finally, set a tab stop at the same position as the paragraph indent. (For example, set the left indent to 0.5-inch, set the first-line indent to 0.25-inch, and set a tab stop at 0.5-inch.) For each entry in the list, type the bullet character, press tab to move the insertion point to the text position, and then type the text. The tab stop will control the beginning of the first line of text; the left indent will align all other lines beneath it.

Don't forget, you can also insert a bullet in front of the first line in a paragraph using the Quick Formats tab on the Paragraph dialog box. This will not tab the line in, but will instead indent. It does, however, give the same appearance.

 TIP: Works can create what is called a hanging indent, where each line but the first in a paragraph is indented. You can do this by placing the insertion point in the paragraph and then using the Ctrl+H key combination to have Works create this format for you.

Working with the Tabs Dialog Box

There's another way to set tabs that involves choosing the Tabs option on the Format menu. When you do this, you will see the Tabs dialog box, as shown here.

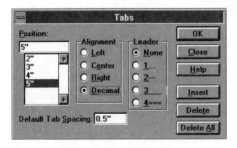

This might be the simplest and most direct way to set tabs. Here's how.

1. Open the Format menu, and then choose Tabs.

2. Click Delete All to delete all the previously set tabs.

3. In the Position box, enter the location of the first tab.

4. Click on the type of tab you want to use.

5. Click Insert.

6. Repeat steps 2 through 5 for as many tabs as you want to set.

7. Click OK.

> **TIP:** You can access the Tabs dialog box by double-click-ing on the ruler.

In the Tabs dialog box, you can see how tabs were set at 2 inches, 3 inches, 4 inches, and 5 inches. When you set tabs, you can also specify whether you want leader characters. Works uses leader characters to fill in the space leading up to a tab stop—the type of characters you would use in a table of contents, as shown here.

To use leader characters, just click on the type of leader you want and Works will incorporate it.

Working with Page Layout

The layout of a printed page is governed by more than the alignment, spacing, and indentation of the paragraphs. You've no doubt encountered form letters or handouts on which the text literally covered the paper, marching down the page in rank after closely spaced rank of small, dark blots of ink.

Such printing might initially save a few dollars, but the money saved can actually be money wasted if no one wants to read what the writer has to say. Conventional wisdom maintains that adequate margins, indents, and paragraph spacing enhance the readability of any document. So do such elements as page numbers, running heads that appear at the top of each page, and controlled breaks that avoid awkward interruptions in words, lines, and paragraphs.

You've already seen how to control various types of spacing in paragraphs. Now you'll learn how to adjust the top, bottom, left, and right page margins. You'll also find out how to

- Select a page size and orientation
- Number pages
- Print footnotes
- Set columns
- Break lines and pages at a specified place
- Keep certain words together on the same line
- Keep all lines of a particular paragraph on the same page

Setting Margins

Works automatically sets reasonable margins for a printed page. To check the margins, choose the Page Setup command from the File menu. When you do this, the Page Setup dialog box is displayed with the Margins tab chosen, as shown in Figure 5-8.

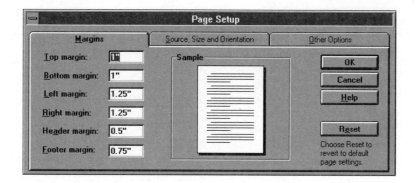

FIGURE 5-8.
The Page Setup
dialog box.

The first four boxes on the left show the current settings for the top, bottom, left, and right margins. They are displayed in the unit of measurement you specified in the Works Settings dialog box. If your setting is in inches, you see top and bottom margins of 1 inch and left and right margins of 1.25 inches. To change any of these, type a new measurement (whole or decimal number). You can omit the unit of measure unless you want to specify a different one. (For example, you can type *5 cm* even though Works displays all other measurements in inches.)

Left and right margins of 1.25 inches are standard for letters and similar documents, but you might want to change one or both to suit a particular layout. For example, if you're planning to print and bind a report, increase the left margin to 1.5 inches, or more, to allow space for the binding. If you're preparing a manuscript or a draft document for review, increase both side margins to allow adequate room for editing or review notes.

The default top and bottom margins, on the other hand, might be a little tight for your purposes. Business documents, especially letters, tend to leave plenty of space at the top and a bit less at the bottom, so a top margin of 1.5 inches might be more appropriate.

You can also set the margins, or positions, of the header or footer. A header is text that appears on the top of each page. A footer is text that appears on the bottom of each page. This book uses headers, which is the text that you see the top of this page. You will learn how to create headers in Chapter 6, page 145.

To set margins, simply click on the margin you want to change and enter the new value. Look to the Sample area to see the effect of the change. Use the Tab key to move from one margin setting to another.

TIP: Press Shift+Tab to move back to the previous setting.

Selecting a Page Size and Orientation

In the Page Setup dialog box, the Source, Size and Orientation tab offers options for changing page size and orientation. These options are especially useful if you need to print on larger paper or smaller (such as postcards) or change the orientation from Portrait to Landscape if you have a very wide document (such as a table).

To work with Source, Size and Orientation, follow these steps.

1. Open the File menu, and then choose Page Setup.

2. Click on the Source, Size and Orientation tab.

3. Select the paper size you want to use.

4. Select the orientation of the paper. In Portrait orientation, the lead edge is the shorter one (just as you see in a simple typewritten page). In Landscape orientation, the lead edge is the longer side.

TIP: If your printer has more than one paper source—such as both a regular paper tray and an envelope feed—you can select your printer's paper source in this dialog box.

5. Check the Sample area to see whether it shows the size and orientattion you want.

Numbering Pages

Finally, using the Other Options tab in the Page Setup dialog box (Figure 5-8 on page 135), you can enter the page number with which you want Works to start numbering the manuscript (be it 1 or 1000).

The page numbering will begin on the page that was active when the Page Setup option was selected. If you want to skip any page, just set the 1st page number box at the page number where you want to start.

Printing Footnotes

Footnotes are used to cite quotations or summaries, or to make comments to supplement the information in the body of your document. Microsoft Works is preset to print your footnotes at the bottom of each page that contains a footnote, but you can choose to print all of the footnotes at the end of the document.

To specify that Works prints footnotes at the end of your document following these steps.

1. From the File Menu, choose Page Setup, and then select Other Options.

2. Select the Print Footnotes At End of Document check box.

3. Click OK.

See Also: For more information about footnotes, see "Creating Footnotes," page 149.

Setting Columns

Columns enhance the appearance of a document and take just a click to create. With this new version of Works, you can create multiple columns as well.

You can create columns by following these steps.

1. Open the Format menu, and then choose Columns. The width of a column is determined by the number of columns on a page, the page margins, and the space between columns (with 0.5 inch as the default).

2. Enter the number of columns you want to appear.

3. Press the Tab key to move to the Space Between box and to see in the Sample area what the columns looks like.

4. Enter the space you want between columns. It's best to leave this setting alone if you are working with only two or three column.

TIP: Don't worry about the space between columns until you have so many columns that the space between them is wider than the columns themselves. Keep in mind that you want your reader's eye drawn to the text, not to the spaces between columns.

5. Click off the Line Between check box if you do not want a line between columns.

In Figure 5-9, you can see the print preview of a page with three columns and lines between them.

FIGURE 5-9.

A print preview of three columns with lines between them.

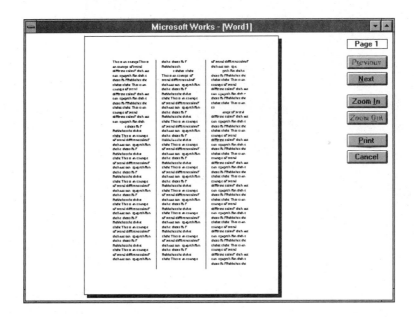

You can select only one column setting for any document. The column format applies to the entire document.

> **TIP:** Columns won't appear on the regular Works screen. You either have to use the Print Preview option on the File menu or choose Page Layout from the View menu. When you are finished with columns work, choose Draft View from the View menu.

Keeping Text Together

Sometimes you want to begin a new page without having to completely fill the previous page. For example, you want to begin Chapter 2 on a new page, but the last page of Chapter 1 only fills up half the sheet. The answer? A page break.

There are other situations in which you might want to keep text together. If a quotation appears at the bottom of a page, you certainly don't want the first line to appear on one page and the remaining lines on subsequent pages. Stay tuned as we show you how to deal with these and other text management issues.

Working with Page Breaks

When you create a multiple-page document, Works keeps track of the document's length. Works also shows you where page breaks occur as you're typing by displaying a new page character (≫) at the left edge of the screen (this symbol appears at the top of a new word-processed document as well).

Sometimes, pages will break where you don't want them to (for example, at the end of a letter, between the closing and your signature). To correct this, you can either insert a manual page break or tell Works that certain paragraphs must appear together on the same page. Here's how you do both.

Inserting a Manual Page Break

To insert a manual page break, follow these steps.

1. Move the insertion point to the place you want a new page to begin.

2. Press the Ctrl+Enter key combination. Works then displays a dotted line showing the page break, plus the ≫ character, as you can see here.

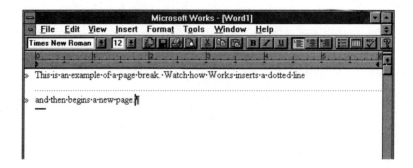

After you insert a manual page break, choose Paginate Now from the Tools menu so that any adjustments in page length are made automatically. To see how other pages might have been affected by the insertion of the page break, view them in Print Preview. If you later decide you don't want a manual page break you inserted, place the insertion point in front of the first character following the page break, and then press the Backspace key.

Keeping Paragraphs Together

You might want to keep paragraphs together. There are two ways do this and keep a Works-initiated page break from interrupting paragraphs in a document. You can do this by having Works keep a line paragraph, such as a list, on one page, or by keeping related paragraphs together on a single page.

In either situation, you use the Breaks and Spacing tab on the Paragraph dialog box you saw in Figure 5-5 on page 124.

To keep all lines of a paragraph on the same page, click the box next to Don't break paragraph. To keep related paragraphs together, click next to Keep paragraph with next.

TIP: Be careful with the commands that keep text together. If, for example, the salutation to a letter is the only thing that carries over to an additional page, go up a few lines and press the Enter key until there are a few lines of text along with the salutation. If you elect to keep the salutation as part of the last paragraph, the previous page will have a significant amount of blank space at the bottom.

Viewing and Printing Documents

Because Works is an integrated program, the printing process is consistent throughout the Works modules. Once you've defined the margins, formatting, running heads, and other elements of a document, the only steps remaining are previewing and printing. We'll cover both of those here. Any special printing functions or operations will be addressed in our discussion of each module.

Print Preview

You've learned about Print Preview and its Zoom feature, so neither needs much additional explanation. Print Preview is great for examining format changes before you print.

For more information about Print Preview and its Zoom feature, see "Shaping and Viewing Text," page 42.

One preview aspect you haven't seen, however, is controlled by the Previous and Next buttons on the Preview window. So far, you've previewed single-page documents. On a multiple-page document, you use the Previous and Next buttons to move from page to page. Previous takes you back one page (if there is one) and Next takes you forward one page.

Previewing a document saves time and paper. More important, it can also reduce your frustration when a printout doesn't look as you thought it would. For example, you might use several page breaks and keep other text together to create a certain effect. The only way to check if these tools served their purpose is to preview the document.

Setting Up for Printing

Before you can print a document, Works has to know that there is a printer available and its kind. In most cases, you needn't worry about this because Windows helps you set up for printing when you install it. And, because Works is a Windows application, it can use the printer setup you have already defined. Once you tell Windows about your printer, printing becomes a simple matter of choosing the Print command from the File menu, where it appears in Works and many other Windows applications.

If you choose the Printer Setup command on the File menu, the Printer Setup dialog box appears, where you select from a list of printers that have already been installed. Why install more than one printer? Some people print drafts on one printer (such as a low-resolution printer), and then print the final versions using a high-resolution printer.

Use the Printer Setup command when you are changing printers; use the Setup option in the Printer Setup dialog box when adding or deleting fonts, or switching to a different printer port, page orientation (portrait or landscape), or paper size. Printer Setup walks you through the process with the aid of detailed dialog boxes customized for your printer. If you need explanations of any of the options, click the Help button in the dialog box for details.

Printing

After your document looks exactly the way you want it to and you've set up your printer, printing is a snap. All you need to do is choose Print from the File menu and you'll see the following dialog box.

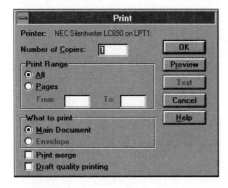

Works proposes to print one copy of the current document. If you want more, type the number you want in the Number of Copies box.

TIP: If you want to print part of a multiple-page document, click Pages in the Print Range box and fill in the From and To boxes with the starting and ending page numbers. For example, to print only page 43 of a document, enter the number 43 in the From box and 43 in the To box, and then click on OK. If you want to print from a certain page to the end of a document, enter the page you want to start with in the From box and a page number greater than the last page (such as 999) in the To box.

Coming Next

The medium is the message, so take advantage of all the formatting tools that Works provides. Practice using them judiciously so that your documents look as good as they read. In the next and last chapter on the Works word processor, we'll introduce some advanced topics such as headers, bookmarks, spelling check, and more.

6

Advanced Word Processing Features

B esides its formatting, graphics, and layout capabilities, the Microsoft Works 3 for Windows word processor offers a number of options that are bound to make your life easier. To finish coverage of this application, we'll take a look at these options. Some, such as the spelling checker, might become regular parts of your word processing routine. Others, such as search and replace, might become occasional assistants you'll appreciate in special circumstances.

Using Bookmarks

Unless you've got a photographic memory, you'll probably find yourself scrolling up and down in long documents, searching for information you want to refer to as you write about another topic.

One way to save a lot of time when you're working on a long document is to insert bookmarks at appropriate sections of the document. For example, you might insert a bookmark at each heading in a proposal or a report, at the top of a price list, or even at the beginning of a graphic.

Creating a Bookmark

Bookmarks are your computer equivalent of real bookmarks, paper clips, dog-eared pages, marking pens, and highlighters. A bookmark is a hidden marker that helps you find specific places in your document. Although your *raingear.wps* document isn't very long, use it in this exercise to see how easily you can create and use bookmarks.

1. Open the file named *raingear.wps*.

2. Scroll down to the beginning of the list of rainwear, which starts with umbrellas.

   You can place bookmarks anywhere in a document, but you'll probably want most of them at or near the beginning of a topic.

3. Place the insertion point at the beginning of the list, as shown here.

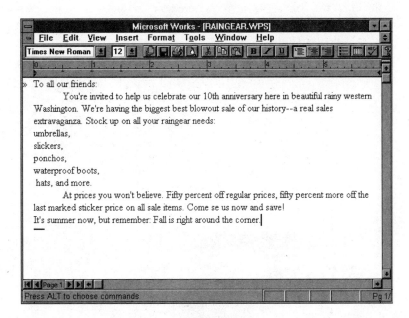

4. Open the Insert menu, and then choose Bookmark Name. The following dialog box appears.

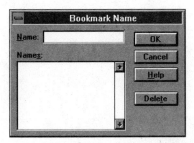

Here you will assign a name to the bookmark. After you have done so, Works will associate the name with the location you've marked, and you can return to that exact part of the document whenever you want.

5. For this example, type *product* in the Name box, and click OK.

Works displays the names of all assigned bookmarks in the Names portion of this dialog box, so when you assign names, try to make them descriptive and distinct. You can include spaces in a bookmark name, but if it is longer than 15 characters, Works will truncate or cut off the name. Even so, you can still use it to jump to the part of the document you marked.

Going to a Bookmark

Bookmarks are not visible on the Works screen, but they are there. To use one, follow these steps.

1. Scroll to the top of the document.

2. Open the Edit menu, and then choose Go To. The following dialog box appears.

This dialog box lists the names of all bookmarks you've assigned to a particular document.

TIP: You can also access Go To by pressing F5.

1. Double-click on the bookmark name that you want to go to. For example, to go to the bookmark you defined in the last section as *product,* simply double-click on the bookmark name, *product.* Almost instantly, Works jumps to the part of the document you marked.

If you create a bookmark and later decide you no longer need it, choose Bookmark Name from the Insert menu, select the bookmark name in the dialog box, click Delete, and then click Close. If you decide to rename a bookmark, go to the bookmark's place in the document, choose Bookmark Name from the Insert menu, and type a new name. When Works asks if you want to replace the existing bookmark, click OK. Once you've assigned a bookmark name, you cannot use that name again in the same document.

TIP: You can create another type of bookmark if you enter a unique set of characters, such as @#, in a document and then use the Works search feature (which you'll shortly learn about) to find them. This is a good away to mark your place—for example, when you quit editing a document. However, this bookmark will print, where a regular bookmark will not appear on any of your printed pages.

Creating Footnotes

Footnotes are an important part of professional papers and academic publications, and they can often be useful in other documents, too. Reports that include statistics, citations from other sources, and facts that you want to document outside the body of your text can easily be created with footnotes.

Typing and numbering footnotes can be a chore without a computer. Works makes the process much easier by taking over the drudgery of referencing them. Works places all the footnotes neatly at the end of the document—even though it does not look that way on the screen. Footnotes are more easily seen than described, so let's create one.

1. Clear the screen or open a new word processor document and type the text exactly as it appears here.

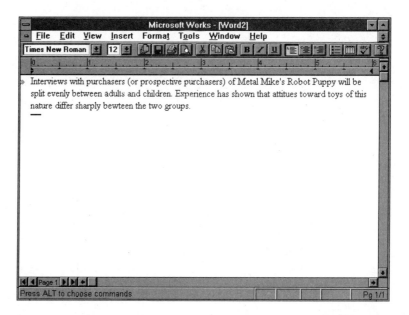

2. To add a footnote at the end, open the Insert menu, and then choose Footnote. The following dialog box appears.

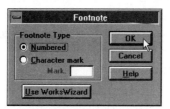

Choose Numbered footnotes (the default Footnote Type). Notice that Works lets you mark footnotes with either numbers or special symbols.

3. Click OK.

Your screen immediately changes to this display, which shows a separate footnote panel in the bottom of the window.

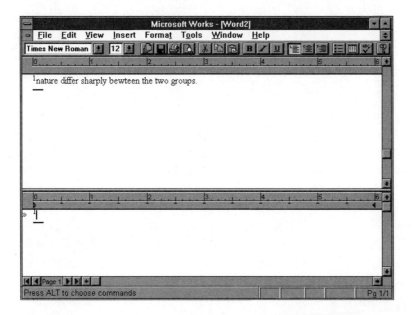

The new window at the bottom is a *footnote window*. Works displays footnotes in their own window, keeping them completely separate from the text to which they are attached. You can make the window larger or smaller by dragging the split bar at the top of the footnote window. You can also make the window disappear altogether by turning off Footnotes on the View menu. For this example, leave the window as it is.

Notice that Works has inserted a superscript 1 in the text and in the footnote window. Works keeps track of the numbering, so if you had already inserted four footnotes, a superscript 5 would have appeared here.

Works applies the font and font size you've chosen for the body of your document to both footnote reference numbers and footnote text. To conserve space and to minimize the visual impact of footnote-reference numbers in the text, you might want to print all footnote-related material in a smaller size.

1. Select the footnote reference mark in your text. Change it to a smaller size, such as 8.

2. Click in the footnote window, or press F6 to jump quickly between windows.

3. Next, type the following footnote text: *Based on prior surveys for SuperFantastic, Inc., manufacturers of the MechanoMiracle line of 25th Century Action Toys.*

After you've created footnotes, you can edit them in the footnote window and move reference numbers by cutting and pasting, just as you do with normal text. If you add or delete footnote references in the body of your text, Works renumbers the remaining footnotes for you.

Works prints the footnote on the current page. By opening the File menu and choosing Page Setup, then Other Options, you can have Works print the footnotes at the end of your document. If you choose to have Works print all footnotes at the end of a document, you'll probably want to preview your finished work and insert a manual page break to start all footnotes on a separate page. You can also add and format a heading, such as "References" or "Citations," at the top of the first footnote page to further distinguish the notes from your text.

Saving Time with Works

The tasks of creating, formatting, and laying out a document are yours, but Works can help you save time when you're grasping for a word that's just out of reach, when you want to check your spelling, when you want to find or replace specific text, and when you want to save formats to avoid duplicating your efforts.

Checking Spelling

Most people have trouble spelling certain words. Does *parallel* have one *r* or *two*? Does *embarrassment* really have all those double letters? Does *broccoli* have one *c* and two *l*'s?

Works has a dictionary of 120,000 words against which it checks the spelling in your documents. You can check an entire document, or you can limit the operation by selecting only the section you want to check.

In a new word processor window, type the following sentence. Be sure to enter the words as they are misspelled here: *Let us go nww, you and eye, where the sunlight drapes the sky. All the way to microsoft.*

Now let's check the spelling.

1. Place the insertion point at the beginning of the sentence.

2. Open the Tools menu, and then choose Spelling. Words automatically starts the spell-checking process.

3. To see a list of possible spellings, click the Suggest button.

   A list of possible word choices appears, among them the correct spelling, *now.*

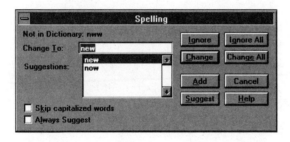

4. To correct the spelling in your document, highlight *now* in the Suggestions box.

5. Click the Change button.

The spelling checker then moves to the next word it does not recognize, telling you it has found irregular capitalization in the word Microsoft. Works knows this word should be capitalized because it is an entry in the Works dictionary.

Notice that Spelling skipped over *eye*, even though it should have been *I*. Works cannot check for correct usage, so remember to always proofread your documents for mistakes like this one.

TIP: Spelling checkers really check your typing, rather than your spelling and usage. Words like *eye* instead of *I*, *to* instead of *too*, *cent* instead of *scent*, and other homonyms (words that sound the same but have different meanings) will not be caught by the spelling checker.

The occurrence of *microsoft* is the last misspelling in your document, so before you correct it, take a moment to look at the remainder of the Spelling dialog box. The eight buttons along the right side let you do the following:

- Ignore: Disregard the spelling currently highlighted. (You'll probably want to do this with proper names.)

- Ignore All: Disregard all instances of that spelling.

- Change: Change the word in the document to the one highlighted in the Suggestions box.

- Change All: Change all occurrences of the highlighted spelling throughout the document.

- Add: Add the highlighted word to the Works dictionary. (You can do this with the names of people and companies that appear often in your documents.)

- Cancel: Quit the spelling checker.

- Suggest: Display a list of variant spellings.

■ Help: Display Help.

TIP: Do be careful with the Add option. If the spelling checker stops on a word and you want to add it to the dictionary, be absolutely sure that it is spelled correctly before you click Add. If you mistakenly add a word that is spelled incorrectly, Works will never identify the word as being unrecognized or spelled incorrectly.

At the bottom of the dialog box, you can also choose to

■ Skip capitalized words: (You might want to do this with proper names.)

■ Always Suggest: Provide alternatives without waiting for you to click the Suggest button.

As you can see, Spelling is both powerful and flexible. To finish up your example, complete the following steps.

1. Click the Suggest button and choose the correct spelling of Microsoft.

2. Click OK when Works tells you the spell check is complete.

The inclusion of Microsoft in Spelling's dictionary isn't rampant egomania. You'll find IBM, WordPerfect, and Macintosh in the dictionary, too.

Finding Synonyms

The Works Thesaurus is a large and nicely cross-referenced collection of synonyms for most common (and some uncommon) words. Let's try it out.

1. Type the following text in an open area of the document window: *Don't desert me now, luck. Serendipity is my middle name.*

2. Place the insertion point on the word *desert*.

3. Open the Tools menu, and then choose Thesaurus. You'll see the following dialog box.

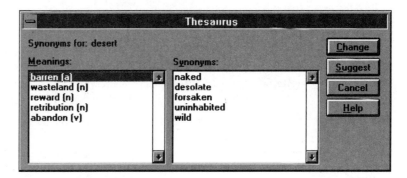

The box titled Meanings lists various definitions for desert, along with the part of speech, such as noun (n), verb (v), and adjective (a), each represents. The highlighted definition in the Meanings box corresponds to the list of words (naked, desolate, forsaken, etc.) displayed in the Synonyms box, all meaning *barren*.

4. Click on the word *abandon* in the Meanings box. The list of synonyms changes immediately.

At the right of the dialog box are four buttons labeled Change, Suggest, Cancel, and Help. These buttons perform the following functions:

❑ Change: Replace the selected word in your document with the highlighted word in the Meanings box.

❑ Suggest: Cause the Thesaurus to produce a new list of possible synonyms for the highlighted word.

❑ Cancel: Quit the Thesaurus.

❑ Help: Provide online help.

5. To finish up with the Thesaurus, highlight *forsake* in the list of synonyms for *desert*.

6. Click Change. The word in your document changes from *desert* to *forsake*.

> **TIP:** Even though Thesaurus can be quite helpful, there are limits to what it can do. If Works cannot find a synonym for a word you select, it will tell you so through a simple dialog box stating the word and No synonyms found.

Finding and Replacing Text

Works has two search commands: Find and Replace. Like bookmarks, Find can be useful when you need to search a document for specific text or for special characters, such as tabs and page breaks. Replace works like the Find command, except that it both finds text and special characters and replaces them with other text or special characters.

When you use Find, Works takes you to the first occurrence of the text you specify that follows the current position of the insertion point. If it is not the occurrence you seek, you can press the F7 key to continue the search.

When you use Replace, Works also takes you to the first occurrence of the text you specify following the insertion point. It then asks if you want to replace the text and, after following your instructions, goes on to the next occurrence, and the next, until it reaches the end of the document.

> **TIP:** Replace can also be used to speed up your typing. If you constantly use a particular word or term, such as *psychological* or *federal* or *Plato*, you can enter *psy* or *fdl* or *plt* and then replace that abbreviation with the complete text.

Unlike Spelling, which asks if you want to continue checking from the beginning when it reaches the end of the document, Find and Replace go to the end of the document and then stop. To search an entire document, be sure to *first* place the insertion point at the beginning of the document. It's a small matter, but one that can mean the difference between a complete and an incomplete search or replace operation. If you want to search just part of a document, highlight the portion to be searched before choosing the command.

Try out the Find command by following these steps.

1. Enter the text you see in the following screen.

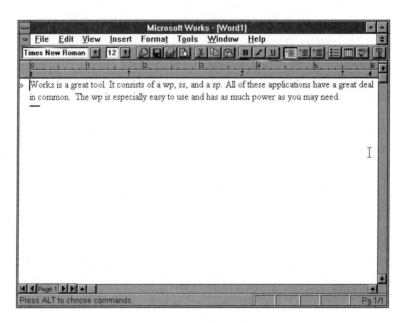

2. Place the insertion point at the top of the document.

3. Open the Edit menu, and then choose Find.

   Works displays this dialog box:

4. Type the text you want to find in the Find What box. In this example, we would enter the characters *wp*. The box is relatively small, but you can type more than it holds. Find searches for the entire set of characters.

5. Click OK. As you can see in the following screen, Works highlights the first occurrence of the characters that were specified in the Find dialog box.

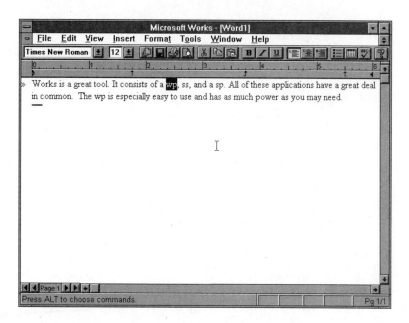

If you want to limit a search to whole words, check the Match Whole Word Only box. Doing this will eliminate those occurrences in which your text is part of a larger word, for example, the *works* in *fireworks* and *gasworks*. To search only for exact matches of uppercase and lowercase letters, click the Match Case box. Doing this finds *Works*, but not *WORKS* or *works*.

Now let's try the Replace command.

1. Move the insertion point back to the beginning of the document and open the Edit menu, and then choose Replace. The Replace dialog box (as you see on the next page) is almost identical to the Find dialog box. Replace, however, includes a Replace With box; here you type the text that is to replace the text in the Find What box. It also includes a Replace All button that you can click to replace, in one step, every occurrence of the specified text in the document. Use this option with care because all replacements

happen quickly. You can reverse all changes with the Undo command, but that will take you right back to where you started.

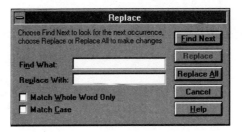

2. In the Find What box, enter *wp*. (This step will not be necessary if you first used Find. Works remembers your last search characters and automatically fills in the Find What box for you.)

3. In the Replace With box, enter *word processing*.

4. Click Replace All.

Works replaces all occurrences of *wp* with the words *word processing*.

Here's a warning well worth heeding. When you replace text, provide as much information for Works to search for as possible. For example, if you want to find the word *in* and replace it with *on*, don't search for the letter *i* and replace it with the letter *o*. In that case, the words *into*, *find*, and *fiction* would become *onto*, *fond*, and *foctoon*! If you do search for words that can be part of larger words (such as *in* or *on*), search for the entire word by placing a space before and after the word in the Find box.

Wildcard Searches

If you're not certain about the spelling of a word you want to find, you can use the question mark (?) as a wildcard character to take the place of any other single character. For example, if you want to find *pin*, *pan*, and *pun*, you can type *p?n* in the Find box. Similarly, to find both *soon* and *seen*, you can type the search text as *s??n*.

To search for or replace special characters, use the following codes in the Find and Replace dialog boxes.

Use This Code	To Find or Replace
^t	Tabs
^p	Paragraph marks
^n	End-of-line characters
^d	Manual page breaks
^s	Non-breaking spaces
^	Caret marks
^?	Question marks
^w	White space (combination of tabs, spaces, and nonbreaking spaces, or non-breaking spaces alone)

You can put these special characters to good use when jumping from page to page of a document. You can also use them to clean up files (such as those that are transferred over phone lines) that contain unneeded paragraph marks or that contain blank spaces instead of tabs. For example, a document might contain two paragraph marks between paragraphs, but you want only one. Type ^p^p in the Find What box, ^p in the Replace With box, and click OK. To delete unwanted characters, type the characters in the Find What box, but leave the Replace With box blank.

The Find and Replace features may take some time to learn, but they can really be worth the investment. Just think about how easy it will be to find extra spaces placed after periods in a 100-page document and change them all to only one space.

TIP: Before using Replace, it is a good work habit to save your document first. Should you make an error, you can easily recover your previous version.

Headers and Footers

A *header* is any text that repeats at the top of the pages in your document. Likewise, a *footer* is text that repeats at the bottom of the pages. You can create a *standard header* (a single line) or a *paragraph header* (multiline). Both are controlled by the same command.

Let's see how both a header and a footer are created.

1. Open the View menu, and then choose Headers and Footers. You'll see the following dialog box.

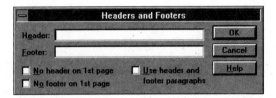

2. Enter the text you want to appear as a header or footer.

3. Click OK.

To create *standard running heads*, you use the Header and Footer boxes. To create *paragraph running heads*, click the box next to Use header and footer paragraphs. When you don't want a header or footer on the first page, click the boxes next to No header (or No footer) on 1st page.

Standard Headers and Footers

Standard running heads are single lines that you create by typing text in the Headers and Footers dialog box. You don't see standard headers and footers as you work, but Works displays them in Print Preview and, of course, it prints them on your documents.

By default, standard headers and footers are centered horizontally on the page. You can, however, use the codes on the following page, each beginning with an ampersand (&), to alter their alignment and to add special elements, such as the page number or the date.

This Code	Does This in the Header
&l	Align left
&r	Align right
&c	Center
&p	Print page number
&d	Print short date (1/01/94)
&n	Print long date (January 1, 1994)
&t	Print time (01:01 PM)
&f	Print filename
&&	Print an ampersand

You can include more than one code in a single header or footer. Even though they might strike you as cryptic, the codes offer considerable flexibility. Alignment codes affect all text that follows; they stay in effect until you type another code. Try this in a clean word processing screen.

1. Open the View menu, and then choose Headers and Footers.

2. Type the following (using either uppercase or lowercase) in the Header box: *&LMY DOCUMENT: &F&C&P&R&D &T.* (Be sure to include the spaces.)

3. Click OK.

This is what you've told Works to do to your header: Left align (&L) the characters MY DOCUMENT: on the page; leave a space and print the filename (&F); center (&C) and insert the page number (&P); and right align (&R) the date (&D) and time (&T).

TIP: You can edit a header or footer just by choosing Headers and Footers from the View menu. The active header and footer will show up in the dialog box and you can edit it as you see fit.

4. To see the result, click the Print Preview button on the toolbar and zoom in.

You should see something like the following illusration.

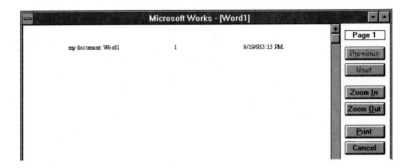

Headers can add lots of information to a document and make it more accessible to readers.

Paragraph Headers and Footers

Standard headers and footers are limited to a single line of text. If you want a multiline running head, or if you simply prefer to see your running heads on screen, create paragraph headers and footers instead.

Let's now create one of those. Be sure you are in Normal view.

1. Open the View menu, and then choose Headers and Footers.

2. In the Headers and Footers dialog box, click the check box next to Use header and footer paragraphs.

3. Click OK.

This time, Works displays two special paragraphs at the top of the document.

4. Following F (for the footer), type *This is an example of a multiline paragraph footer*. Press Shift+Enter. Type *Here's the second line*.

You do not have to include both headers and footers simply because Works displays a paragraph for each. If you don't want one of these elements, simply leave the paragraph blank or delete any text that appears there.

Header and footer paragraphs are formatted by default with left alignment and two tab stops, one centered in the middle of the page and another right aligned at the right margin. You can add others if you want.

5. Click the Print Preview button on the toolbar and switch to the Page Layout View to see the multiline footer.

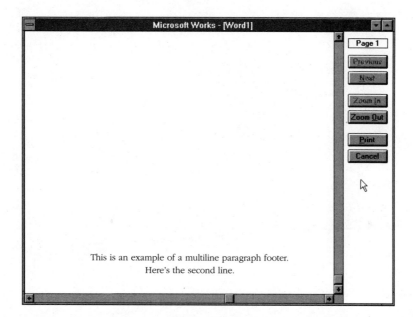

There is one other important difference between standard running heads and paragraph running heads. In a paragraph header or footer, you don't use the special codes, such as &P. If you try, Works simply prints those characters.

There's another way to format a paragraph header or footer so that you can use special characters. It's easier than using codes; we're about to show you how to do it now.

Special Characters

Page numbers, the date, the time, and filenames are useful items of information for a running head (or for other parts of a document, for that matter). Works has special internal codes for these items, which you can add to a document whenever, and wherever, you choose. Here's how to use them.

1. Open the Insert menu, and then choose the Special Character command. The Special Character dialog box appears, as shown here.

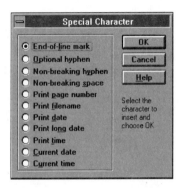

2. To insert any of these special characters in a running head, or elsewhere in a document, select the one you want.

3. Click OK.

The following table lists the characters and describes what they do.

Character	Meaning
End-of-line mark	Start a new line; displayed if All Characters is on (Keyboard: Press Shift+Enter)
Optional hyphen	Hyphenates a word if it must be broken at the end of a line; displayed as a hyphen; appears if All Characters is on (Keyboard: Press Ctrl+Hyphen)
Non-breaking hyphen	Prevents a hyphenated word from breaking at the end of a line; displayed the same as the optional hyphen (Keyboard: Press Ctrl+Shift+Hyphen)
Non-breaking space	Prevents related words from being broken at the end of a line (Keyboard: Press Ctrl+Shift+Spacebar)
Print page number	Inserts the current page number in a document; displayed as *page*; always shown on screen

Character	Meaning
Print filename	Inserts document's filename; displayed as *filename*; always shown on screen
Print date	Inserts the date, in short form (for example, 1/01/94), that the document is printed; displayed as *date*; always shown on screen
Print long date	Inserts the date, in long form (for example, January 1, 1994), that the document is printed; displayed as *longdate*; always shown on screen
Print time	Inserts the time of printing; displayed as *time*; always shown on screen
Current date	Inserts current date in short form (Keyboard: Press Ctrl+Semicolon)
Current time	Inserts current time (Keyboard: Press Ctrl+Shift+Semicolon)

These special codes can be used to dress up your documents. For example, a letter might contain the special character for inserting a date. That way, whenever you print the letter, the date of the printing (not the *writing* of the letter) will be inserted. The time and date in a header can help you distinguish between different drafts of a document.

Header Margins

Increasing the default values for the top and bottom margins can be especially important if you plan to include running heads in a document. Works prints running heads and footers within the top and bottom margins. If you use the defaults, it will print a top running head, or header, 0.5 inch from the top of the page and a bottom running footer 0.75 inch from the bottom.

To see an example, follow these steps.

1. Open the View menu, and then choose Headers and Footers.

2. Type the text for the header in the Header portion of the Headers and Footers dialog box.

3. Click OK.

Nothing appears on your screen if you are in the Draft View, but don't worry. Works will print the word *header* at the top of every page.

4. To see this header in relation to some text, center the following text: *This is a sample line of text I'm typing to see how close it will be to my new header.*

5. Now click on the Print Preview button on the toolbar. To see a close up, click the Zoom In button. You can also switch to the page layout view.

6. To see how the preview page corresponds to a printout, verify that your printer is on and click the Print button.

7. Click OK in the Print dialog box that appears.

To change the spacing between the header and the text, open the File menu, choose Page Setup, and then select Margins. Specify a larger or smaller value for the header margin so that it prints closer to or further from the top of the page. The footer margin is adjusted the same way.

TIP: On some printers, such as the Hewlett-Packard LaserJet, headers and footers don't print exactly where the margin settings indicate because the printer has small "unprintable" regions at the top and bottom (and sides) of the page. Check your printer manual or experiment a little to determine how close your printer comes to the actual edge of the page.

Working with Hyphens and Spaces

You know about word wrap, that wonderful feature that automatically places full words that can't fit on one line on the next line. But not all lines end conveniently. For example, an especially long word that cannot fit on one line will have to go to the next, and depending upon the justification you select, the initial line might look quite odd. A fully justified line consisting of a few long words will have extra space between the words and letters.

Normally, if Works cannot fit an entire word at the end of a line, it simply moves the word to the next line. Sometimes, however, you want to hyphenate words at the end of a line to make the line endings less ragged or to decrease extra space between words in a justified paragraph. Chances are you won't need to do this type of fine-tuning very often, because most documents look fine without such niceties. A little tinkering, however, can be useful when an important document, proposal, business plan, or prospectus must look as good as possible.

Hyphens

A hyphen by any name might seem like a hyphen but, as you can see from the list of special characters shown previously, Works actually recognizes three different types of hyphens:

- Those you normally type, as in the word *double-click*

- Those you want to use only if a word cannot fit at the end of a line

- Those you want to use at all times to prevent a hyphenated word from being broken at the end of a line

To see how these hyphens work, set your current font and font size to Times New Roman 12. Check that the right margin is at 6 inches and verify that All Characters in the View menu is turned on. Now type the following paragraph:

It·was·a·dark·and·stormy·night.·The·wind·howled·through·the·bleak·bones·of·the· willow·trees.·Hollow·branches·clicked·in·frantic·rhythm,·the·long,·skeletal·fingers·of· departed·misers·clutching·for·their·lost·gold.·Sad·and·tired,·Mrs.·Haversham- Bavisham·hurried,·bent·and·bundled,·along·the·winding·road·while·will-of-the-wisp· ghost·lights·danced·madly·in·the·fog·rising·from·the·slough.¶

If the text on your screen doesn't break in the same places as the example, you should change the right paragraph indents with the mouse or change the margins with the Page Setup command, Margins tab, from the File menu.

Now let's fiddle with the line endings. Suppose you decide that Haversham-Bavisham, a hyphenated name, should not break at the end of a line, as it does now. Here's how to fix it.

1. Select the hyphen in the name.

2. Delete it.

3. Replace it by inserting a non-breaking hyphen from the Special Character list.

The non-breaking hyphen tells Works to keep the name together, which it does by moving the entire name to the next line. Now, however, you've got a considerable gap to fill at the end of one line. One way to fix this is by hyphenating words. Here's how to do that.

1. Move the insertion point before the word *fingers*.

2. Insert an optional end-of-line mark from the Special Character list.

That did it. The text looks much more attractively formatted. As you saw in this example, displaying special characters can produce inaccurate line breaks on the screen because more space is needed to display them. If you insert a lot of optional hyphens in a document, check the finished layout before printing by turning off All Characters or by using Print Preview or the page layout view.

Creating Tables

By far, the easiest way to create a table in Works is to use the spreadsheet application, then transfer it into the word processor. Although you'll find the Works spreadsheet much easier for creating tables, you might want to use the word processor for simple tables or for those in which one column contains multiple lines of text.

To create columns in a table, set tabs where you want them. Depending on the type of table you create, you can make each line a separate paragraph or, for ease of handling, you can make the body of the table a single paragraph, ending each line with an end-of-line character. Here are two short examples.

To create a simple table in which headings form one paragraph and the body forms another, follow these steps.

1. Move the insertion point to an open area of the screen and press Enter to create a new paragraph.

2. Insert left-aligned tab stops at 2 inches and at 4 inches.

3. Type the table shown here.

Breed	Color	Price¶
German·Shepard	Black/Tan	$300¶
Collie	Brown/White	$250¶
Boxer	Tan	$275¶

To create a table in which one column contains more lines than the others, make each line of the table a separate paragraph and use paragraph indents to align the lines of one column correctly.

1. Create a new table with the same tab stops as in the preceding example.

2. To allow for a multiple line column, open the Format menu, and then choose Indent and Spacing.

3. Give the body paragraph a left indent of 4 inches and a first-line indent of 4 inches.

4. Type the following table.

Breed	→	Price	→	Description¶
German·Shepard	→	$300	→	Active,·alert,· protective··yet· gentle·with·its· family¶
Collie	→	$250	→	Quiet,·devoted,· needs·considerable· grooming¶
Boxer	→	$275	→	Easy·to·care·for,· active,·good· playmate¶

In some tables, you'll probably want to create headings as separate paragraphs. By doing this, you can center or otherwise align them separately above the columns.

Coming Next

We're done with the word processor. Now you should know enough to create a stunning wedding invitation, that final term paper, or the growth report your boss has been hounding you about. Now it's time to move on to the Works spreadsheet, and learn how to manipulate and organize numbers and produce show-stopping graphs of those numbers.

Using the
Spreadsheet

7

Getting Started with the Spreadsheet

Working with Numbers 199

The main attraction. Just as with text, we can work with numbers and change the way they appear (for the better, we hope).

Formatting Your Work 205

You will explore ways to organize rows of information and find text or numbers that need to be modified, and will look at the new Works shading feature.

Printing a Spreadsheet 212

Finally, you'll find out how to print the entire Works spreadsheet or a particular section.

TFrom the time you're small, you use both words and numbers to communicate. Eventually, words become your primary vehicle for communicating thoughts and ideas; numbers satisfy the need to organize, understand, and communicate data. In business, at home, and at school, the Works spreadsheet can help you manage the ever-growing quantity of numbers that sometimes seem to dominate our everyday activities. With the Works spreadsheet, you are in control of the numbers!

This chapter takes you into the world of the spreadsheet—an electronic ledger sheet that you can use to build, organize, and print numerical information without resorting to pencils and erasers. You'll find the basics here—entering, editing, and printing data. In Chapter 8 (page 215), you'll learn how to work with formulas and functions. In Chapter 9 (page 251), you'll see how to turn data into charts.

Say Hello to the Spreadsheet

Because Works is a Windows application, you've already seen and used many of the procedures in word processing, such as copying and moving data, that you'll use in working with spreadsheets. The best way to learn is by doing, so let's start right now with some illustrative examples of what the spreadsheet can do.

1. If necessary, start Works.

2. Click on the Spreadsheet button in the Startup dialog box to start the spreadsheet with a blank workspace.

3. Maximize the application and document windows.

   Works displays a blank spreadsheet like the one on the next page.

   As you can see in the illustration on the next page, Works assigns the name Sheet1 to the as-yet unsaved spreadsheet.

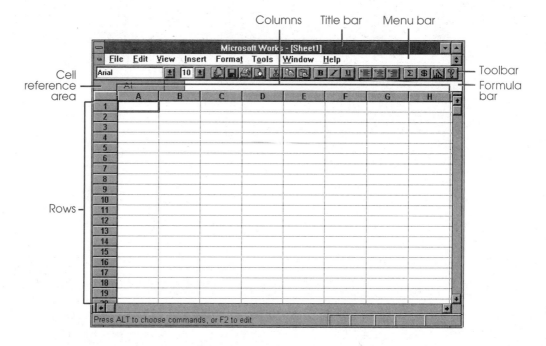

The Spreadsheet Cell

At first glance, the spreadsheet window appears a lot busier than a word processor window, primarily because the spreadsheet displays a grid of cells. Each cell is capable of holding text, a numeric value, a date, or a formula used to calculate new values.

Each cell in a spreadsheet has a unique *address*, composed of its column letter and row number (for example, A1, A2, B1, B2, and so on). Altogether, a single Works spreadsheet contains 256 columns and 16,384 rows, for a total of 4,194,304 cells. The first 26 columns are lettered A through Z; succeeding columns are lettered AA through AZ, BA through BZ, and so on, ending with column IV at the extreme right edge of the sheet. Rows are numbered sequentially; the last row is 16384, and the last cell in a sheet, in the bottom right corner, is cell IV16384, which represents the junction of column IV and row 16384.

Think about it: The number of rows and columns in a Works spreadsheet allows for the entry of data into more than 4,000,000 (4,194,304 to be exact) cells! That's a lot of information. You may never use all these cells, but some people do. The size of a worksheet alone will give you some idea of the capabilities the Works spreadsheet offers.

Using the Toolbar

Many window elements in the spreadsheet—scroll bars, the title bar, control buttons, and the status bar at the bottom of the window—are identical to the window elements in the word processor.

The toolbar in the spreadsheet also is similar to the toolbar in the word processor. But, three of the buttons differ, to give you easy access to often-used spreadsheet features. Here's what the toolbar looks like.

Specifically, the three toolbar buttons to the left of the Learning Works button are different. The Autosum button adds the values in the rows or columns. The Currency button formats in currency. Finally, the New Chart button creates a visual image of selected spreadsheet data.

Remember that, as with any toolbar, you can remove existing buttons, or add new ones, by using the procedures described in Chapter 3 (page 57).

Using the Formula Bar

Another important element in the spreadsheet window is the formula bar, located below the toolbar. The formula bar consists primarily of a space where Works displays whatever text, value, or mathematical formula will be inserted into the currently highlighted cell. You can both view and edit cell contents in the formula bar.

To the left of the formula bar are several related elements. The Cancel button and the Currency button are visible only after you type letters or numbers that appear in the formula bar.

The cell reference area displays the address of the currently active cell. The Cancel and Enter buttons let you use the mouse in place of the Esc or Enter keys to cancel or accept what you've typed into the cell.

To see how the formula bar and the Cancel and Enter buttons work, do the following.

1. Click on any blank cell. It doesn't matter where you click, because you'll clear the screen later.

2. Type *1234567890*.

   As you type, notice that the characters in the cell "scroll" to make room for new numbers. Works will remember everything you type and assign it to the proper cell, even if the cell is too narrow to display all your typing at once. The formula bar, however, displays all of the cell's contents.

3. Cancel the entry by clicking the X on the Cancel button. The text disappears. (You can also cancel the entry by pressing the Escape key.)

Now let's try the Enter button and, at the same time, see what happens to an entry that's too long to display in a cell.

1. Type *Pepperoni Pizza* in any cell.

2. Click the check mark on the Enter button to complete the entry. (You can also complete the entry by pressing Enter or Tab.)

Works displays your text in both the highlighted cell and the cell to its right. You can see all of a cell's contents if the adjacent cell is vacant. Now try something else.

1. Click in the cell to the right of the one in which you entered text.

2. Type *12345*, and click the Enter button.

The original text now appears only in its own cell. You haven't lost any text, even though the cell displays only a small portion of it; the formula bar displays the entire contents of the cell when you highlight it

In general, you can enter data in a spreadsheet cell by using the following steps.

1. Place the mouse pointer on the cell where you want to enter data.

2. Click once to make the cell active. It will appear with a dark border.

3. Enter the data as shown here.

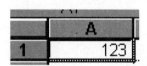

4. Click on the Enter box (the one with the check mark) or press the Enter key.

Editing Cell Contents

When you use the spreadsheet, you edit the contents of cells only in the formula bar, not in the cells themselves. You can clear, replace, or edit the contents of a cell by following these procedures.

- To clear a cell, select it and press the Del key.

- To replace the contents of a cell, select the cell and simply type the new entry.

- To edit the contents of a cell, select the cell and click in the formula bar or press F2. When you do this, the mouse pointer becomes an insertion point (which puts you in the EDIT mode, as the status bar at the bottom of the window will show).

When you're editing cell contents, you can position the insertion point simply by pointing to the location you want and clicking. The procedure is just like the one you learned when you practiced editing text in the word processor. You can drag the mouse to highlight one or more characters for deletion or replacement. You can also use the keys in the following table to control the insertion point and to highlight characters in the formula bar.

Key	Effect
Home	Move to beginning of entry
End	Move to end of entry
Left and Right arrow keys	Move the insertion point one character left or right
Ctrl+Left arrow and Ctrl+Right arrow	Move the insertion point to the beginning or end of a word
Shift+Left arrow and Shift+Right arrow	Extend highlight over one or more characters
Del	Delete selected characters or (if no characters are selected) delete the next character to the right

TIP: A single cell can hold up to 255 characters, so even the formula bar isn't wide enough to display the entire contents in some circumstances. When that happens, you can jump back and forth in the formula bar using the Home and End keys, plus the Left and Right arrow keys.

Now it's time to work with the spreadsheet itself. To clear existing entries and start over, follow these steps.

1. Highlight all the cells containing what you've typed so far by clicking and dragging the mouse

TIP: To select all the cells in a spreadsheet, you can also click in the cell above row 1 and to the left of column A.

2. Open the Edit menu, and then choose Clear.

3. Click on cell A1 to reduce the highlight to a single cell.

Working with Cell Ranges

Building a spreadsheet lets you organize data so that it is easy to compare, contrast, summarize, and calculate information. You often work with values in groups of cells, called a *range*, that encompasses as few as two cells to all the cells in the spreadsheet.

To select all the cells in a spreadsheet, open the Edit menu, and then choose Select All. (When you want to deselect, you click anywhere in the spreadsheet.)

Even though you can't see it, Works is highlighting the entire spreadsheet. In the cell reference area, you see the notation A1:IV16384. When a range of cells is selected, Works identifies the range by displaying an address of the top left cell, a colon, and the address of the bottom right cell. Because the entire spreadsheet is selected here, Works displays the range as A1 through (:) IV16384 as you see in Figure 7-1.

FIGURE 7-1.
The cell range.

A range is any group of cells that forms a rectangle. Each cell in the range must share at least one border with another cell. You can't highlight cells in a diamond shape, an L shape, or any other nonrectangular shape. Nor can you select more than one range at once. If you try to do this, the first range of cells you have selected will be deselected as soon as you start to create the second range.

A range can be as small as two adjoining cells or as large as all cells in the spreadsheet. You'll use ranges for many tasks, including adding columns of numbers, applying formatting, choosing values to chart, and especially creating formulas that perform calculations.

To put the Works spreadsheet module to work, build a sample spreadsheet by entering the headings and numbers shown in the following illustration. You can use the Tab and arrow keys to move easily from cell to cell. Be sure you press Enter to complete the last entry of the sample.

Your screen should look like the one shown here.

	A	B	C	D	E	F	G	H
2		Small	Medium	Large	Total			
3	Cheese	57	32	29				
4	Sausage	97	143	168				
5	Pepperoni	102	169	185				
6	Anchovy	23	17	9				
7	Vegetarian	49	73	53				
8								
9	Price							
10	Small	7.95						
11	Medium	9.95						
12	Large	12.95						

Microsoft Works - [PIZZA.WKS]

File Edit View Insert Format Tools Window Help

Press ALT to choose commands, or F2 to edit.

As you can see in the title bar, we saved the file and named it *pizza*. Works attaches the extension .WKS to a spreadsheet when it saves it for the first time. Save the worksheet you created.By the way, just like the word processor, the spreadsheet offers the spelling check option. You can find it on the Tools menu; now would be a good time to try it.

Working with Data

There's a lot to learn about using a spreadsheet. Let's begin with how to move around. Then we'll look at how to copy and move data; we will finish with some ideas about working with cells, columns, and rows.

Moving Around

Many spreadsheets are too large to display on a single screen. One easy way to move from place to place in a large spreadsheet is to use the Go To command, located in the Edit menu. Using this command (or the F5 function key) you can move directly to a cell. Go To is a natural with named cells, but it can also be used to jump to specific cells or cell ranges. Instead of typing a name, you simply type the cell reference, as shown here.

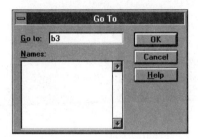

When you carry out the command, Works will jump to the cell or cell range you specified and highlight it.

As you work with a spreadsheet, you'll also want to scroll or move from place to place. The scroll bars are obvious mechanisms for moving quickly, but you can also use the keyboard. The following table lists useful keys for moving around in a spreadsheet. Notice that these keys can be used for moving in the spreadsheet only if you aren't currently editing in the formula bar.

Key	Result
Left arrow or Right arrow	Left or right one cell
Up arrow or Down arrow	Up or down one row
Home	First cell in current row
End	Last column containing data in any row

Key	Result
Ctrl+Home	Top left corner of the spreadsheet
Ctrl+End	Last cell in the bottom right corner. This cell is in the last row and the last column that contain data or formatting. The cell itself does not necessarily contain data or formatting
PgUp or PgDown	Up or down one screen
Ctrl+PgUp or Ctrl+PgDown	Left or right one screen
Ctrl+Left arrow or Ctrl+Right arrow	Left or right to the beginning or end of the current or next block of cells
Ctrl+Up arrow or Ctrl+Down arrow	Up or down to the beginning or end of the current or next block of cells.

Moving and Copying Data

Moving information on a spreadsheet is generally synonymous with organizing or reorganizing a spreadsheet. Although copying is as easy as moving information, it is a little harder to define because there are several ways to copy spreadsheet information. You might want to enter the same data or formula in a number of cells, you might want to copy cell contents to another part of the same spreadsheet, or you might want to copy all or part of one spreadsheet to another.

Entering Data in Multiple Cells

There's another way to fill cells with the same information, using the keyboard shortcut Ctrl+Enter. You can use this key combination to enter data or formulas. When you use the Fill command, Works copies the information of the top cell in the selection to the highlighted cells below it. You can use this command to fill adjacent cells in a column or row. For example, suppose you want to fill a set of cells with the number 123. Proceed as follows.

1. Open a new spreadsheet.

2. Select cells A1 through D7.

3. Type *123* but don't click the Enter button or press a key. Instead, press Ctrl+Enter.

Works immediately fills the selected cells with the same data as you can see here.

Moving and Copying Values

You can move and copy values to any area in the same spreadsheet or a different spreadsheet. It doesn't matter if the values are those you've entered as data or those you've calculated with formulas.

To move or copy data to the Clipboard, you use the Cut and Copy commands, which work exactly as they do in the word processor. You can copy cells or cell ranges in either rows or columns, but you can't alter the orientation of a range. If the cells you copy are in a column, you can't duplicate them in a row, nor can you reorient a row to become a column. Try copying values, using the 123 data you just entered by following these steps.

1. Select cells A1 through A7.

2. Copy the selected cells to the Clipboard by opening the Edit menu, and then choosing the Copy command, or by using the Ctrl+C key combination.

3. Select cell E1.

4. From the Edit menu, choose Paste.

Works copies the contents of the Clipboard to column E, placing the first of the copied cells in E1 as you see here.

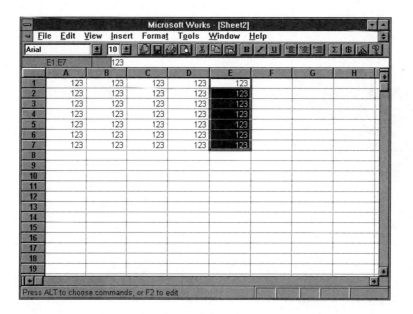

When you copy or move a range of cells, remember that Works uses the selected destination cell as the top left corner of the incoming range. Be sure that there are no cells containing data or formulas within the area to be filled by the copy. If cells in this area do contain data or formulas, the information they hold will be overwritten by the contents of the copied cells.

Working with Cells, Columns, and Rows

You can control the appearance, display, and behavior of your spreadsheets in several ways. By default, Works displays the toolbar; it also displays gridlines on the screen, although it doesn't print them unless you choose to do so with the Page Setup command, Other Option tab, on the File menu. The following sections describe the commands you use to control Works.

Displaying Gridlines

If you find that the dotted gridlines on the screen get in your way, you can turn them off and on at will. Here's how we turned off the gridlines in the *pizza.wks* spreadsheet you see here.

■ From the View menu, choose Gridlines.

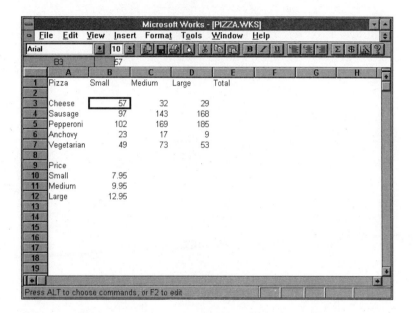

Even though the gridlines are turned off, the rectangular cell highlight encloses the cell's total area and jumps from cell to cell, as it does when gridlines are turned on. You can see that cell B3 is highlighted.

Freezing Row and Column Titles

When you're working on or printing a large spreadsheet, you can *freeze* row and column titles. Doing this keeps the titles on screen at all times and causes Works to print them on each page of a multiple-page spreadsheet. If you didn't freeze the titles, once you scrolled you would see rows and columns without their titles.

To freeze column titles, follow these steps.

1. Select a cell in column A, below the titles you want to freeze.

2. Open the Format menu, and then choose Freeze Titles. No matter how far down the spreadsheet you scroll, the frozen column titles will remain on screen.

To freeze row titles, follow these steps

1. Select a cell in row 1 to the right of the last title you want to freeze.

2. Open the Format menu, and then choose Freeze Titles. No matter how far to the right you scroll, the frozen row titles will always be displayed.

To freeze both row and column titles, follow these steps.

1. Select a cell below and to the right of the last column and row title you want to freeze.

2. Open the Format menu, and then choose Freeze Titles. No matter how far down or to the right you scroll, the titles will remain on screen.

Working with frozen titles can feel awkward at first because you cannot scroll into or select the titles, although you can use the Go To command to highlight them. Clicking on a frozen title causes Works to scroll to that location and display both the title and its associated data, but outside the frozen area of the screen.

The first time you try this, you might think you are seeing double as Works duplicates the frozen area elsewhere on the screen. All told, however, freezing provides a terrific way to view both titles and the offscreen data related to them. To see what freezing does, follow these steps.

1. Open or return to your *pizza.wks* spreadsheet.

2. To freeze the titles in row 1, select cell A2 and open the Format menu, and then choose the Freeze Titles command.

3. Use the vertical scroll bar to scroll downward. No matter how far you go, the titles remain on screen.

4. To freeze the titles in column A, turn off the Freeze Titles command (by choosing it again), select cell B1, and choose the Freeze Titles

command from the Format menu again. Now the titles remain on screen, no matter how far to the right you scroll.

5. To freeze both the row and column headings, turn off the Freeze Titles command, select cell B2, and choose the command again. Now both row and column titles remain on screen as you see in Figure 7-2. Notice that column B is not shown because it is scrolled behind the frozen column A.

	A	C	D	E	F	G	H	I
1	Pizza	Medium	Large	Total				
2								
3	Cheese	32	29					
4	Sausage	143	168					
5	Pepperoni	169	185					
6	Anchovy	17	9					
7	Vegetarian	73	53					
8								
9	Price							
10	Small							
11	Medium							
12	Large							
13								
14								
15								
16								
17								
18								
19								

Microsoft Works - [PIZZA.WKS]
File Edit View Insert Format Tools Window Help
Arial   10
B2
Press ALT to choose commands, or F2 to edit

FIGURE 7-2.
Freezing both row and column titles.

6. Turn off the Freeze Titles command again for now.

Another way to view different parts of a large spreadsheet is to split the window and scroll to the areas you want to view. You've already split a window and scrolled in a document with the word processor. It works the same way in the spreadsheet. Drag on the split bar (the mouse pointer changes to a bar labeled Adjust) until you create the approximate size of the second spreadsheet window.

Protecting Spreadsheet Information

Protecting information is vital in certain spreadsheets. When you protect or "lock" data or formulas, you ensure that they can't be changed or deleted accidentally. Essentially, protected cells become what is known as *read-only cells*, whose contents cannot be changed. To protect information, you use the Protection command from the Format menu.

To see how locking works, use the *pizza.wks* spreadsheet and do the following.

1. Select the values in cells B3 through D7.

2. Open the Format menu, and then choose Protection. When Works displays the dialog box you see here, verify that the Locked option at the top of the box is checked to indicate it's turned on. Select Protect Data and click OK.

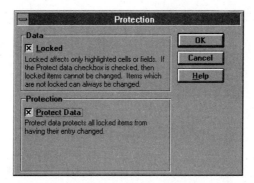

Now cells B3 through D7 are secure from change. To see what happens and to test the protection, do the following.

1. Select locked cell B3.

2. Type the value *32*.

3. Click the Enter button.

Instead of changing the value as it normally would, Works displays the following dialog box.

Now to unlock or unprotect the data, do the following.

1. Click OK to eliminate the dialog box.

2. Select cell B3.

3. Open the Format menu, and then choose Protection.

4. Click the Locked check box to deselect it.

5. Click OK.

6. Now try to enter a value in cell B3. It works!

As you can see, you can change some data while protecting other data.

That's all it takes. You can selectively lock or unlock one cell or all the cells in a worksheet.

TIP: Don't use cell protection unless you need it, because there is no way to tell what cells are protected once that process is complete. If you are in doubt, select all the cells in the spreadsheet and then unlock them.

Hiding Cells

Another way to protect data and formulas, or at least remove them from open view, is to actually hide the cells in which the data or formulas appear. Although this approach is less effective than locking, it is useful when you want to temporarily eliminate columns that intervene between two or more sections of a spreadsheet where you want to work. Even when columns are hidden, Works remains aware of their contents and accurately calculates any formulas.

To hide columns, simply reduce their width to nothing. To hide a single column by using the mouse, do the following.

1. Point to the boundary between any two columns. The mouse pointer changes to a bar labeled Adjust, with a two-headed arrow running through it, as shown here.

FIGURE 7-3.
The mouse pointer, changed to a bar labeled Adjust.

2. Drag the boundary left, all the way to the edge of the next column. Release the mouse pointer, and the column disappears.

When you "hide" columns, Works does not change the remaining column letters. In our example, column C is now missing from the column labels. Because of this, hidden columns should not be considered a true security measure. Anyone who knows Works will detect that a column is hidden and will know how to redisplay the missing columns.

To hide more than a single column, follow these steps.

1. Select more than one column by dragging across the column headings.

2. Open the Format menu, and then choose the Column Width command. Works will display the following dialog box.

You use this dialog box not only to hide columns, but also to change their widths. Simply type the width (in number of characters), and click OK.

To reduce the column widths to nothing in this example, type 0 (zero), and click OK.

To redisplay the columns once they have been hidden, follow these steps.

1. Open the Edit menu, and then choose the Go To command.

2. Enter the cell references you want to redisplay, for a single cell or multiple cells. For example, in the *pizza.wks* spreadsheet, if you hide columns B and C, then enter *B1:C12* in the GoTo dialog box.

3. Click OK.

Although the columns are hidden, Works displays a small, double-thick gridline between columns A and D in our example. This indicates that the hidden columns are now selected; you can return them to a visible width by doing thhe following.

1. Open the Format menu, and then choose Column Width.

2. Either click OK to accept the default width of 10 or type a new width and then click OK.

The hidden columns return to the screen.

Inserting and Deleting Rows and Columns

A spreadsheet doesn't spring into being at the click of a mouse button. It takes time, patience, and experimentation before you get it right. Suppose you've been entering data and you suddenly realize you forgot to allow an extra column or row for a needed element.

Chances are this will happen to you more than once because you'll be concentrating on what you want the spreadsheet to do, rather than on how you want it to look. As the spreadsheet takes shape, you'll find places where you could use an extra row or column for displaying information you hadn't originally thought about including. Conversely, you'll sometimes want to delete extra rows or columns that you allowed for but now don't need. You might also want to select and delete rows or columns to "erase" information or cell formatting.

When you need to add or delete rows or columns, you can do so with the Row/Column and Delete Row/Column commands on the Insert menu. You can use these commands at any time.

To insert or delete a row or a column, you must first tell Works where you want the insertion or deletion to be. You do this by selecting a row or column.

To select an entire row, point to the row number and click. Works highlights the row.

To select an entire column, point to the column letter and click. Again, Works highlights the column.

To try inserting and deleting columns, return to our favorite *pizza.wks* spreadsheet (hungry, yet?). If the file is still open, choose its name from the Window menu; if part of the file is visible, just click on it. If you've closed the file or quit Works after saving the file, either choose its name from the bottom of the File menu (if it is displayed there) or open it with the Open Existing File command.

We will insert a new column named Special to the left of the column named Total by following these steps.

1. Point to column E and highlight it by clicking once in the column heading.

2. Open the Insert menu, and then choose Row/Column.

As you see in Figure 7-4, Works adds the new column to the left of what was column E (now column F) and it relabels the column to the right to avoid any break in the numbering sequence.

FIGURE 7-4.
Inserting a column.

	A	B	C	D	E	F	G	H
1	Pizza	Small	Medium	Large		Total		
2								
3	Cheese	45	32	29				
4	Sausage	97	143	168				
5	Pepperoni	102	169	185				
6	Anchovy	23	17	9				
7	Vegetarian	49	73	53				
8								
9	Price							
10	Small	7.95						
11	Medium	9.95						
12	Large	12.95						
13								
14								
15								
16								
17								
18								
19								

Microsoft Works - [PIZZA.WKS]

File   Edit   View   Insert   Format   Tools   Window   Help

Arial   10

E1:E16384

Press ALT to choose commands, or F2 to edit

While you're at it, add the Onion model right after the Anchovy pizza. This means inserting a new row. Here's how to do it.

1. Point to row 7 and highlight it with one click in the row heading.

2. Open the Insert menu, and then choose Row/Column.

You have just added a column and a row to the spreadsheet.

> **TIP:** If you had selected a cell rather than an entire row or column, the result would have been the same, but because Works would not know whether you meant to insert a row or a column, it would have displayed a dialog box to ask which you wanted. Selecting the entire row or column is faster than selecting a cell, because the additional dialog box query does not appear.

Working with Text

The spreadsheet you've been working with, like most others, includes two types of information: text and values. The distinction between the two is simple: Text is nonnumeric information that cannot be used in calculations; values are numeric data and always begin with a numeral (0 through 9), a plus sign (+), a minus sign (-), or a currency symbol. Cells containing dates and times actually contain numeric values, but they can be displayed in standard date or time formats.

Most text is easily distinguished from numbers, but on occasion you might include numeric information, such as years (1991, 1992, and so on) or ID numbers, as headings or descriptive text. If the spreadsheet is complex, you can ensure that Works treats these numbers as text by beginning each entry with a quotation mark. Because Works treats a number preceded by a quotation mark as text, the number won't accidentally be calculated.

Formatting Text

To format text in the spreadsheet you follow the same steps as in the word processor. The only real differences are (1) you select cells instead of words or paragraphs and (2) when you choose to align text, you do so in relation to the cell borders, not the margins of the page. To see how this works, boldface and underline the column headings in cells A1 through E1 by doing the following.

1. Drag the mouse to select the cells.

2. Click the Bold (B) and Underline (U) buttons in the toolbar.

Works aligns text at the left edge of a cell by default. You can change this with the alignment buttons on the toolbar. Right align the headings in cells B1 through E1, by following these steps.

1. Select the cells.

2. Click the Right Align (R) button, in the toolbar.

To "unformat" the cell, select it and remove the formatting. You remove the formatting by clicking on the buttons on the toolbar.

Using the Font and Style Dialog Box

As with the word processor, the spreadsheet offers a Font and Style dialog box as you see here.

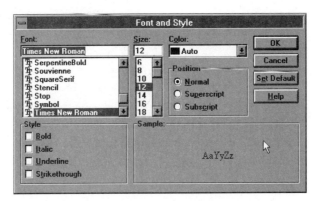

You can select the font you want to use, its size and style, and see a preview of how the characters will appear. This dialog box provides one-stop shopping.

Working with Numbers

Numbers are at the heart of any spreadsheet. You can type in numbers with the row of keys at the top of the keyboard (not the function keys) or, when the Num Lock key is turned on, you can use the numeric keypad at the right of the keyboard. Works always right-aligns numbers in cells, unless you specify otherwise, and normally displays partial values as decimals if the cell is wide enough (up to eight decimal places).

TIP: Remember the wonderful UNDO feature from the word processor? It's alive and well in the spreadsheet (and the database). Use it *immediately* after the operation you want to undo.

You can type in and calculate both positive and negative values, indicating negative numbers either by preceding them with a minus sign (-) or by enclosing them in parentheses, for example, ($500.00). Works displays negative values in both forms, depending on the format you choose to use.

Using Number Formats

Because numbers can represent so many different types of values, such as quantities, currencies, and percentages, Works offers many different formats for numbers. When you apply number formats, you don't format the number itself. As with text, you format one or more selected cells to display numbers in a specific format. Formatting "sticks" to a cell even after you've changed or deleted the number it contains.

We assume you have set up Windows to run with the default numeric settings for the United States. If you have selected International from the Windows Control Panel and made any changes, Works will display different formats.

To see the available number formats, open a new spreadsheet with the Create New File command and type in the headings and numbers as shown below.

	A	B	C	D	E	F	G	H
1								
2	General	1.1	-1.1	1234	0.95			
3	Fixed							
4	Currency							
5	Comma							
6	Percent							
7	Exponential							
8	Leading Zeros							
9	Fraction							
10	True/False							
11	Date							
12	Time							
13	Text							
14								
15								
16								
17								
18								
19								

Each row label in column A represents a different format option. Now do the following:

1. Select cells B2 through C13.

2. Open the Edit menu, and then choose Fill Down.

The Fill Down command duplicates information by copying it into selected cells that appear below the cells to be copied. You'll find the Fill Down command and the complementary Fill Right command particularly useful in repeating formulas for calculating similar values.

Let's look at the number formats. The first two, next to General, show the default format (the format Works uses unless you specify otherwise) for numbers. Works always tries to display any number as precisely as possible. This is what the General format will do for you.

TIP: Type a currency symbol ($) before a number and Works will recognize the currency format. You can also type a percent symbol (%) and Works will recognize the percent format.

To select other number formats, use the Number command from the Format menu. Here's how to select the first format.

1. Select the cells B3 and E3, next to the row's label, Fixed.

2. Open the Format menu, and then choose Number.

   Works now displays the Number dialog box, as you see here.

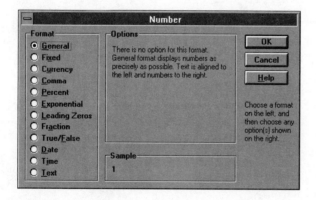

3. Click the Fixed option in the Format area.

4. In the Options area of the Number dialog box, leave 2 as the number of decimals you want to uses.

5. Click OK.

6. Select the cells B4 and E4, and use the Currency button on the toolbar to apply the currency (U.S.) format.

Now use the same procedures, relying on the Number dialog box, to apply the formats described in column A to succeeding pairs of cells. We left some date and time cells (such as negative time) blank because reformatting them would be meaningless.

When you're finished, the different formats should appear as they are shown in Figure 7-5.

FIGURE 7-5.
The different formats available in the Number dialog box.

	A	B	C	D	E	F	G	H
1								
2	General	1.1	-1.1	1234	0.95			
3	Fixed	1.10	-1.10	1234.00	0.95			
4	Currency	$1.10	($1.10)	$1,234.00	$0.95			
5	Comma	1.10	(1.10)	1,234.00	0.95			
6	Percent	110.00%	-110.00%	########	95.00%			
7	Exponential	1.10E+00	-1.10E+00	1.23E+03	9.50E-01			
8	Leading Zeros	00001	-00001	01234	00001			
9	Fraction	1 1/10	-1 1/10	‑1234	0 19/20			
10	True/False	TRUE	TRUE	TRUE	TRUE			
11	Date		########	5/18/03	########			
12	Time	2:24 AM	########	12:00 AM	10:48 PM			
13	Text	1.1	-1.1	1234	0.95			

Microsoft Works - [Sheet1]

File   Edit   View   Insert   Format   Tools   Window   Help

Press ALT to choose commands, or F2 to edit

TIP: If you format a row or a column in a specific number format, Works will remember the format. Even if you extend beyond the range of entered values, that format will stick.

General formats cells to display numbers as integers (whole numbers) or as decimals. If a number is too long to be displayed in a cell, Works uses the exponential notation (the scientific notation described later in this section). A minus sign indicates a negative number.

Fixed formats cells to display numbers with the number of decimal places you specify. If a number must be truncated, this format rounds the decimal portion up or down accordingly, but Works remembers the actual value. For example, 3.456 formatted for two decimal places would be displayed as 3.46, whereas 3.454 would be displayed as 3.45. A minus sign indicates a negative number.

Currency formats cells to display numbers as currency values and includes commas if necessary. If you type a currency symbol with the number, Works automatically assumes the currency format. Negative amounts are enclosed in parentheses.

Comma formats cells to display numbers with comma separators. For example, 111111 would be displayed as 111,111. As with the currency format, negative numbers are shown in parentheses.

Percent formats cells to display numbers as percents. This format multiplies a number by 100 and displays it as a percentage to the number of decimals you specify. When you type values into cells formatted for displaying percents, type the decimal equivalent of the percent: The spreadsheet multiplies the value by 100. Thus, 70 becomes 7000.00%, whereas .7 becomes 70.00%. A minus sign indicates a negative percentage.

Exponential notation, often used in science and engineering, formats cells to display numbers as a "root," such as 1.10, plus the power of 10 by which the number is multiplied to create its "long" form. In Figure 7-5, the E indicates exponential notation, 1.10 is the number to two decimals, and +00 shows that the number (originally 1.1) is not multiplied by any power of 10.

Leading Zeros formats cells to pad numbers with zeros on the left to fill them out to the required number of digits (five in the example). If the number already consists of the required number of digits, no leading zeros are added.

Fraction displays values as fractions with a 0 in front so that .2 becomes 0 1/5 and .78 becomes 39/50. You can also round fractions in the Round to area of the Fraction box.

True/False formats cells to display numbers as logical values in which any nonzero number produces TRUE and 0 produces FALSE. The True/False format is useful when you want to check spreadsheet cells for 0 and nonzero values, without regard to the actual values. For example, you would use the True/False format to see if calculations that depend on other calculations work as expected.

Date and *Time* format cells to display numbers as dates or times in any of the forms listed in the Date and Time areas of the Number dialog box. The Date box is shown here.

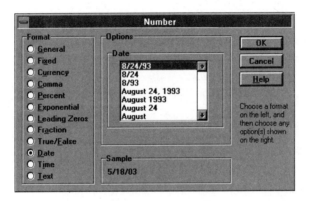

The Date and Time formats are useful in several different situations. You can use them to enter a series of dates or times and to "stamp" spreadsheets with the date and time of creation. You can also use the format to calculate elapsed times. Works can calculate with dates from January 1, 1900, to June 3, 2079. Dates outside this range are displayed as text.

You won't normally type a five-digit number and later turn it into a date as you did here, but the example serves to show the format. Figure 7-5 also shows a set of symbols you might see: a set of number signs (#########). These symbols appear because Works was unable to display 1.1 as a date or because the cell value is too large to fit into the cell.

Text sorts entries including those with numbers or special characters. "Special characters" can include hyphens, such as the ones that occur in postal codes and phone numbers. To display values as text, apply the Text format to blank cells before entering values into them.

The Too-Small Cell

Often, when you see a set of number signs, Works is telling you that a number is too large to be completely displayed in a cell. The solution is simple. Widen the column with the mouse (the easy way), or use the Column Width command on the Format menu. To try this, do the following.

1. Select a blank cell, and apply the Fixed format with two decimal places.

2. Type *1234567890*.

3. Press Enter or click the Enter button. Works displays #########.

4. Place the mouse pointer on the right boundary edge of the column header in which you typed the number. The mouse pointer turns into a vertical bar with a doubleheaded arrow through the middle, as you saw in Figure 7-3.

5. To widen the cell, press the left mouse button and drag to the right. Or, from the Format menu, you can choose the Column Width command.

    That's all there is to it.

Formatting Your Work

You can enhance or clarify a spreadsheet by using formatting. As in the word processor, Works gives you a variety of options: fonts, font sizes, alignments, and borders. All of these options should be familiar from your work with the word processor. You can apply different fonts, styles, and sizes to different parts of the spreadsheet. You can use the toolbar to make font and size selections, or you can use the Font and Style command on the Format menu.

When it's time to print your spreadsheet, be sure to use the Print Preview command to see how the information fits on the page. To improve the overall layout, remember that you can juggle column widths, fonts, and font sizes to open up a cramped spreadsheet or condense one that sprawls too much.

Simple as it sounds, a small change in font or font size may make a dramatic difference in your printed documents. This is especially true when you change from a monospace font such as Courier, in which a lowercase *i* requires as much space as a capital *W*, to a proportional font such as Helvetica, in which characters take up only as much linear space as they need. This chapter won't walk you through an example of text formatting because it's done in the spreadsheet the same way it is done in the word processor. You might want to try using different fonts, font sizes, alignments, and borders on one of your sample spreadsheets to see their effects.

We made some adjustments to the *pizza.wks* spreadsheet, removing gridlines, centering text, changing size, and creating a border (on the Format menu) at the bottom of the selected range of cells. You can see the final results here.

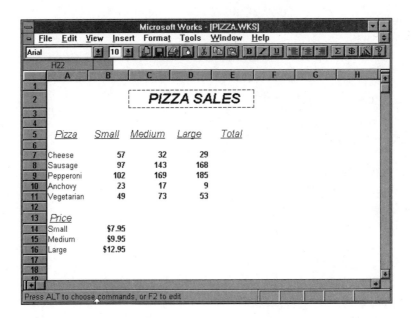

Using Patterns and Shading

Let's experiment some more with the *pizza.wks* spreadsheet to see how to use Works Patterns to highlight a set of cells. With a few clicks, you can use patterns to highlight particular areas of a spreadsheet, as you see here.

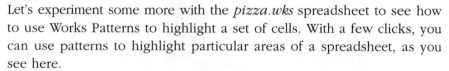

	A	B	C	D	E	F	G	H
1	BlueBird Diner Daily Sales, week of August 23, 1993							
2								
3		8/23/93	8/24/93	8/25/93	8/26/93	8/27/93	8/28/93	8/29/93
4	Dinner #							
5	1	5	8	11	14	17	20	23
6	2	12	15	18	21	24	27	30
7	3	9	12	15	18	21	24	27
8	4	15	16	17	18	19	20	21
9	5	22	24	26	28	30	32	34
10	6	3	5	19	9	11	13	15
11	7	11	12	13	14	15	16	17
12	8	7	8	9	10	11	12	13
13								
14	Total	84	100	128	132	148	164	180
15								
16								
17								
18								
19								
20								

Here's how to do this.

1. Highlight cells B5 through H12.

2. Open the Format menu, and then choose Patterns. When you do this, you will see the Patterns dialog box, shown here.

3. From the Pattern box, select the widely spaced dots. You can see the pattern that was selected as well as a sample of how it will appear in the Sample area of the Patterns dialog box on the next page.

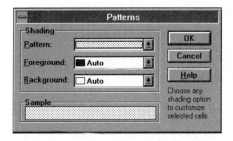

4. Click OK.

Sorting Rows

The Works spreadsheet can sort information, arranging in alphabetic or numeric order the rows of entries you've selected. Works sorts based on the information in a column (A, B, C, and so on); you can specify up to three columns, in order of importance, for it to consider. During the sort, Works checks the contents of the first column and arranges the rows to match the sort you specified (ascending or descending). If you've specified a second and, possibly, a third column, Works turns to them to refine the result by sorting entries that are duplicated in the previous column(s). The following example sorts a list of expenses alphabetically in column A, then by amount in column B.

1. Open a new spreadsheet and enter the text and values shown here.

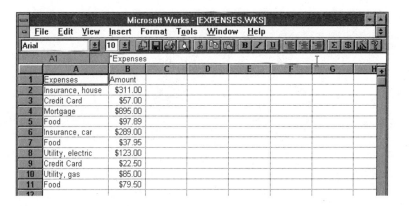

2. First, tell Works which rows you want to sort. You don't want to include the column titles, so select cells A2 through B11.

3. Open the Tools menu, and then choose Sort Rows. Works displays the following dialog box.

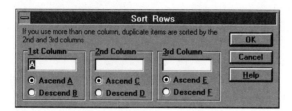

This is where you tell Works which columns to use for the sort and the order in which to sort them. For the first column, Works always proposes using the first column in your selection. In this case, it's column A. Notice, too, that Works proposes to sort in ascending order: A to Z or lowest (0) to highest (9). If the settings were not correct, you would type the column letter and choose the type of sort you wanted.

You also want Works to consider column B if it finds duplicates in the sort.

4. Click in the box headed 2nd Column, and type *B*. Once again, ascending order is fine, so click OK to begin the sort.

Almost instantly, Works sorts the entries and modifies the spreadsheet, as shown on the next page.

Here you can see how categories were sorted in alphabetical order, then within categories, with values going from lowest (such as Food $37.95) to highest (Food $97.89).

Sorting is fast and useful for arranging any type of alphabetic or numeric information. If you want to preserve both the original and the sorted versions, save the original under one name and the sorted spreadsheet under another. Use a "key" when naming the files so you'll be able to tell that they are related and that they represent sorted and unsorted data. The preceding example, for instance, could be saved in its original form as *exp.wks* and in sorted form as *expsort.wks*.

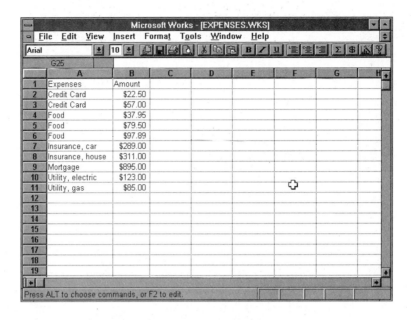

The AutoFormat Command

AutoFormat makes Works very easy to use. It allows you to select a group of cells and then choose from one of 14 different predesigned formats. In Figure 7-6, you can see two examples of these formats.

FIGURE 7-6.
Different
AutoFormat
options.

Here's how to use AutoFormat.

1. Select the range of cells you want to format.

2. Open the Format menu, and then choose AutoFormat. When you do this, you will see the AutoFormat dialog box shown in Figure 7-7. You can see a list of all the different available formats.

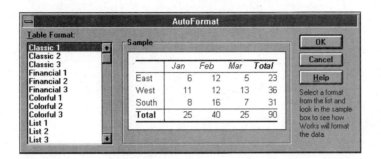

FIGURE 7-7.
The AutoFormat dialog box.

3. Select the Format you want to use. You can view what it will look like in the Sample area before you click OK.

4. Once you find the one you want to use, click OK.

In Figure 7-6, you can see two samples of formatting created by using the AutoFormat command. The first is Financial 1; the second is 3D Effects 1. They both look attractive and were accomplished simply by selecting the cells and then selecting a format style. Easy, neat, and impressive.

The Find Command

The Go To command provides a quick way to jump to a specific cell, regardless of what it contains. But what do you do if you know the value you want, but don't know where the cell is? You use the Find command on the Edit menu.

The Find command in the spreadsheet works much like Find in the word processor, with one exception. The word processor lets you refine a document search by limiting the command to whole words or upper and lower case, but the spreadsheet lets you refine a search by specifying direction (left to right by row, or top to bottom by column). If you're searching a large spreadsheet, specifying a horizontal or vertical scan can speed the process by tailoring the search to the orientation of the spreadsheet.

You can select columns, rows, or cell ranges to limit the search to a particular part of the spreadsheet, or you can select any cell and have Works search the entire spreadsheet. To see how simple it is, use the *pizza.wks* spreadsheet as an example and do the following steps.

1. Open the Edit menu, and then choose the Find command.

2. Type *7.95* in the Find What box.

3. Works proposes to search by rows, rather than columns. Your spreadsheet is small enough that the search direction doesn't matter, so click OK.

Almost immediately, Works selects cell B10, which contains the value $7.95.

The Replace Command

Remember how, with the word processor, you could search for and then change text? You can do the same with the spreadsheet. This is a great tool for changing a simple value or a set of incorrectly entered ones.

To use this option, from the Edit menu choose Replace. Just as with the word processor, Works will ask you for both the string of characters you are searching for and those that will replace them.

Printing a Spreadsheet

Because printing in Works is uniform throughout the three applications, this section deals only with features unique to the spreadsheet. If you need more information about headers, footers, or other topics, see Chapter 6, page 145.

When it comes to printing, a spreadsheet can differ from a word-processed document in one important way. Although it is a single document, the spreadsheet can be either too wide or too long to fit on a single page. This means you might find yourself doing some fine-tuning before you print.

If you create a document that is both too wide and too long to print on one page, Works breaks up the spreadsheet and prints it on separate pages. It does this in the following order: upper left section first, lower left second, upper right third, and lower left fourth.

To control page breaks at the bottom, you can use the Page Break command on the Insert menu. To control page breaks from side to side, you can insert a page break between columns with the Page Break command, or you can adjust column widths or insert a blank column wide enough to force the column to its right onto a new page.

As in the word processor, you can add headers, footers, and page numbers to a printed spreadsheet. You can also adjust page and header margins and, of course, preview the spreadsheet before printing (always a good idea)

If your printer can print sideways (landscape orientation), you can reverse page length and width in the Page Setup dialog box. In this set of tab dialog boxes, you can change margins, orientation, and even (under Other Options) select whether to print the gridlines that are visible on the screen version of the spreadsheet. One other option is different from the word processor in the spreadsheet: In the Page Setup dialog box, you can direct Works to print (or not print) the row and column headings.

Printing Part of a Spreadsheet

You can choose to print all or part of a spreadsheet. This is one area in which the spreadsheet differs significantly from the word processor. To print part of a word-processed document, you specify the starting and ending pages in the Print dialog box. To print part of a spreadsheet, you specify the area to print with the Set Print Area command on the Format menu. Using the command is simple.

To print a range of cells, follow these steps.

1. Select the cells you want to print.

2. Open the Format menu, and then choose Set Print Area.

3. Click OK in response to Works' confirmation that you want to select a range to print.

TIP: To see the cells before printing, click the Print Preview button on the toolbar. Only the print area you specified appears.

To deselect a print area, select the entire spreadsheet and choose Set Print Area again. (To quickly select the entire spreadsheet, either choose All from the Select menu or click on the unlabeled, rectangular box above row 1 and to the left of column A.)

Coming Next

That's just the beginning of what the spreadsheet can do for you. In the next chapter you'll learn about creating formulas and using the powerful set of built-in functions that accompanies Works. Let's turn to both of those now.

8

Working with Formulas and Functions

The Microsoft Works 3 for Windows spreadsheet has lots of handy tools that make working with numbers easy. Among its most powerful features are the ability to create new formulas and the set of built-in formulas, called *functions*. Using formulas, you can develop your own calculations based on the relationship between different variables. To use a function, you simply select the one you want from a Works menu and click it into your worksheet. Want to know when that loan will come due? The mean and standard deviation of a set of numbers? How much you owe on the house? You'll find how to answer these questions and more.

Working with Formulas

You know about formulas. They compute such things as the area of a square (l^2, or the length of one side squared) or the amount of time it takes for an investment to double ($S=P(1+i)^n$) or the semi-interquartile range ($Q=(Q1-Q3)/2$). A *formula* is set of calculations that you want Works to perform. No matter what your task, using Works to compute formulas can be a great help.

There are two types of formulas: those you create yourself and those that are preprogrammed. You use the first type to create custom calculations designed for a very specific purpose. The second type, called *functions*, are built-in equations that perform useful tasks, such as calculating averages, depreciation, and loan payments. Works comes with 76 functions that are simple to use.

When referring to cells containing formulas, you can specify a single cell or a range of cells. Even better, you can refer to a cell by its usual address, or you can give it a descriptive name and use the name in your formulas. Let's create a sample formula to demonstrate.

Building a Formula

You tell Works that you are about to build a formula by first typing an equal sign (=) in the cell where you want the formula to reside. If you don't type an equal sign, Works will consider the entry to be text, plain and simple.

If you still have it, open the *pizza.wks* worksheet. Or, create this worksheet as shown below. We'll use *pizza.wks* to create several types of formulas.

As you can see, the *pizza.wks* worksheet includes a number of values that would provide useful totals. Let's start by building a simple formula that adds the number of small, medium, and large cheese pizzas.

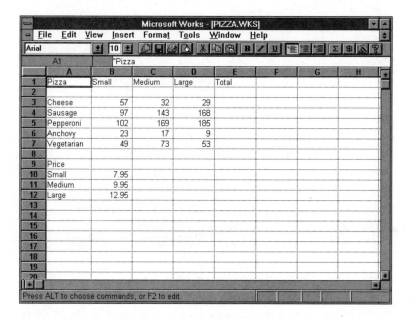

This illustration will help clarify the basics of entering a formula and explain, by contrast, how useful Works built-in functions can be.

We are going to compute the total number of each type of pizza, beginning with cheese. The values you want to add are in cells B3, C3, and D3. Here's how to tell Works what to do:

1. Click on cell E3 to select it.

2. Type an equal sign to let Works know you are starting a formula.

3. Enter the cell reference *B3* or click on cell B3. As you can see, Works immediately displays the cell reference in the formula bar, indicating that it will use the value in B3 in its calculations.

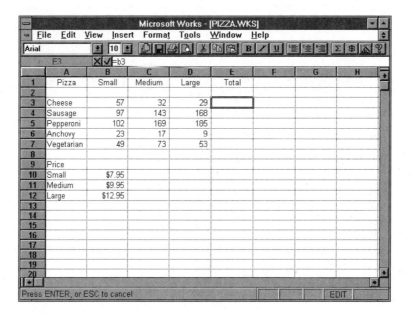

4. Type a plus sign. The plus sign appears in the formula bar.

5. Click on cell C3, type another plus sign, and then click on cell D3. Each of these moves adds another cell reference to the formula.

6. Click the Enter button, or press Enter to complete the formula.

As soon as you're done, the total for cells B3 through D3 appears in cell E3. Whenever you want to refer to cells in a formula, simply point and click at those cells. Works does the rest.

Results Automatically Updated

Try this: Change the value in cell C3 from 32 to 12 and press Enter. What happens? The Total value in cell E3 changes from 118 to 98. The value in cell E3 is dependent on the values in cells B3, C3, and D3, and when one of the three is changed, the total must change as well.

This is no small deal. Imagine working with a complex spreadsheet in which hundreds of values are interconnected and wanting to see how changing this or that value affects the final outcome. This "what if" feature, which we will explore later in this chapter, is one of the primary reasons why spreadsheet programs are so popular in the business world. They allow you to play out several different scenarios and examine the impact of changing variables.

It's easy to check the contents of a cell by selecting it and checking the formula bar. You can see, in the illustration below, how cell E3 shows the total number of cheese pizzas sold and not the formula, which you see in the formula bar.

	A	B	C	D	E	F	G	H
1	Pizza	Small	Medium	Large	Total			
2								
3	Cheese	57	32	29	118			
4	Sausage	97	143	168				

Microsoft Works - [PIZZA.WKS]

File Edit View Insert Format Tools Window Help

Arial   10

E3   =SUM(B3:D3)

TIP: Formulas and functions can be edited like any other cell entry. Use the F2 function key or click in the formula bar and move the insertion point to the location where you want to make the edit.

When building related formulas in a spreadsheet, be careful not to create a circular reference, that is, one in which formulas refer to one another. A circular reference has no start and no end, so Works cannot calculate it correctly. If you see the notation CIRC in the status bar at the bottom of the screen, check your formulas for a circular reference.

Using Operators

When you build a formula, you use mathematical operators, such as + and -, to tell Works what to calculate and how. You can use these operators, shown in the following table, in formulas in both the spreadsheet and the database.

Operator	Meaning
^	Exponent, as in 2^3 for 2^3
+ and -	Positive and negative
* and /	Multiplication and division, as in 2*3 and 6/2
+ and -	Addition, as in 2+2, and subtraction, as in 2-1
= and < >	Equal, as in PROFIT = INCOME, and not equal, as in PROFIT < > LOSS
< and >	Less than, as in COST < PRICE, and greater than, as in PRICE > COST
<= and >=	Less than or equal to, as in SUPPLIES <= BUDGET, and greater than or equal to, as in INCOME >= EXPENSE
~	Not, as in ~(PROFIT < INCOME)
|	Or, as in FIXED COST | VARIABLE COST
&	And, as in ADS & BROCHURES

Some of these operators perform arithmetic calculations and are equally applicable to both the spreadsheet and the database. Others, such as the tilde (~), the pipe (|), and the ampersand (&), are known as logical operators because they help with comparisons and searches.

Controlling When Works Calculates Formulas

In our example, we showed you how Works calculates formulas again whenever you change the spreadsheet. Sometimes, however, you might want to put a hold on the calculations until you've made a series of changes to a spreadsheet. In other words, you want to change more than one value and then examine the impact of all the changes at once, rather than one at a time. You might also find that this constant recalculation on large spreadsheets can become time-consuming.

You can control when Works calculates formulas by using two commands on the Tools menu. Manual Calculation tells Works not to update the spreadsheet each time you make a change that affects a formula, but to wait until you are ready to have all the calculations occur. Calculate Now gives Works the go-ahead to recalculate all the formulas in a spreadsheet.

The Manual Calculation command affects only the spreadsheet that's active at the time you choose the command. If you have three spreadsheets open and specify Manual Calculation for the active spreadsheet, Works still recalculates on the other two whenever you make a change that affects a formula. Works overrides Manual Calculation only when you enter a new formula. In that case, Works calculates the formula whether Manual Calculation is turned on or off.

In a small spreadsheet like the one we have been working with, whether manual calculation is on or off will not make much difference in the way you work with the results you get. However, if you are using many formulas of increasing complexity, this feature can be a time-saver. You need not wait for one formula to finish its work before you create another one.

Controlling the Order of Calculation

Formulas often perform several calculations to achieve a desired result. Calculating an average, for example, requires totaling a group of items and then dividing by the number of items. Many formulas include more than one operator; Works needs to know which order of operations to follow to get the desired outcome.

The standard order of calculation is:

Order	Operator
First	^
Second	+ and - (positive and negative)
Third	* and /
Fourth	+ and - (addition and subtraction)
Fifth	= and < >, < and >, <= and >=
Sixth	~
Seventh	| and &

If more than one operator with the same "rank" appears in a formula, Works evaluates them from left to right.

To see how this order of evaluation can affect a formula, select an empty cell in your spreadsheet and follow these steps:

1. Type an equal sign to start a formula.

2. Now type the formula *8+8/4*3^3*.

3. Click the Enter button.

Works calculates the result as 62 because it follows its internal rules for evaluating mathematical operators. These are the steps it follows:

1. It evaluates the exponent: 3^3 (or 3^3), or 27.

2. It evaluates the division and multiplication operators from left to right: 8/4, or 2, followed by 2*27, or 54.

3. It evaluates the addition operator: 8+54, or 62.

To override the normal order of calculation, use sets of values in parentheses. If you want to control more than one calculation, you can nest one set of parentheses within another to determine the order in which their contents are calculated. Works evaluates sets of parentheses before it does any other calculating, working out from the innermost set.

Using the same formula as before, you can produce an entirely different result by enclosing values in parentheses. In another cell in a practice spreadsheet, try this:

1. Type the formula *=(8+(8/4)*3)^3* and click the Enter button.

   This time the parentheses control the order of evaluation, so the result is 2744.

2. The inner set of parentheses produces 8/4, or 2.

3. The multiplication operator takes precedence over the addition operator in the outer set of parentheses to produce 2*3, or 6, followed by 6+8, or 14.

4. The exponent is evaluated to produce 14^3, or 2744.

Using a Built-In Function

Now for the shortcut—and for the fun. You can create formulas galore, but why go to all that trouble when you can use one of the built-in functions that comes with Works?

As we said earlier, there are 76 built-in functions available in Works. Quite frankly, it is very unlikely that you will ever use all of these functions in your spreadsheets. You are more likely to use just a few, based on the work you want to do. Of course, all of the functions are ready for your use at any time.

Functions save time and work. They are also a necessity in some spreadsheets. Consider this problem: Suppose you have 100 employees, and you want to total the weekly payroll. Your spreadsheet starts at cell A1 with the employee's name, and cell B1 shows the employee's salary. Your spreadsheet would look something like this:

	A	B
1	Mary Smith	$335.00
2	John Jones	$287.50
3	Pam Shapp	$380.00
...	...	...
99	Susan Apple	$500.00
100	Fred Bucher	$325.00

To add the total salaries, you would probably think that you should move to cell B101, and begin typing the following formula:

```
=B1+B2+B3+B4 ... +B99+B100
```

But, consider how much work this would be. It would take a lot of time and effort. Because of all the typing, you could easily make a typo, which would give you an error.

But there is another major problem that you might have forgotten. Do you remember the maximum width of a spreadsheet cell? The maximum width of a cell is 254 characters. If you think about it, you cannot type this formula into a cell because it is too long. For cell addresses such as B4, you must type three characters—*+B4*. And the problem becomes worse when you move to cell addresses such as *B11*. Including the plus sign, it takes four characters to identify a cell. With a list of 100 names, it would take well over 300 characters to create the formula. And this cannot be done because of the maximum cell width.

The solution, of course, is to use a Works function. By using the function, you need only type a few characters. It saves time, eliminates mistakes, and of course, easily fits into the width of a cell. Functions might seem confusing at first, but they will save you a lot of work, and make the Works spreadsheet much easier to use.

In this example, all you need to do is to move to cell B101 and type =SUM(B1:B100). Works automatically totals all of the values in each cell from B1 through B100 and places the result of the summation in cell B101. You can use the SUM function to total not only columns, but also rows.

The SUM function is the one you will probably use most often. Works includes an Autosum button [Σ] on the toolbar. By using this button, you can total columns or rows automatically.

You can type a function directly into any cell. Works also helps you by including the Functions command on the Insert menu, which brings up a dialog box called Functions. This dialog box displays all the available functions in Works. You can also display only certain functions, such as those used for statistical calculations. The Insert Function dialog box is shown in Figure 8-2, on page 227. It will be discussed further under the heading "Selecting Built-in Functions," on page 226.

Using the *pizza.wks* example once again, to compute the total number of cheese pizzas, we can use the SUM function, a much more efficient means of totaling values. You can use the SUM function by typing it or by clicking the Autosum button [Σ] on the toolbar. We'll use the easiest method first, using the Autosum button.

Let's start again with the original *pizza.wks* spreadsheet. If you have a value in cell E3, delete it. To use Autosum, follow these steps:

1. Highlight cell E3.

2. Double-click on the Autosum button on the toolbar, which is an uppercase sigma (Σ).

TIP: Be sure to double-click. If you click instead of double-click, you must press Enter to accept the formula. The sum function should then be placed in the cell. You can also press Delete to remove the contents of the cell, and then start over, double-clicking again.

That's all you need do. The total—the sum of the values in that row— is inserted in the cell that was selected.

The same total appears in cell E3, but as you can see in Figure 8-1, a new and different formula is displayed in the formula bar.

	Microsoft Works - [PIZZA.WKS]						
File	**Edit**	**View**	**Insert**	**Format**	**Tools**	**Window**	**Help**
Arial	10				B I U	Σ $	
E3	=SUM(B3:D3)					Autosum	

	A	B	C	D	E	F	G	H
1	Pizza	Small	Medium	Large	Total			
2								
3	Cheese	57	32	29	118			
4	Sausage	97	143	168				
5	Pepperoni	102	169	185				

FIGURE 8-1.
Using the Autosum button.

Double-clicking the Autosum button caused a number of sophisticated operations to take place very quickly. Works scanned the spreadsheet, "decided" that cells B3, C3, and D3 were the logical cells to total, highlighted those cells, built the formula, calculated the total, and displayed the result in cell E3.

TIP: If you want to verify the cells Works will total, click the Autosum button once. After highlighting the cells and building the formula, Works waits for you to click the Autosum button again to confirm that it chose the correct cells.

Let's look at the formula shown in the formula bar in Figure 8-1. Although the results of the formulas (B3+C3+D3 and SUM(B3:D3)) are the same, the formulas reach their results in a different way. Built-in functions follow the same basic design, regardless of the calculations they perform. The SUM function, as an example, can be broken down as follows:

1. The formula starts with an equal sign, as do all Works formulas.

2. The word SUM names the function. Other functions have other names. When you type functions on your own, remember to always start them with the function name.

3. A set of parentheses surrounds the cells that Works proposes to total. Whenever you use a function, you must enclose values or cell references within parentheses.

4. The cells chosen by Works are displayed as a range beginning with B3 and ending with D3. The references in the range are separated by a colon. Ranges are the easiest method of specifying continuous groups of cells in a formula or a function.

The Sum button is a great tool when you've built a spreadsheet and the cells you want to total are grouped in an obvious set (either down a column or across a row). Sometimes, however, you'll want to add values from cells scattered around the spreadsheet. Works is not smart enough to pick individual cells for the formula, so in those cases, type in the SUM function, using the same format Works uses here, and then enter the exact cells.

Selecting Built-in Functions

You can find a list of all the Works functions in Appendix A (page 509).

Or, you can use the Insert Function dialog box you see in Figure 8-2, which allows you to select from a specific group of functions on the Category list.

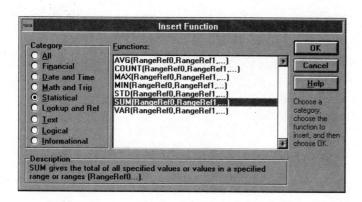

FIGURE 8-2
The Insert Function
dialog box.

Each of the categories available in the Insert Function dialog box contains a set of functions. For example, to use the SUM function using the Insert Function command, follow these steps:

1. Place the insertion point in the cell where you want the results of the function to be located.

2. Open the Insert menu, and then choose Function. When you do this, you see the Insert Function dialog.

3. Click on the Statistical category.

4. Click on SUM(RangeRef0,RangeRef1,...).

5. Click OK.

6. Enter the range of cells between the parentheses in the formula bar.

7. Press Enter.

In step six, you are advised to enter the range of cells you want SUM to add together to give you the total of the values. This range of cells is actually called the *argument*. This is a computer term for the values the function needs to perform its task.

The big advantage to using the list of functions from the Insert Function dialog box is that you can review all the available functions and also look at the structure of the argument you will have to provide. With functions that you use often, you probably don't need any additional information, but for rarely used (but important) functions, the list can be indispensable.

Duplicating Formulas

When you work with spreadsheets, you'll often need to perform the same calculation on different groups of cells. In our example *pizza.wks*, you need totals for the other types of pizza, and totals for the different sizes, too, would be helpful. Start by using the Autosum button to total all the small pizzas in cell B8:

1. Select cell B8.

2. Double-click the Autosum button to see the total number of small pizzas.

Now let's duplicate the formulas. In Chapter 7 (page 175), you used the Fill Down command to copy information to selected cells. You can use this command with formulas as well. To see the results more clearly, do the following:

1. Open the View menu, and then choose Formulas.

    The Formulas command tells Works to display formulas in those cells that contain them. To accommodate the command, the columns suddenly expand until your Total column is almost off the screen. Don't worry about it. Scroll to the right so you can see columns B through E.

2. Select cells E3 through E7.

3. Open the Edit menu, and then choose Fill Down.

4. Select cells B8 through D8.

5. Open the Edit menu, and then choose Fill Right.

Notice the formulas, in Figure 8-3 on the next page, that now appear in cells C8 and D8 and in cells E4 through E7. In each, Works has adjusted the cell references so they refer not to the cells in the original formula, but to cells in the same position *relative* to the new formula. The formula in E4 refers to the cells in B4 through D4, the formula in E5 refers to B5 through D5, and so on. Works modifies cell references in this way, so you don't have to adjust them manually.

You might not always want cell references to change, however. For example, you might want each formula to refer to a value in one particular cell. You do this by using absolute or mixed cell references, rather than the relative cell references you've been using.

If you want to get back to the normal spreadsheet view, choose Formulas from the View menu.

FIGURE 8-3.
Filling cells down and right.

	B	C	D	E
1	Small	Medium	Large	Total
2				
3	57	32	29	=SUM(B3:D3)
4	97	143	168	=SUM(B4:D4)
5	102	169	185	=SUM(B5:D5)
6	23	17	9	=SUM(B6:D6)
7	49	73	53	=SUM(B7:D7)
8	=SUM(B3:B7)	=SUM(C3:C7)	=SUM(D3:D7)	
9				
10	7.95			
11	9.95			
12	12.95			
13				
14				
15				
16				
17				
18				
19				
20				

Microsoft Works - [PIZZA.WKS]

File   Edit   View   Insert   Format   Tools   Window   Help

Arial   10

E24

Press ALT to choose commands, or F2 to edit

Moving and Copying Formulas and Functions

Works lets you move and copy formulas as well as data, but you must be careful when you do this. Works does the best it can, but both moving and copying formulas can produce unexpected and even bizarre results.

In general, when you move or copy a range of cells containing one or more formulas that refer to cells outside the range, Works does the following:

- When moving, Works keeps the original references to non-moved cells. The references to moved cells reflect their new location.

- When copying, either within the same spreadsheet or from one spreadsheet to another, Works alters all relative references to reflect the new location of the copied cells.

Here are some sample exercises to show you how copying works:

1. Create a new spreadsheet.

2. Type the value *1* in cell A1, *2* in cell A2, and *3* in cell A3.

3. Use the Autosum button to total the three values in cell A4. Notice that the formula bar displays =SUM(A1:A3).

4. Enter the formula *=A4*2* in cell A5, and enter the formula *=A5*3* in cell A6.

5. Select cells A4 through A6, and then copy them to the Clipboard using the Copy command on the Edit menu.

6. Select cell D6, and then choose Paste from the Edit menu. Your screen should resemble this illustration.

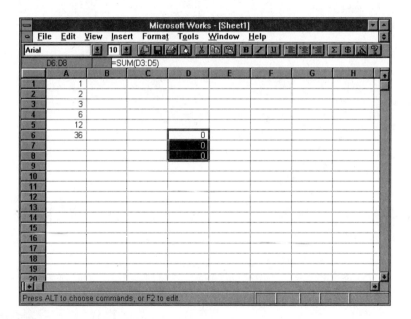

Notice that the formula bar tells you cell D6 contains the formula =SUM(D3:D5). Works has adjusted all references to reflect the cells' position after the copy. As you can see, the values the formulas return are 0 since the relative references refer to cells (D3 through D5) that contain no values.

230

Now let's see what happens during a move:

1. Select cells A4 through A6, open the Edit menu, and then choose Cut.

2. Select cell C6, open the Edit menu, and then choose Paste. For comparison, also paste the cut cells back into cells A4 through A6.

3. Select cell C8 so you can see its contents in the formula bar. Your screen should now resemble the one below.

	Microsoft Works - [Sheet1]							
File	Edit	View	Insert	Format	Tools	Window	Help	
Arial		10						
C8		=C7*3						
	A	B	C	D	E	F	G	H
1	1							
2	2							
3	3							
4	6							
5	12							
6	36		6	0				
7			12	0				
8			36	0				

Press ALT to choose commands, or F2 to edit.

This time Works retains the original cell references in the SUM function, the first of the three formulas you moved. If you select cell C7, however, the formula bar displays C6*2. Works has altered this formula so that the cell reference is relative to the formula's new location. If you check cell C8, you'll find an altered reference there, too.

The logistics of moving and copying formulas, especially within or between spreadsheets that contain other formulas and data, can make you feel like Hannibal taking elephants across the Alps. If you're not a puzzle fancier, your best bet is to copy or move data, not formulas.

Such precautions are particularly important in spreadsheets with sensitive information, like your annual income taxes. Sometimes reinventing your formulas is preferable to untangling masses of relative cell references.

To move or copy *values* calculated by formulas, start with the same Cut and Copy process, but use the Paste Special command to insert the contents of the Clipboard. The Paste Special command lets you insert values from cut or copied cells that contain formulas. You can choose to insert the values (with the Values only option), add the incoming values to those already in the selected cells (Add values), or subtract the incoming values (Subtract values).

Working with Relative, Absolute, and Mixed References

Relative cell references refer to a cell's position relative to another cell. A relative reference is comparable to saying, "Go one block east and three blocks north." When you build a formula using relative references, you're telling Works to use the value in the cell that is X columns and Y rows away from the current cell. That's what happened when Works created the SUM formulas with the Fill Down and Fill Right commands. The operation is the same relative to the cell where the results of the formula are returned. The contents of the formula change as the cell where the results will appear changes.

Absolute cell references refer to a specific cell in a spreadsheet. An absolute reference is comparable to saying, "Go to the intersection of State and Main." No matter what the starting point, there is only one intersection of State and Main.

To distinguish an absolute cell reference from a relative cell reference, insert a dollar sign ($) before the column letter and row number. For example, the notation $A$5 in a formula would tell Works to use the value in cell A5, regardless of that cell's location relative to the formula cell. If this cell were part of a formula that was moved, the cell reference would remain $A$5. Typing dollar signs is tedious, even if a spreadsheet is not large. Works provides a simple alternative: Press the F4 key to change any cell reference from relative to absolute.

Absolute cell references are particularly useful in spreadsheets where a single value, such as an hourly wage or a loan rate, is used in multiple formulas scattered throughout the spreadsheet, or when you move or copy formulas to new locations but want to retain a reference to a particular cell. Depending on how your spreadsheet is constructed, you can also create mixed cell references by inserting a dollar sign before the absolute portion (either the column or the row) of the reference. For example, you could type $A1 when the column is always A but the row number can be any row, or you could type A$1 when the column is not necessarily A but the row is always row 1.

In the following spreadsheet, you can see how Larry, Moe, and Sam all worked different hours, but the hourly rate (in cell C3) remains the same.

```
┌────────────────────────────────────────────────────────────────────┐
│ —                    Microsoft Works - [Sheet1]              ▼ ▲    │
│ □  File  Edit  View  Insert  Format  Tools  Window  Help       ▲    │
│ Arial          ▼ 10 ▼  ▢▣▤▥ ▦▧▨ B I U ▤▤▤ Σ $▨▨            │
│    D57.E57                                                           │
│        A            B              C              D           ▲     │
│  1                                                                   │
│  2                                                                   │
│  3            Hourly Rate     6.72                                   │
│  4                                                                   │
│  5                                                                   │
│  6   Employee     # Hours     Pay                                    │
│  7   Larry        43          =$C$3*B7                               │
│  8   Moe          51          =$C$3*B8                               │
│  9   Sam          39          =$C$3*B9                               │
│ 10                                                                   │
│ 11                                                                   │
│ 12                                                                   │
│ 13                                                                   │
│ 14                                                                   │
│ 15                                                                   │
│ 16                                                                   │
│ 17                                                                   │
│ 18                                                                   │
│ 19                                                              ▼    │
│ ◄►                                                              ►    │
│ Press ALT to choose commands, or F2 to edit                         │
└────────────────────────────────────────────────────────────────────┘
```

Look at the formulas in cells C7, C8, and C9. Because Pay is computed as the number of hours worked times the hourly rate, and we want to keep the hourly rate constant, the hourly rate is represented by $C$3 in each formula in each cell.

Naming Cell Ranges

Let's go back to the *pizza.wks* spreadsheet to experiment with naming cells and cell ranges. Even though cell references become second nature and are easier to interpret after you gain a little experience with Works, they're still somewhat cryptic at first glance. Names, which you can assign to any cell or range of cells, are much easier to decipher than numbers, if only because they are closer to "real" language and can more clearly describe cell contents.

Cell and range names are especially useful in the following types of spreadsheets:

- Large or complex spreadsheets containing specific information to which you want to refer

- Spreadsheets from which you want to extract or link information for use in another document, such as a word-processed document

- Spreadsheets in which descriptive formulas would be a real help

Naming cells and ranges is easy and one of the more entertaining features of the spreadsheet. Here are some of the ways you can assign a name to a range of cells:

1. Open *pizza.wks*. Begin by highlighting cells A3 through D7, the pizza names and sales figures by size.

2. Open the Insert menu, and then choose Range Name. You will see a dialog box like the one below.

   Notice that Works proposes the name Cheese, which corresponds to the text in the top left corner of the selected range. That's not terribly appropriate.

3. To change the name, be sure the highlight is in the Name box.

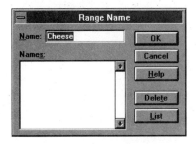

4. Type Pizza Sales and click OK.

   Now the fun begins.

5. Click on any cell outside the Pizza Sales range.

6. Open the Edit menu, and then choose Go To or press the F5 function key. Works displays a new dialog box similar to the one it uses for assigning names, with the name Pizza Sales (and the range A3:D7) listed in the Names box.

7. Double-click on the name Pizza Sales.

   Works highlights the range you named Pizza Sales.

 TIP: You can name an individual cell as easily as a range; simply select that one cell and go through the steps listed above.

Even though you've assigned a name to cells A3 through D7, those cells are not off-limits as far as other names are concerned. You can assign different names to sets of cells within the named range, as well as to sets of cells partly in and partly out of the range. Let's try that.

1. Select cells B3 through B7 and assign them the name Small, using the same steps that we went through above.

2. Assign the name Medium to cells C3 through C7, and assign the name Large to cells D3 through D7.

3. Assign the name Price-Small to the price in cell B10, Price-Medium to the price in B11, and Price-Large to the price in B12.

4. Assign the name Total-Small to the total in cell B8, Total-Medium to the total in C8, and Total-Large in D8.

All these names are overkill for such a small spreadsheet, but there's a point to this exercise. Even in large spreadsheets that you create, you might find that you've named so many groups of cells that you're beginning to lose track of what's what. To refresh your memory, use the List button in the Range Name dialog box.

1. Find an empty group of cells below or to the right of any cells containing text or data. In this case, select cell G11.

2. Choose the Range Name command, and click the List button in the dialog box.

Works inserts a list of names and the cells they represent, beginning with the list in the cell you selected before choosing the command. Notice that Works requires two adjoining columns and the number of rows that corresponds to the number of names you've assigned. If you started the list where there was insufficient room, Works would overwrite existing data with the list of names. This is why it's so important to find a vacant area of the spreadsheet large enough for listing names.

If you want to insert the list well away from your working area, and yet you want to be able to consult it freely, scroll to an empty part of the spreadsheet, select a cell, and request the list. Next select the list and assign it a name before scrolling back to your workspace. When you want to consult the list, use the Go To command from the Select menu. Before you print the spreadsheet, however, be sure to check for the list and either delete it (with the Clear command) or omit it from the print area.

Range Names and Formulas

Now that you know about cells and cell ranges, you can see how helpful descriptive formulas can be. To make things a bit clearer, we made some terms bold, added a new row label in cell A8, and added an empty row above *Price*. See Figure 8-4 on page 237.

To start, select cell B8 (the cell in which you created a formula that totals the cells you just named Small). Notice the formula in the formula bar. Without prompting, Works has replaced the original cell designation (B3:B7) in the formula =SUM(B3:B7) with the name you assigned those cells: =SUM(Small).

You'll see this happen whenever you assign a name to a cell or a range of cells incorporated in a formula. If you select cells C8 and D8, you'll see that they now contain formulas showing range names, instead of range references.

You can use assigned names in creating formulas as follows:

1. Select cell C11 and type an equal sign to begin a formula.

2. Click on cell B8 (named *Total-Small*) to tell Works you want that cell in the formula.

3. Type the multiplication operator (*), and click on cell B11 (the price).

4. Click the Enter button to complete the command. You can see the results in Figure 8-4 below.

If you hadn't assigned names to these cells, your formula would be =B8*B11. Useful, but not very descriptive. Instead, the formula bar reads ='Total-Small'*'Price-Small.' Much better. (Works adds the single quotation marks enclosing the names.)

Now let's create similar formulas for medium and large pizzas by selecting cells C11 through C13, opening the File menu, and then choosing the Fill Down command.

It looks as if you've made a mistake here. Works displays 0 as the totals for medium and large pizzas. Let's see why. Select cell C12, and look at the formula bar.

There's the problem: Works treats names as *relative* references. It found the totals for each size pizza because the original formula simply referenced the cell directly above the formula cell. However, Works expected to find the price for medium pizzas in cell C11, and the price for large pizzas in cell D11—the cells in the same relative position as the price for small pizza in the original formula.

FIGURE 8-4.

Using descriptive formulas.

	Microsoft Works - [PIZZA.WKS]						
File Edit View Insert Format Tools Window Help							
Arial	10			B I U	Σ $		
C11	='Total-Small'*'Price-Small'						
	A	B	C	D	E	F	G	H
1	Pizza	Small	Medium	Large	Total Type			
2								
3	Cheese	57	32	29	118			
4	Sausage	97	143	168	408			
5	Pepperoni	102	169	185	456			
6	Anchovy	23	17	9	49			
7	Vegetarian	49	73	53	175			
8	Total Sales	328	434	444	1206			
9								
10	Price		Total Cost					
11	Small	$7.95	2607.6					
12	Medium	$9.95						
13	Large	$12.95						

You need to edit the formulas as follows:

1. Select cell C12.

2. Select the cell reference C11 in the formula bar.

3. Click the price for medium pizzas.

   Works replaces the highlighted portion of the formula with the cell reference you clicked. The formula is now correct, so do the following:

4. Click the Enter button to finish.

5. Edit the formula for totaling large pizzas in the same way.

   For the grand finale, do the following.

6. Select cell F8 and use the Autosum button to total the amounts in cells B8 through D8.

   Here are your pizza numbers!

	A	B	C	D	E	F	G	H
1	Pizza	Small	Medium	Large	Total Type			
2								
3	Cheese	57	32	29	118			
4	Sausage	97	143	168	408			
5	Pepperoni	102	169	185	456			
6	Anchovy	23	17	9	49			
7	Vegetarian	49	73	53	175			
8								
9	Total Sales	328	434	444		1206		
10	Price	$2,607.60	$4,318.30	$5,749.80		$12,675.70		
11	Small	$7.95						
12	Medium	$9.95						
13	Large	$12.95						
14								
15								
16								
17								
18								
19								
20								

Microsoft Works - [PIZZA.WKS]

File   Edit   View   Insert   Format   Tools   Window   Help

Arial   10   H22:J22

Press ALT to choose commands, or F2 to edit

Creating a Series

One element common to many, if not most, spreadsheets is that values and formulas (and even text) repeat. Because of its columnar format, a spreadsheet is ideal for laying out sequential sets of data such as sales by month, salaries by week, operating expenses by quarter, and so on.

We know that it's easy to fill cells either to the right or down. It is also easy to have Works generate a sequence of spreadsheet entries, such as four months in a row, 12 years, or 30 days.

The Fill Series command on the Edit menu is particularly useful in creating headings. It can take a starting value and generate a series of numbers or dates in selected cells, increasing them by the interval you specify.

To see how this works, do the following:

1. Open a new spreadsheet and maximize the document window as you have done in the past.

2. Enter the text shown in the following illustration.

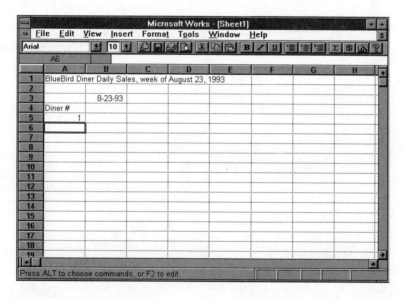

3. Select cells A5 through A12. You must include A5 in the selection. Works needs a "seed" number to start the series. Without a starting point, Works cannot carry out the Fill Series command.

4. Open the Edit menu, and then choose Fill Series. When you do this, you see the following dialog box.

You use this dialog box to choose a numeric series (such as 1, 2, 3, 4) or a series of dates (such as 4/1/93, 4/2/93, 4/3/93). The Step by box lets you choose the intervals within the series. For example, stepping by two creates the series 1, 3, 5, 7, and so on.

For this example, the only series choice available is Number, because your starting value, 1, can only be part of a numeric series.

5. Click OK to create the series.

Now create the second series you need, the days of the week, across the top of this small spreadsheet by doing the following:

6. Select the seven cells B3 through H3.

7. Open the Edit menu, and then choose Fill Series.

This time, Works suggests Day, which is the logical choice.

8. Click OK.

You could have chosen Weekday if you wanted to skip Saturdays and Sundays. The other possible choices for a date are Month, which fills the series with monthly intervals, and Year, which steps through the series by year.

Let's do more.

1. Type the following numbers in cells B5 through B12: *5, 12, 9, 15, 22, 3, 11*, and *7*.

2. Fill cells C5 through H12 with numbers by using the Fill Series command. Specify different step intervals, such as 3 and 7, to make the entries seem somewhat random.

3. Type *Total* in cell A14.

4. Select cell B14, and use the Autosum button to total the numbers in column B.

5. Use the Fill Right command to copy the formula from cell B14 into cells C14 through H14.

6. Select cells B12 through H12.

7. Choose the Border command from the Format menu, and click in the box to the left of the word Bottom to create a border line along the bottom of each cell.

8. Click OK to carry out the command.

9. Select cells A1 through A14 and click the B button on the toolbar to boldface all entries.

10. Select cells B3 through H3 and make them bold.

11. Select the word *Total*, and italicize it.

12. Open the File menu, and then choose Save. Then type *eats!.wks* and press Enter

13. Click the Print Preview button on the toolbar. Here's what you've created.

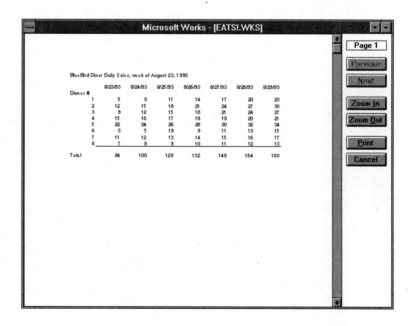

What If?

Far and away, the most valued feature of a spreadsheet program is its ability to test different values to see the effect they will have on your calculations.

Using the built-in function named IF, you can create a formula that tailors the result to conditions you define. For example, *IF* we sell 10,000 gizmos, *THEN* our profit will be X, *ELSE* our profit will be Y. IF produces one of two results, depending on whether the condition you specify (If we sell 10,000 gizmos) is true (our profit will be X) or false (our profit will be Y). The following examples show you the basics of using the IF function. Experiment with this function. You'll learn how to use it quickly and find its use invaluable.

The format of the IF function is as follows:

`IF(`*Condition,* `TrueValue,` `FalseValue`*)*

In this function's argument, *CONDITION* represents a value or the result of a calculation, *TrueValue* represents the result produced if the condition is true, and *FalseValue* represents the result if the condition is false.

Welcome to the Gizmo company sales report for January and June. The following example uses the sales from four Gizmo, Inc. stores to determine how much of each month's total represents profit. The example assumes that gizmos sell for $0.99 each and that Gizmo, Inc. makes 18 percent per gizmo on sales over 10,000, and 14 percent per gizmo on sales of 10,000 or less. To create the example, do the following:

1. Create a new spreadsheet with the Create New File command on the Edit menu. If necessary, maximize the window. See Chapter 7, page 175.

2. Create the spreadsheet shown on the next page.

3. Format cells B10 through G10 and cells B12 through G13 for currency and two decimal places.

4. Use the Autosum button to create a total in cell B9, and use the Fill Right command to copy the formula through cell G9, as shown on the next page.

```
=                    Microsoft Works - [GIZMOS.WKS]              ▼ ▲
─  File  Edit  View  Insert  Format  Tools  Window  Help          ▲
Arial            ▼ 10 ▼  ▭▭▭▭  ▭▭▭  B I U  ▭▭▭  Σ $ ▨ ?
        H59
        A         B         C        D        E        F        G        H
1   Gizmo Sales January-June
2
3              January  February   March    April     May     June
4   Store 1      2500     1983      3345     4121     1398     2765
5   Store 2      1750     2576      1522     1893     2175     3021
6   Store 3      3456     3602      2043     1087     2890     2998
7   Store 4      2892     1923      2980     3056     2901     2795
8
9   Total Sales
10  $$ Volume
11
12  Profit
13
14
15
16
17
18
19
20
Press ALT to choose commands, or F2 to edit
```

5. To derive the income values, enter the formula *=0.99*B9* in cell B10. Use the Fill Right command to copy the formula through cell G10.

   Now that you've finished the preparation, enter an IF function in cell B12.

6. Select cell B12.

7. Type *=IF (*or select the If function from the Function list discussed earlier.

8. Click on cell B9 to add it to the function.

9. Type *>10000,*

10. Click on cell B10 to add it to the function.

11. Type **18%,*

12. Click on cell B10 again to add it to the function.

13. Type *14%,

    The formula is complete; it should look like this:

    `=IF(B9>10000,B10*18%,B10*14%)`

14. Click the Enter button.

15. Use the Fill Right command to copy the formula through cell G12.

    Notice that in the formula bar Works converts the numbers you typed as percentages into their decimal equivalents: 0.18 for 18% and 0.14 for 14%.

What Does IF Mean?

An IF function isn't the easiest set of characters to interpret. This is what your formula means, piece by piece.

- *=IF(B9>10000* is the conditional part of the formula. This is the part Works evaluates to check whether the condition is true or false.

- Here, the condition tells Works to find out if the value in cell B9 is greater than 10,000.

- *B10*0.18* is the result if the condition is true. If sales are greater than 10,000 for the month, Gizmo, Inc. makes a profit of 18 percent per gizmo. If the condition is true, Works calculates 18 percent of the income shown in cell B10.

- *B10*0.14* is the result if the condition is not true. If sales are 10,000 or less for the month, Gizmo, Inc. makes only 14 percent profit. If the condition is false, Works calculates 14 percent of the income shown in cell B10.

IFs Within IFs

Sometimes you'll want to evaluate conditions that can have more than one true/false outcome. When this happens, you can place one IF function inside another, in the same way you place sets of parentheses inside others when controlling the order of calculation.

In this example, for instance, Gizmo, Inc. might find that profits are 18 percent for sales of 10,500 or more, 14 percent for sales between 10,001 and 10,500, and 12 percent for sales of 10,000 and less. To calculate profits for all three situations, you have to expand the formula. Do that by following these steps:

1. Type the following formula in cell B13:

    ```
    =IF(B9>10500,B10*.18,IF(B9>10000,B10*.14,B10*.12))
    ```

2. Use the Fill Right command to copy the formula through cell G13.

Here's what the formula does. If the value in cell B9 is greater than 10,500, multiply the income in cell B10 by 0.18. If the condition is false, but the value in cell B9 is greater than 10,000, multiply the income in cell B10 by 0.14. Otherwise, multiply the value in cell B9 (now down to any value of 10,000 or less) by 0.12.

> **TIP:** If you enter information incorrectly in the formula bar, Works will try to point out the error and give you a chance to edit the entry.

Functions like IF are very powerful, if a bit intimidating at first sight. Be patient and practice. You'll find that these functions will become everyday tools.

Calculating with Dates and Times

Although numeric values are the most common entries in spreadsheets, dates and times can be valuable, too. Date and time values can be used for "stamping" spreadsheets, tracking progress, and calculating elapsed times.

Works gives you two ways to use dates and times. The first is as a fixed value. The second is as an entry that is updated when you open the spreadsheet.

To display the date or time, Works starts with a serial number based on your computer's internal clock and calculates the appropriate result. Dates are formatted in long or short form, and times are formatted on the basis of a 12-hour or a 24-hour clock. Here's how Works presents each of these formats.

Time	12-Hour	24-Hour
Hour, minute, second	02:26:31 P.M.	14:26:31
Hour, minute	02:26 P.M.	14:26
Date	Long Format	Short Format
Month, day, year	January 1, 1992	1/1/92
Month, year	January 1992	1/92
Month, day	January 1	1/1
Month only	January	No short form

Open a new spreadsheet and try entering the time and date in each of these formats.

Entering Any Date or Time

One way to enter times and dates is to simply type them in. Use this method when you want one or more entries that do not represent the current time or date. You can follow one of the formats shown in the preceding table, or you can type the time or date in one form and then use the Number command on the Format menu to change the format. Follow these steps:

1. Select a cell and widen it to accommodate about 15 characters.

2. Type *1/1/93* and click the Enter button. You entered the date in its short month/day/year form. Now let's change it to the long form.

3. Open the Format menu, and then choose Number.

4. Click Date in the Format area of the Number dialog box.

5. Click on the style you want to use in the Date area.

6. Click OK to carry out the command. The date changes to the style you selected, such as January 1, 1993.

Entering the Current Date or Time

You can use two other methods to enter the current date or time. One method, which makes use of the NOW function, inserts a serial number in the cell. When you use the NOW function, Works updates the serial number whenever you reopen the spreadsheet and, in doing so, recalculates and updates the time or date as well.

After you use the NOW function, you can use the Number dialog box to convert the serial number to either a time or a date, in whatever format you want. You can also switch the format from time to date, or vice versa. To try the NOW function, follow these steps:

1. Select an empty cell, and type *=NOW()*.

2. Works inserts a number in the cell, such as 34206.93848, which corresponds to August 25, 1993 and 10:31 PM.

3. Open the Format menu, and then choose Number.

4. Click the date or time format you prefer, and then click OK.

Another way to enter the current date or time is to use the keyboard shortcuts Ctrl+semicolon for the date and Ctrl+Shift+semicolon for the time. When you use this method, Works inserts the date or time as a fixed entry that will not be updated, unless you specifically change it. To enter the current date and time:

1. Select a cell and press Ctrl+semicolon.

2. Press Enter to insert the current date.

3. Use the Number dialog box on the Format menu to format the date if you want. (If a set of number signs (#) appears because you chose the long format, remember that you can widen the column simply by pointing to the boundary between column labels and dragging to the right.)

4. Select another cell, and press Shift+Ctrl+semicolon.

5. Press Enter to insert the current time. Use the Number dialog box to format the time if you want.

Using Dates and Times in Formulas

The Works spreadsheet can even stretch its wings a bit and pretend to be a project-management program of sorts. Because Works can use dates and times in calculations, you can use the spreadsheet to track elapsed times.

When you use dates and times as part of a formula, you can either refer to the cells that contain them, or you can type the dates or times as part of the formula. If you choose the latter approach, however, enter dates in short form. Also, be sure to enclose the date or time in single quotation marks (for example, '1/1/92'). If you don't, Works will not recognize the entry as a valid date or time. The following example shows a simple tracking spreadsheet that uses time and date information.

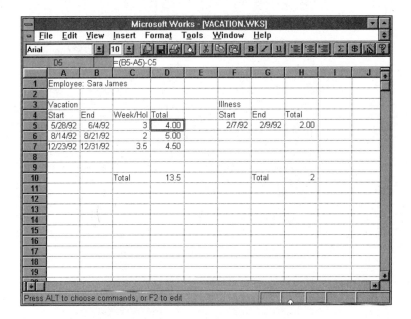

If you want to create this spreadsheet or a similar one, keep the following points in mind:

- The formula for calculating days elapsed subtracts the start date from the end date, not vice versa. Because Works does not compute weekends and holidays in its calculations, column C gives the number of weekends and holidays to subtract from the total. (The complete formula is shown in the formula bar.)

- A SUM function totals the number of vacation and sick days in columns D and H. The Autosum button could have been used instead.

- Extra cells are left blank for additional entries. Entering additional formulas is a simple matter of filling the extra cells. If you want, you can omit the extra columns and add new ones as needed with the Insert Row/Column command.

All other parts of this spreadsheet should be old news now that you're an accomplished Works worker.

Using Templates

Chances are that your spreadsheets will tend to follow certain forms and patterns. When you find yourself repeating layouts and formatting, remember that Works allows you to set up and save templates. To create a single spreadsheet template that opens whenever you start the Works spreadsheet, do the following.

1. Create the layout you want.

2. To save it as a template, open the File menu, and then choose the Save As command. The Save As dialog box appears.

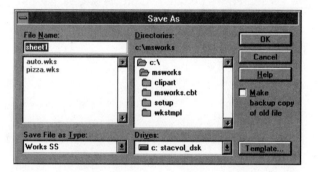

TIP: Always check to make sure that WORKS SS is displayed in the Save File as Type box. If it is not displayed, select it.

3. Select Template. The Save As Template dialog box appears:

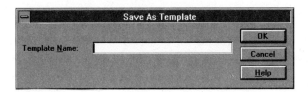

Any template you create can be opened by choosing Templates from the File menu.

You can also save a template for occasional use. First save the layout and formatting as a normal spreadsheet file. Open the file whenever you want to use the template. Save the finished spreadsheet under a different name to keep the template unchanged.

Coming Next

A picture is often worth much more than a thousand words. Much of the data that you work with in a spreadsheet can convey information more effectively if it is presented in a chart. Chapter 9 shows you how to create those charts.

Creating Charts

Would you like to have someone read the following two series of numbers to you: 5, 7, 11, and 17 versus 1, 4, 9, and 16? Or, would you rather look at the following chart? From which presentation of information do you learn more?

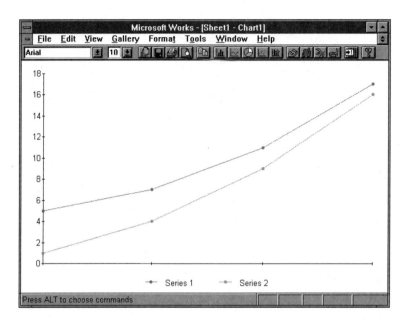

The corresponding numbers in these two series differ by 4, 3, 2, and 1 with succeeding pairs of numbers coming closer and closer together. You probably saw the pattern more quickly in the chart than you did when hearing the numbers recited; patterns are easier to recognize in graphics than they are in independent sets of numbers, letters, symbols, or other characters. A picture is still worth a thousand words.

When you work with numbers, charts can be invaluable in helping to visualize patterns of any type, including trends, comparisons, ranges, or fluctuations. Look at business or academic documents and you'll find that they're often filled with impressive charts.

One scatter chart can be clearer than pages of data to the scientist trying to figure out how many starfish are on the bottom of the sea as a function of sea depth. A set of bar charts or line charts can be more useful than piles of printouts in helping an economist interpret the effects of gasoline prices on the cost of fruit and vegetables.

Because of the importance of charts, we'll devote an entire chapter to their creation and modification. Besides, many people feel that creating and working with charts is the most enjoyable aspect of using Works.

Creating a Chart

Works can chart spreadsheet data with the click of the mouse button on the New Chart button on the toolbar. All you need to do is use a spreadsheet to provide the values you want charted. You created a number of spreadsheets in Chapter 7, so you can use them as a starting point. We'll continue to use the *pizza.wks* worksheet.

To create a chart, you begin by selecting the range of cells containing the data you want charted. A range can consist of as many as six consecutive rows or columns. Although you can include blank rows or columns of cells in the range, it's best not to because Works will plot the "values" of those empty cells or treat text differently from the way you might expect. At best, the chart might look unprofessional. At worst, it could be misleading.

In the *pizza.wks* spreadsheet, you have a made-to-order range of cells to chart (A3 through D7), which list sales of five types of pizza in three sizes. To turn this data into a chart, follow these steps.

1. Start Works and if necessary, open the file *pizza.wks*.

2. Select cells A3 through D7.

3. Click the New Chart button on the toolbar. Works shows the New Chart dialog box shown here, where you can select the type of chart you want to use and make adjustments.

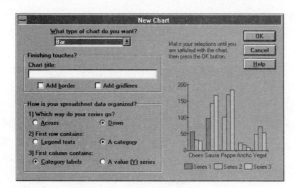

4. The default chart type Works uses when you click the New Chart button is a bar chart. Let's stick with the bar chart. Click OK. Almost immediately, Works opens a new window, named *PIZZA.WKS*, and displays Chart1, as shown in Figure 9-1.

FIGURE 9-1.
The default bar chart.

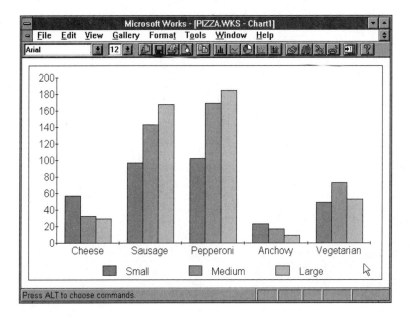

This is a bar chart, the default chart type Works uses when you click the Chart button. Notice that Works has turned text into labels along the horizontal axis of the chart. When the first column or top row of a range of cells contains text, Works turns the text into labels, as shown in the illustration.

The New Chart dialog box allows you to select from 12 different types of charts; add a title, a border, and gridlines; and provide information so that Works charts the data in the proper direction. Best of all, you can see everything you have specified (in the Sample area) and make changes before you click OK to get the final chart.

Some Charting Terminology

Even though charting is easy, knowing how Works "views" a chart and the data in it can help you create a chart easily and quickly. The best way to develop a feel for the charting process is to display the chart and spreadsheet side by side. To do that, choose Tile from the Window menu.

When you compare the cells you selected with the chart Works produced, you can see that Works rotated the spreadsheet cells 90 degrees. This happens when the selection includes more rows than columns. When the selection includes more columns than rows, Works keeps the original orientation. Works was designed to make data as visually informative as possible.

Except for circular pie charts, all charts have both a horizontal, or X, axis and a vertical, or Y, axis. Works refers to the X axis as the *category axis* (the type of pizza in Figure 9-1) and the Y axis as the *value axis* (the number of pizzas in Figure 9-1). The category axis identifies the values being charted. The value axis is the measure against which values in a line, bar, or scatter chart are plotted.

The value axis of the chart is divided into units against which Works plots the values in the cells you selected for charting. Works determines the lowest and highest values for you, depending on the smallest and largest values in the range. As you will learn later in this chapter, you can change these values to modify the way the charted data appears.

See Also: For more information, see "Modifying a Chart," page 283.

When you chart more than one set of data, as you did in Figure 9-1 with small, medium, and large pizzas, Works uses a different color or pattern to represent the values in each set.

Finally, note that each series of values is given its own color (or pattern). A *series* (such as small, medium, or large) is a related group of values from a single row or column in the range selected for charting. The number of small pizzas forms one series in the chart, just as *Glop, Son of Glop*, and *Return of Son of Glop* would form a recognizable (if uninspiring) series of films.

 TIP: You can easily tell which cell range is included in each series. In the chart window, choose GoTo from the Edit menu.

Saving a Chart

Saving a chart can be so simple you literally don't have to think about it. Works links charts to the spreadsheets from which they're created, so saving one or more charts is simply a matter of saving the spreadsheet file through a standard Save dialog box. Even if you forget about a new or changed chart and proceed to close the spreadsheet, Works reminds you when you choose the Close command. Because the chart is part of the spreadsheet, when you open one, you also open the other.

The Chart Toolbar

In Figure 9-1 on page 254, you can see the Chart toolbar at the top of the work area. Like any other toolbar, it contains a set of buttons that makes working with charts fast and efficient.

You will find many of the same features on this toolbar that you have seen on the word processor and spreadsheet toolbars, but here you will also find a set of icons, each representing a particular type of chart. Keep these in mind as we now discuss changing charts types and the different kinds of charts.

Changing Chart Types

Although Works creates a bar chart by default, you can choose from several other types of charts, all of which are available through the New Chart dialog box, on buttons on the charting toolbar, or through commands on the Gallery menu. Here are the charting buttons on the toolbar.

The last button on the right (the Go To 1st Series button) is used to modify a series in the spreadsheet from which the chart was generated.

All of the charts are available through the New Chart dialog box shown on page 253, but not all of these are available on the Gallery menu or the toolbar. If you can't find the particular type of chart you want on the toolbar, look to the Gallery menu. Or, open the New Chart dialog box by choosing the Create New Chart command from the Tools menu.

After you've created a basic bar chart from the spreadsheet, you can change chart types at any time to see which type best suits the data you're charting. Before you get more involved in the whys and wherefores of charting, you might like to see what your chart looks like in other formats.

TIP: You already know about font junk, where different fonts, sizes, and styles are mixed beyond repair (or understanding!). The same thing can happen with charts. Not all data is compatible with all types of charts; certain data must be illustrated using only one type of chart. Be careful, and be sure your chart says what the data says, not just what you want it to say.

Let's see what the pizza data looks like as a line chart. Click the toolbar button for the Line Chart, and as with all chart types, you'll see the type of dialog box shown here.

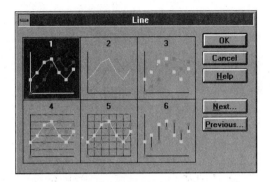

This dialog box expands your choices even further. The toolbar button for each chart type produces a dialog box like this one, showing variations of the basic chart you selected. The two buttons at the right, labeled Next and Previous, take you from one chart type to another without having to close the current dialog box and choose a different chart type.

In the following sections, you'll transform your chart several times to see how the same data is represented in some of the different chart types.

Bar Charts

Bar charts are often used for comparing such values as:

- Total sales of Arbor Shoes, by region, for the last four quarters
- The U.S. national deficit compared to tax revenues for the years 1980 through 1990
- Consumption of electricity by your household for each of the last 12 months

Works produces six types of bar charts. To see them, follow these steps.

1. Click Cancel if the Line dialog box is still displayed.

2. Click the Bar Chart button. Here's what you should see.

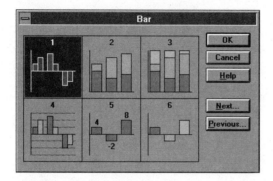

Notice from the examples in the dialog box that Works charts positive values above the X axis and negative values below it. To make values easier to interpret, the bar chart can include horizontal gridlines (option 4) or it can print the actual value above or below each bar (option 5).

The stacked bar charts in options 2 and 3 "add" series values to produce a single bar for each category on the X axis. To see how this works, follow these steps.

1. Double-click option 2 to stack the series values. This creates a bar equivalent to the sum of its parts for each category.

2. Click the Bar chart button again, and double-click option 3 to represent the parts of each bar as a percent of the total for each category.

Line Charts

Line charts are useful for showing trends and fluctuations over time, such as:

■ Atlantic and Pacific tuna catches over the last decade

■ Number of travelers per month on three major airlines

■ Ice cream sales in Phoenix and Minneapolis from January through December

There are six types of line charts. To see them again, click the Line Chart button on the toolbar. Most of the line charts use markers to indicate individual values and distinguish one series from another by color or shape. Works uses different-colored circles on a color screen and solid shapes, such as circles, squares, and diamonds, on a black-and-white screen. If you want, you can change the markers with the Patterns and Colors command on the Format menu.

For more information about the Paterns and Colors command see "Working with Patterns and Colors," page 281.

If markers are not important to your chart, you can choose option 2 to display lines alone. Conversely, if the lines are not important, you can choose option 3 and display markers only. Options 4 and 5 are standard line charts, but with horizontal or both horizontal and vertical gridlines.

Option 6 looks a bit odd for a line chart, but it is well suited for stock prices and similar values in which highs and lows are as important as or more important than trends over time. This chart differs from the others in using markers and a straight line to show the range between the lowest and highest values in each set. If you have intermediate values, Works adds markers on the line to show the position of each intermediate value, relative to the lowest and highest.

To turn the *pizza.wks* chart into a line chart, double-click on the option you want to see.

Whole and Sliced Pies

Pie charts, familiar to any reader of the local newspaper, show a single set of values as ratios or as slices of an entire pie. Pie charts are commonly used for demographic reports such as:

■ Percent of households in various income ranges that have one or more computers

- Proportion of Republicans who voted

- Percent of total time spent with clients

Both eye-catching and easy to interpret, pie charts are useful in any situation in which the parts need to be seen in relation to the whole, such as poll results, census results, federal spending, state spending, city spending, and personal spending.

Creating a pie chart is straightforward and works like this.

1. Click the Pie Chart button, and you'll see the following dialog box.

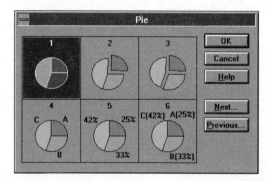

Notice that you can create a pie chart with category labels, percents, or labels and percents.

2. Double-click option 5 to create a pie chart that shows the percentage each slice represents.

So far, so good. But there's something subtle going on here. When you create a pie chart, Works uses only a single set of values—in one row or one column of cells. If you choose more than a single row or column, as you did in the *pizza.wks* spreadsheet, Works creates a pie chart from the first value series. This one-series limit applies only to pie charts. There's an easy way to check.

1. Open the Window menu, and then choose *pizza.wks*. Select cells B3 through B7 in the *pizza.wks* spreadsheet.

2. Click the New Chart button to create a chart. Choose Pie, and click OK.

3. Now click the Pie Chart button, choose option 5, and click OK.

4. Tile the windows so you can see both pie charts. They're identical because both charts are based on the same cell ranges, even though you might have assumed that the original pie chart represented a compilation of all selected values.

   You don't need the duplicate chart anymore, so click in the chart window, and choose Delete Chart from the Tools menu.

5. When the Delete Chart dialog box appears, click the Delete button, and then click OK to complete the command.

6. Tile the windows again to make the display neat.

   Aside from whether to add labels, the biggest decision when creating pie charts is whether and what part or parts to explode, or separate, from the rest. If you choose option 2 from the Pie dialog box, Works explodes the first value outward. If you choose option 3, Works simulates the Big Bang and explodes the entire pie.

   If you don't want to explode the entire pie, but you do want to explode a slice other than the first, create a standard pie and choose the Patterns and Colors command from the Format menu. The dialog box in Figure 9-2 will appear.

FIGURE 9-2.
The Patterns and Colors dialog box for a pie chart.

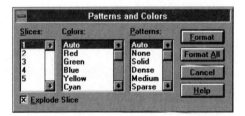

Now you can select the pattern and color you would like applied to each slice. Choose the slice you want to explode from the Slices box, click Explode Slice, and then click the Format button. You can repeat this procedure to explode additional slices. When you have finished, click the Close button. You can also use the Patterns and Colors command to create an exploded pie chart with labels, percentages, or both, something you cannot do directly from the Pie Chart dialog box.

Stacked Line Charts

Stacked line charts are line charts with a dash of stacked bar chart tossed in. Instead of plotting values independently, stacked line charts add or subtract the values in each series so that the marker in the topmost line reflects the combined total. Sound confusing?

Take a look by choosing the Stacked Line chart in the New Chart dialog box. (There is no Stacked Line button on the toolbar.) Then do the following steps.

1. Double-click option 2 to turn your *pizza.wks* chart into a stacked line chart with horizontal gridlines that make it easier to read.

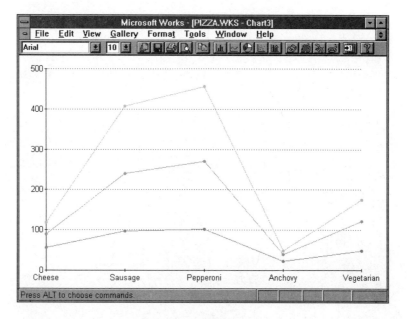

2. Click in the spreadsheet window, and scroll to the right so you can see the totals in column F.

By comparing the chart with the totals for each type (category) of pizza, you can see that Works has added the values for each series (small, medium, and large) in constructing the line chart, and the markers in the topmost line correspond to the combined total for each category. In contrast, a regular line chart for the same range of cells would plot values (and lines) independently.

X-Y (Scatter) Charts

Scatter charts show relationships between sets of data by plotting values against both the horizontal and vertical axes of the chart. Bar, line, and stacked line charts use the X axis for categories, whereas scatter charts use both the X and Y axes as scales for numeric values. Each corresponding X and Y point is graphed.

Typical examples of data used in scatter charts show the relationship between the following items:

- Height and weight

- Education and income

- Amount of ice cream consumed and daily temperature

Other charts might compare age with auto accidents or sick time reported against overtime worked. If you were a scientist, you might use scatter charts to see if a relationship exists between hours of light and flower production for geraniums.

You can see the options for scatter charts in the dialog box shown here.

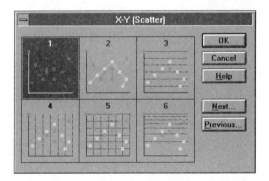

Because both the Y and X axes must be scaled, the data in the spreadsheet has to be prepared in a particular fashion and the chart must be created following some very specific steps. Here's how to create a scatter chart.

1. Select the column of data you want to chart on the X axis. Ignore the Y axis values for now. Remember that the data must be numeric and can not include text.

2. Open the Edit menu, and then choose Copy. This will save the data to the Clipboard.

3. Select the data you want to chart on the Y axis.

4. Click the New Chart button on the toolbar.

5. Click OK. Works will produce a bar chart with the values scaled against the Y axis.

6. Open the Edit menu, and then choose Paste Series. When a dialog box appears, click the series you copied to the Clipboard belongs on the category (X) axis. Click OK.

7. Click the Scatter Chart button on the toolbar, and double-click the type of scatter chart you want. Here's what an X-Y chart (sometimes called a *scattergram*) looks like.

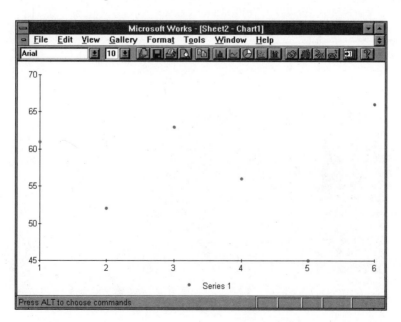

A bit roundabout, but not bad. If necessary, you can fine-tune the scale of the X axis with the Horizontal (X) Axis command on the Format menu.

 See Also: For information about how to fine-tune the scale of the X axis, see "Changing the Scale of an Axis," page 277.

Combination Charts

A combination chart is, as its name indicates, a combination of a bar and a line chart. Because you can include a second vertical axis on the right of a chart, the combination chart is especially useful when you want to chart two differently scaled series. Combination charts are also valuable when you want a clear distinction between two series of values. You might, for example, choose this type of chart when plotting:

- The asking and selling prices for homes

- Sales volumes for new and used cars

- Average loan amounts during periods of different interest rates

As you can see in the following dialog box, there are four types of combination charts.

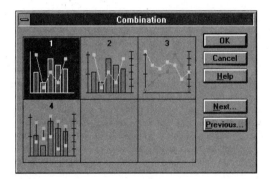

Options 2 and 3 are useful for displaying differently scaled values. Option 4 is a likely candidate for financial data, for example, bars showing stock volumes and range lines showing high, low, and closing prices.

Let's create a combination chart, using the spreadsheet of average new and used car prices over a five year period as shown in Figure 9-3. We'll save it as *cars.wks*.

FIGURE 9-3.
A spreadsheet to use to create a combination chart.

	Microsoft Works - [CARS.WKS]	
File Edit View Insert Format Tools Window Help		

Arial   10

H23:I23

	A	B	C	D	E	F	G	H
1		Used	New					
2	1989	$4,345.00	$12,342.00					
3	1990	$5,434.00	$13,445.00					
4	1991	$5,432.00	$14,323.00					
5	1992	$4,564.00	$14,898.00					
6	1993	$5,676.00	$15,787.00					
7								
8								
9								
10								
11								
12								
13								
14								
15								
16								
17								
18								
19								

Press ALT to choose commands, or F2 to edit

1. Select cells A1 through C6.

2. Click the New Chart button.

3. In the New Chart dialog box, choose Combination from the What type of chart do you want? area.

4. Click OK.

The result of this effortless feature is shown here.

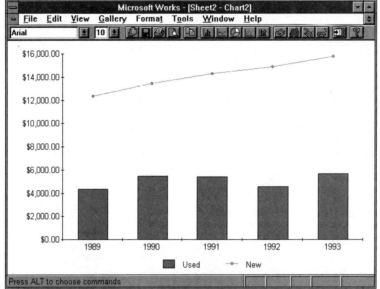

Dressing Up a Chart

After you've created a chart, you can do many things to make charts more informative. You can add titles, include legends that identify series within categories, and insert labels that clarify some or all of the data points in the chart. You can also add a second Y axis, as well as define or change the intervals and scales Works uses for both axis. To change a chart's appearance, you can change fonts, add boldface and other character styles, and choose or change colors and patterns.

We'll deal with all of these in the remainder of this chapter.

Working with Titles

Titles may be the primary way to make a chart more informative. Works lets you add a main title, a subtitle, and titles for the X axis, the Y axis, and (if you include one) the right vertical axis.

To include any or all of these on a chart, you use the Titles command on the chart module's Edit menu. Remember that you are working in the Chart window when you make these modifications.

The chart you first saw in Figure 9-1 on page 254 will help illustrate what Works can do with titles and labels. Be sure that you have a clean screen; retrieve the *pizza.wks* worksheet and chart.

1. Open the View menu, and then choose Chart. When you do this, you will see a listing of all the charts associated with the *pizza.wks* spreadsheet.

2. Click the chart you want to use. If necessary, click the document window's Maximize button to take full advantage of the screen.

3. To add a title, a subtitle, and a title for the vertical axis, open the Edit menu, and then choose Titles. You will see the Titles dialog box shown here.

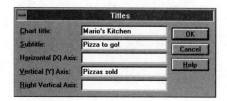

4. Fill in the dialog box, as shown above.

5. Click OK.

As easily as that, you can add titles to your charts, without worrying about spacing or alignment. You simply type the title you want. To delete a title, reverse the command: Choose the Titles command, select the title you don't want, press the Del key, and then click OK.

Take a look at the chart on the next page to see how the titles look and how much more informative the chart is.

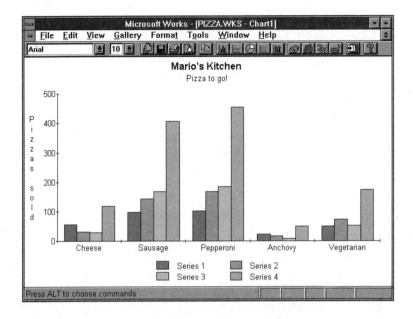

Creating a Title from Existing Text

You can also add a title to a chart without having to enter any new text, simply by using text that already exists on the spreadsheet. Instead of typing the title in the Titles dialog box, type the address of the cell containing the text you want. Then when Works carries out the Titles command, it will use the text in the cell you specified as a title on your chart.

You can also use range names instead of cell references. If a name refers to more than a single cell, however, Works will use the contents of the first cell in the range as the title. In the *pizza.wks* spreadsheet, you assigned the name Small to cells B3 through B7. If you were to type *small* in the Titles dialog box, Works would use the first value, 57, as the title of the chart.

If you are going to use range names, keep in mind that Works treats them as references to cells. If you want to use a name as text, rather than as a cell reference, precede the name with a double quotation mark (").

For example, the name Pizza Sales refers to cells A3 through D7 in the spreadsheet. To use the name as the title for the vertical axis, you would type *"Pizza Sales* in the Titles dialog box. The double quotation mark would tell Works to treat the name as text. This situation is comparable to typing a double quotation mark in front of a number when you want to enter the number in a cell as text, not a value.

Working with Legends

A legend is the key to the color, pattern, or marker used for each series in a category. In *pizza.wks*, the three different series (small, medium, and large) are each different colors. They could just as well be different textures or patterns.

Like the marks, symbols, and colors on a map, a blueprint, or a diagram, legends help the reader interpret the material correctly and with the least amount of effort. You can include legends on all but pie charts. (You identify slices on pie charts by choosing the chart option that includes percents, categories, or both when you create the pie chart.)

Works now has an Auto Legend feature. It automatically assigns legends to a chart if no legends were specified when the chart was created. It uses the names Series 1, Series 2, etc.

When you select a range of cells to turn into a bar, line, or scatter chart, Works creates the appropriate legends for you if the range includes row or column titles for each series being plotted. Note that this is not the same as creating category labels on the X axis. Category labels (such as cheese and anchovy in the *pizza.wks* chart) identify the categories Works is charting.

On the other hand, legends identify the values (such as small, medium, and large) that are plotted. To see the difference, and to create some legends of your own, follow these steps.

1. Open the Format menu, and verify that a checkmark appears next to Add Legend. Works lets you turn the display of legends on and off. Right now, you want it on.

2. Open the chart's Edit menu, and then choose the Legend/Series Labels command.

3. Type the cell references you see here in the Legend/Series Labels dialog box.

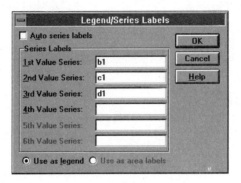

If you tile the windows, you can see that the references refer to cells containing the text for each of the legends.

 TIP: If the Auto series labels check box at the top left of the Legend/Series Labels dialog box is checked, Works will automatically insert Series 1, Series 2, etc., labels as part of the Auto Legend feature. To enter different legends, be sure this box is not checked.

As in creating titles, you can use cell references, rather than typing the text you want to create legends. To use text that is also a range name, insert a double quotation mark before the range name to indicate that the name is to be treated as text, not as a cell reference.

4. Click OK to create the legends.

At the bottom of the chart, below the category labels, Works creates three legends next to three small boxes showing the color or pattern used for the values plotted for small, medium, and large pizzas. If this were a line chart, Works would display markers, rather than colors or patterns, but the result would be the same—more information to help you better understand the contents of the chart.

Using Labels

Titles, legends, and labels form a descending sequence for identifying chart elements. Titles identify all or part of the chart. Legends identify key elements. Labels identify actual values. You can label values on a bar or line chart, but not a pie chart. For a pie chart, select the chart option (4, 5, or 6) that includes labels.

The easiest and most common way to label data is to include the actual value for each data point. You can also label data with text or other information by using existing entries from the spreadsheet or by typing new entries for use as labels. In some stand-alone spreadsheets like Microsoft Excel, you can insert such labels directly on the chart, but you cannot do that in Works.

To create labels, follow these steps.

1. With a chart window active, open the Edit menu, and then choose Data Labels. The following dialog box appears.

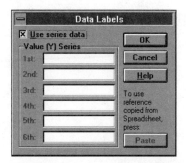

The check box at the top, titled Use series data, is all you need to label a chart with the actual values plotted.

2. Click the Use series data check box.

3. Click OK to carry out the command. Choosing this label option overrides any others you specify in the rest of the dialog box.

The Value (Y) Series box is where you enter the references of cells containing the labels you want to use. To ensure that values are labeled correctly, be sure you understand which values are included in the first, second, and subsequent Y series. If you need to check, cancel this command

and choose Go To from the Edit menu. Works will display the cell ranges for each series in the Go To dialog box.

The OK, Cancel, and Help buttons in the dialog box work as you would expect, but the Paste button is new. When you want to use cell contents other than plotted values as data labels, you can copy the information from the spreadsheet to the Clipboard and then use the Paste button to insert the copy in one of the Value (Y) Series boxes.

To experiment with data labels, add the plotted values to the bars in your *pizza.wks* chart as follows:

1. Open the chart module Edit menu, and then choose Data Labels.

2. In the Data Labels dialog box, click the Use series data box.

3. Click OK to carry out the command.

   Your chart should look like this.

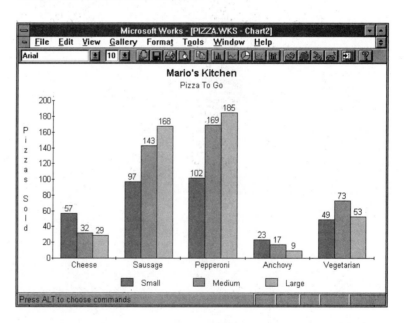

Now let's assign a different type of label.

1. Return to the spreadsheet. Type *S* in cell B2, *M* in C2, and *L* in D2.

2. Copy the contents of the three cells to the Clipboard.

3. Return to the chart. (Select it from the Window menu.)

4. Open the chart module Edit menu, and then choose the Data Labels command.

5. Click the Use series data checkbox to turn the option off.

6. Type *B2* for the 1st Value (Y) Series, type *C2* for the 2nd, and *D2* for the 3rd.

7. Click OK.

The value labels disappear and are replaced by *S*, *M*, and *L* at the top of the three series bars in the first chart category.

Adding a Second Vertical Axis

In bar, line, and scatter charts, Works displays a single Y axis by default. You can add a second vertical axis at the right edge of the chart when it is needed to improve readability or when you want to show two different scales.

To add a second vertical axis, you use the Two Vertical (Y) Axes command on the Format menu. To use this command to create a second vertical axis on the *pizza.wks* chart, follow these steps:

1. Open the Format menu, and then choose Two Vertical (Y) Axes. You'll see the following dialog box.

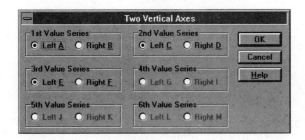

The dialog box might seem a bit cluttered at first, but the contents are easy to interpret. There are boxes for six series, the most Works can handle in a single chart. For each series, you can choose an axis on the left or on the right. (The letters A through M represent the keys you press to choose each of the options if you don't use a mouse.) Notice that only the first three boxes are darkened and active because there are only three series in the *pizza.wks* chart.

When you have a single vertical axis, Works automatically turns on the Left option for each plotted series. To create a right vertical axis scaled to the values in a particular series, click the Right option in that series box. Here are the steps:

1. Click the Right option in the 1st Value Series box.

2. Click OK to create the right vertical axis. Here's the new chart with a right axis added.

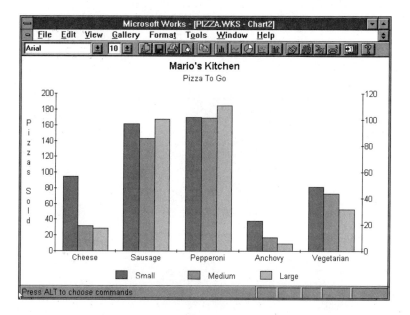

Notice that the new axis has a different maximum value (120), even though it defaults to the same 20-pizza intervals used on the left axis. This happened because Works used the maximum and minimum values in the first value series to create the scale. This series, which contains the number of small pizzas sold, has a smaller range (23 to 102) than do the other series; thus, Works has created a "smaller" scale.

Notice, too, that creating a right axis that is scaled differently from the left one can have some potentially confusing results. The bars for the first value series are no longer proportional to the bars in the other series, even though they all represent the same basic information. That is because Works has to fit in the same amount of information in an even smaller space (with the new axis on the right).

A better approach would be to create a right axis that is identical to the left one. You follow the same steps as before, with one minor change: Click the Right option in *all three series boxes*. You'll end up with two identical axes because Works will fit the largest range for a series.

Let's make the chart even more readable by clicking the Bar chart button on the toolbar and selecting option 4 to display gridlines. Here's the latest version of the chart.

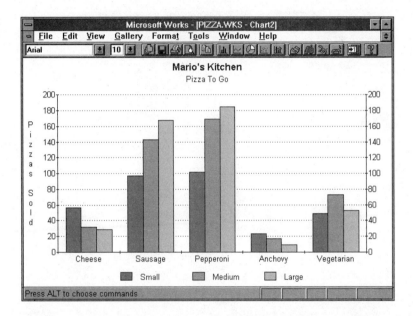

Changing the Scale of an Axis

Even though Works excels at figuring out an appropriate scale for the values it plots, you'll sometimes want to change an aspect of the scale.

For example, you might want to unclutter the Y axis by leaving larger intervals between measures or to change the proportions of the bars in a chart by using a logarithmic scale based on a multiplication factor, rather than a set of equal values.

By changing the extreme values on the Y axis, you can artificially increase or decrease differences represented by lines. In Figure 9-4 you can see two charts that plot the same information. The one on the left has a range from 30 to 70, and the one on the right has a range of 0 to 70. You can see how the differences on the chart with the larger range *appear* to be larger than those shown on the other chart, even though they are actually the same.

FIGURE 9-4.
Changing the scale of an axis.

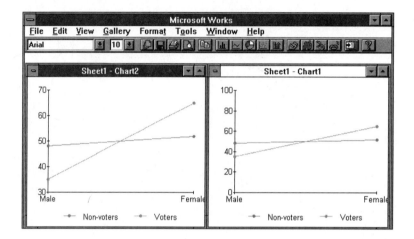

The Vertical (Y) Axis and (if you've added a second axis) the Right Vertical Axis commands on the Format menu let you change the scale of the left and right Y axes on a bar or line chart.

The Horizontal (X) Axis and Vertical (Y) Axis commands, again on the Format menu, do the same jobs on a scatter chart. All of these commands produce a dialog box similar to this one.

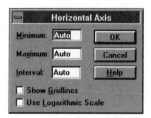

Note the following aspects of this dialog box:

- The Minimum and Maximum boxes let you set the smallest and largest values on the scale. The Auto setting lets Works determine these values.

- Interval lets you specify how large the steps between measurements should be. Again, the Auto setting lets Works do the work.

- The entries in the Type box set the type of scale:

  ❑ Normal for charts like the current one.

  ❑ Stacked for stacked bar or stacked line charts in which each value contributes to a total.

  ❑ 100% for stacked bar charts in which each value is represented as a proportion of 100 percent.

  ❑ Hi-Lo for line charts in which you display high and low ranges, as in stock values.

  ❑ 3-D for rows in which a three-dimensional element is created within the chart.

- Show Gridlines is another way (besides chart-type options) of displaying gridlines.

- Use Logarithmic Scale sets the scale to a logarithmic rather than linear measure.

- No Vertical Axis deletes any vertical axis in the chart. Why would you want to do this? Sometimes you can increase clarity by reducing clutter.

Suppose you want to simplify the scale on the vertical axes of your *pizza.wks* chart. You've added data labels, so you really don't need the closely spaced intervals Works has provided.

1. Open the Format menu, and then choose Vertical (Y) Axis.

2. Type *50* in the Interval box.

3. Click OK.

Works immediately changes both scales. When you have identical left and right axes, as you do here, use the Right Vertical Axis command to change both at the same time. If you have different scales, use the Vertical (Y) Axis command to change the left axis and the Right Vertical Axis command to change the right one.

Working in Fonts

With the Works charting feature, you can now use many fonts, in any style and size that you choose.

You use the Select Title Text command on the Edit menu to select the chart's title, and then use the Font and Style dialog box to change the font used in the title. Follow the same steps to change the font used in the chart.

As in the other Works applications, however, the actual fonts and font sizes available to you depend on your computer and, even more so, on your printer, its capabilities, and the way you've defined it to Windows.

So far, your chart looks pretty good, but it could use a little sprucing up. Let's change the title's font to 14 point, italic.

1. Open the Edit menu, and then choose Select Title Text or double-click on the title to select it.

2. Open the Format menu, and then choose Font and Style.

3. Select a font, size, and style you want to use. Here you can see how we changed the title (but not the subtitle) to make it bigger, bold, and italic.

Mario's Kitchen
Pizza To Go

Now for the rest of the chart. Click anywhere in the chart to deselect the title.

4. Open the Format menu, and then choose Font and Style.

5. Choose a font for the rest of the chart, and, if you would like, a style and size.

6. Click OK.

Your chart is constantly changing. Evaluate its appearance carefully. We encourage you to try all the charting options that Works provides to gain experience working with the software.

Working with Patterns and Colors

The Patterns and Colors command can provide more fun than any one chart maker deserves, but don't go overboard by using too much of a good thing.

With this command, you can specify screen and print colors (the latter only if you have a color printer), patterns for different series in bar and pie charts, and markers for data values in line charts. As mentioned earlier, you can also use this command to explode the slice of your choice in a pie chart.

When you choose the Patterns and Colors command from the Format menu, Works displays a dialog box that looks like this.

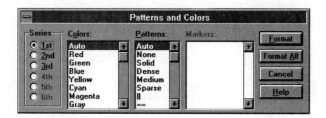

Works tailors the options in the dialog box to suit the type of chart you're working with. For example, this dialog box shows the options available for a bar chart. When you work with a line chart, you see many options in the Markers box because a line chart uses them. When you work with a combination chart, Works displays a choice of markers if you select a series (in the Series box) represented by a line in the chart.

Here's a rundown of the options included in the dialog box and their purposes:

- The Series option lets you choose the value series to format.

- The Colors option lets you pick a color for the series. Auto tells Works to use a predefined set of colors (red for the first series, green for the second, and blue for the third).

- The Patterns option lets you choose a pattern for the bar or line representing the selected series. If you work with a color monitor, but print in black and white, Auto tells Works which predefined patterns to use in place of color during printing. (You can see these patterns on screen by choosing Display as Printed from the View menu.)

- The Markers option lets you choose the type of marker used for data points in a line chart. Auto again sets the markers for you when you display or print the chart in black and white.

- The Format button in the dialog box tells Works to apply the choices you've made to the selected series. Use this button if you want to make additional changes to other series.

- The Format All button applies one or more choices you've made to all series in the chart. Use this button, for example, to change all lines in a line chart from solid to dotted, or to change all bars in a bar chart from multicolored to magenta. (In the latter case, Works changes to a different pattern or marker for each series, so you can still distinguish one bar or line from another.)

- The Close button is labeled Cancel until you make a formatting change. Cancel, as usual, cancels the command. Close tells Works you've finished formatting. When you click Close, Works updates the chart with the changes you specified.

Here are the steps to follow in working with the Patterns and Colors dialog box.

1. Open the Format menu, and then choose Patterns and Colors.

2. If you have a color monitor, select a new color for the first series, and then click the Format button. Do the same for the other two series, clicking the Format button for each.

   As you make these changes, you'll see them occur in the chart, located behind the dialog box.

3. Now select a single color, and click Format All. Click Close to make the changes. Notice that Works displays different patterns to distinguish one bar in the chart from the next.

4. Return the formatting to Auto unless you prefer the display you've produced.

A more noticeable difference in the dialog box appears when you're working with a pie chart. Works then displays the dialog box you saw in Figure 9-2 on page 262.

Here, you choose slices, rather than series. You can change colors and patterns as you did in the preceding example, and you can use the Explode Slice checkbox at the bottom of the dialog box to explode the piece of the pie you select in the Slices box.

Here's a pie chart with an exploded slice (of pizza?).

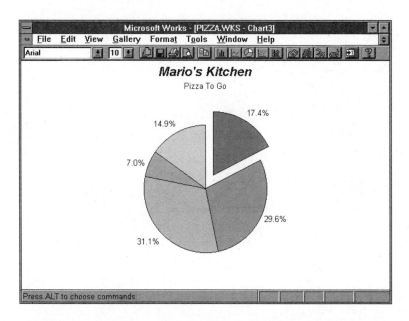

Modifying a Chart

After you've created a chart, you don't have to worry about updating it whenever you change data in the spreadsheet. Works does that automatically because the two documents are so closely linked. You might, however, want to change category labels, alter the definition of a series, add a new series, or delete an old one from a chart. Then, too, you might find that you want to create or change a chart by including one or more series from separate (nonadjacent) locations on the spreadsheet. You can do all this with the Series and Paste Series commands on the Edit menu.

Changing Category Labels

Category labels, like data labels, must already exist on a spreadsheet before you can incorporate them in a chart. After you've entered them on your spreadsheet, however, you can simply select them and copy them into place. The orientation of the copied cells doesn't matter, so you can copy a row of labels into a chart whose categories are based on column titles, and vice versa. For example, suppose Mario has developed a political consciousness and has decided to name his pizzas. We would accomplish this as follows.

1. Switch to the *pizza.wks* spreadsheet, and type the following entries in cells B18 through F18: *Purist, Conservative, Liberal, Independent,* and *Grassroots*. The titles won't show completely in the cells, but that's no problem.

2. Select the titles and copy them to the Clipboard using the Copy command on the Edit menu.

3. Return to the chart and open the Edit menu, and then choose Paste Series.

4. Click Category, and then click OK.

   Your old categories are replaced by the new names.

   Another way to accomplish the same task is to use the Series command, instead of Paste Series. The Series command produces a dialog box that looks like this.

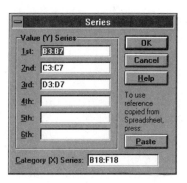

To turn the cell contents you copied in the last procedure into category labels on the X axis, do the following.

1. Click the Category (X) Series box.

2. Click the Paste button to paste the range into the box.

3. Click OK to complete the command.

Changing Series

Changing the Y series is similar to changing category labels. Once again, you use cell references and either the Paste Series or Series command. For example, suppose Mario adds a giant-sized pizza to the menu and wants to include it in the chart. We could do so by following these steps.

1. Return to the pizza spreadsheet by choosing it from the Window menu.

2. Type *X-large* in cell E1.

3. Type *20, 13, 17, 1,* and *15* into cells E3 through E7.

4. Copy the contents of cells E3 through E7 to the Clipboard.

5. Return to the chart.

6. Open the Edit menu, and then choose Series.

7. Click in the box next to 4th series.

8. Click the Paste button.

9. Click OK to add the new series.

10. Now choose the Format menu, and then choose Two Vertical Axes. Notice that the Left option is turned on in the 4th Value Series box. Because you created two vertical axes, and this is the only Left option selected, the new series controls the left axis.

11. Click the Right option.

12. Click OK to bring everything into line.

13. Now use the Legend/Series Labels command on the Edit menu to label the fourth series X-Large. If you've been following along, your chart should look something like this.

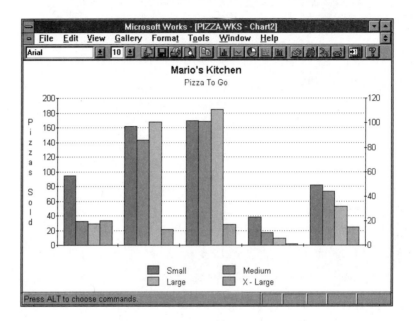

Charting Nonadjacent Ranges

You can use the Series and Paste Series commands to create a chart from nonadjacent ranges. Because ranges don't have to be oriented in the same directions, these commands can be useful if you want to chart related values that are laid out horizontally in one range, but vertically in another.

The examples we just showed you used these two commands, so here we'll outline this new procedure.

1. If you're creating a new chart, select the first range.

2. Click the spreadsheet's New Chart button on the toolbar to create the chart.

3. Click OK in the New Chart dialog box.

4. From the new chart, return to the spreadsheet and select the second range to chart.

5. Copy it to the Clipboard.

6. Return to the chart.

7. Use the Paste Series or the Series command to turn the references for the copied cells into the second value series.

8. Click OK to update the chart.

You might need to return to the spreadsheet and repeat the procedure for additional cell ranges.

That's it. Horizontal, vertical, close together, or widely spaced, you can turn the cell ranges of your choice into the chart you want to see.

Setup and Printing

Setting up and printing a chart is very similar to those processes in other Works applications. We'll review the differences you need to understand to get the job done right.

Previewing a Chart

If you work with a color monitor but print in black and white, the colors you see on screen are replaced by patterns and differently shaped markers in print.

There are several ways to see what the printed chart will look like. The easiest method, and the one designed for this purpose, is to choose the Display As Printed command from the View menu. You'll see the chart as it will appear when printed. At this point, works replaces color with patterns if you don't have a color printer.

If you don't feel like using this command, click the Print Preview button on the toolbar. You'll see a smaller, but otherwise identical, "printed" version of your chart. If you don't want to use either of these methods, you can also choose Black as the color for the entire chart in the Patterns and Colors dialog box. This last approach is pretty roundabout, but it is available.

Page Setup and Printing

When you're ready to finish up and print a chart, you can add running heads, page numbers, and other information with the Headers and Footers command on the View menu. When you create running heads, you can use any of the special characters you use with spreadsheets: &P for the page number; &F for the filename; &D or &N for the date in short or long format; &T for the current time; && for an ampersand; and &L, &C, and &R to left-align, center, or right-align any text that follows.

To set up your margins, you use the Page Setup command from the File menu. As usual, this command displays a tab dialog box (as you see below) with several different options including Margins, Size, Source and Orientation, and Other Options.

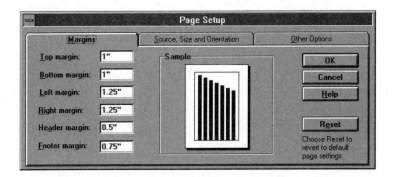

Normally, Works sets up a chart so that it prints on a full page. If you select the Source, Size, and Orientation Size option here, Works reduces the chart to the size one screen would occupy, which is about one-quarter of a page. This is a useful option when you're printing small or uncomplicated charts. If you use it, be sure to check all text and labels before printing to verify that they will be reproduced completely and without appearing too cramped.

Under Other Options, you can also select to print on a full page but keep the chart dimensions proportionate in both height and width.

Keep the original proportions if what the chart "says" is more important than the way it looks. For example, do this if relative heights of bars or relative placement of lines is critical to the chart's impact. Use a full page if the overall appearance of the chart is more important than exact ratios of height to width, and if you don't mind the chart being shortened or widened to accommodate the page size. Use the full page, proportional, if you want an exact duplicate of what you see on screen on one page.

Printing a chart is, as usual, a simple matter of choosing the Print command and specifying the number of copies you want. If you switch between portrait and landscape mode for printing, however, Works might tell you that the printer setup description needs to be modified, even if you've switched the page length and width measurements in the Page Setup & Margins dialog box.

If you have to modify your printer setup, check the dialog box that appears for options that let you toggle between portrait and landscape mode. Be sure to reset the printer when you're finished, to avoid surprises when you try to print your next "normal" document.

Coming Next

That's the end of the spreadsheet discussion. You now have two of the Works modules well in hand and are ready to learn about managing information through the use of a database. So get out your coin collection, comic books, or latest stock report, and let's go to work.

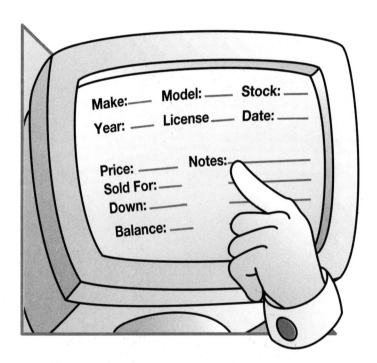

Using the
Database

10

Getting Started with the Database

n Part 2 of *Running Microsoft Works 3 for Windows,* you learned how to work with words using the Microsoft Works 3 for Windows word processor. In Part 3, you learned how to work with and manipulate numbers using the Works spreadsheet. In this part of Running Works, you'll learn how to work with the Works database, a tool for organizing and controlling information.

This chapter and chapters 11 and 12 describe ways to use the Works database module to create and manage information, such as inventories, price lists, catalogs, and collections. Because "data is data," *how* you can work with it makes all the difference in the world. That's where the Works database comes in.

What Is a Database?

A *database* is a collection of information organized according to certain criteria. The phone book is a database; so are a teacher's grade sheet and your collection of baseball cards. A *database management system* is the tool used to create a database. For our purposes, though, we'll speak of the two as the same. Therefore, Works is a database, and what you organize using Works is a database as well.

Database programs require more structure than most other types of applications because they provide fast access to any fact in a collection of information. Like a librarian who must be able to find any single book in a collection of unrelated books, a database program must be able to find the one record you seek in an entire collection of related, but independent, entries. Neither the librarian nor the database program can anticipate what you'll request, so both must rely on a structure or form to make searching quick and effective.

Using the database program is a two-step process. First you design a form for your data and enter the information you want it to hold. Later you use the database program to search, sort, and create a printed report of the data you've compiled.

Forms, Records, Fields, and Files

The Works database relies on *forms, records, fields,* and *files*. A form is the on-screen equivalent of a paper data-entry form. For example, it could be the form you would use to catalog each individual car for a used car business. A record is one completed form or one set of information about a particular entry in the database. For example, record #23 might contain the make, model, year, serial number, and price of a particular Toyota Celica. A field is one item of information within a record, such as the price of the Celica. Finally, a file is a collection of records, which can be called a database.

Here's how forms, records, and fields relate to one another:

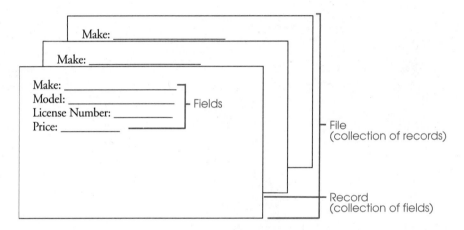

In this chapter, you'll create two databases: a simple record of stock prices and a record of cars. The record of cars is a more detailed database that you will experiment with to see how Works operates.

Start Works, if necessary, and click the Database button in the Startup dialog box to create a new database document. Maximize the application and document windows.

When you start the database, Works presents the opening screen shown in Figure 10-1.

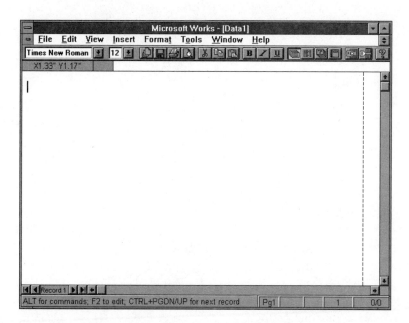

FIGURE 10-1.
The database opening screen.

This window shows the Works database in the mode called *form view*. (Database views will be covered in the next section.)

As you can see, the database window has many things in common with other Works windows, such as the familiar menu across the top, the toolbar, and a large work area. There are some different elements as well.

In the upper left corner below the toolbar is a set of coordinates used to place objects in the work area. The spreadsheet has a cell reference in this area; for the database, Works displays the current location of the insertion point along X and Y axes that begin at the top left corner of the page. In form view, you can precisely control the placement of database fields. The location of the insertion point can help you move or insert fields with an accuracy of up to 0.01 inch. Working with the default settings of 1.00 inch for the top margin and 1.25 inches for the left margin, the insertion point in form view starts out slightly below (1.17 inches) and to the right (1.33 inches) of the top and left margins. The coordinates "X1.33 Y1.17" appear, as shown in Figure 10-1.

At the bottom of the window, toward the left, are the navigation buttons, which allow you to move from record to record with a click of the mouse. Here's how they work:

- The [|◄] takes you to the first record in the database.

- The [◄] takes you to the previous record in the database.

- Record indicates the current record.

- The [▶] takes you to the next record in the database.

- The [▶|] takes you to the last record in the database.

The "perforated" line running down the right edge of the screen marks the right margin of the page in form view. If your form extends beyond the margin, Works might not be able to print all of it; this line helps you see how an evolving form fits on the paper you'll use for printing. To move the margin line left or right, use the Page Setup command on the File menu.

Below the navigation buttons on the status bar are tips on commands that you can use in the database. To the right of these tips are three sets of numbers. The first, Pg1 in Figure 10-1, is the current page (the page on which the insertion point appears). Next is the record number (which is 1 in Figure 10-1). Finally, the fraction in the lower right corner (0/0 in Figure 10-1) represents the current record over the total number of records in the form. For example, the numbers 24/879 indicate the 24th record of 879. These handy numbers can help you keep track of your work in the database.

Database Views

The database is as simple to use as any of the other Works modules. However, one aspect of the database may be confusing for beginners: its ability to work with data in different *views*.

Using views is comparable to using a set of lenses on a camera. If you use a regular lens and look through the camera at a tree, you see one image. If you switch to a wide-angle lens and look through the camera at the same tree, you see something different. One view of the tree can show its entire structure, another can show the leaves in great detail, and yet another can filter the light so that you see one particular aspect of the tree, such as different colors that correspond to warm and cool areas.

It's the same with a database; each view shows your data from one of four different aspects. In the *form view*, you enter, view, and modify database records one at a time. You generally use form view to create the form into which you'll enter database records.

In *list view*, you enter, view, and modify database records on a spreadsheetlike grid that shows many entries simultaneously. You generally use list view for scanning and editing a database or for viewing selected records in it.

In *query view*, which looks like form view, you formulate criteria that tell Works which specific records you want to see. You use query view to ask Works a question about your data; the answer comes back in this view. Because you must have data to ask a question, query view doesn't come into play until you've created a form and entered your data.

The *report view* shows you just what a hard copy of your database will look like when it is printed. The report feature of Works can provide some powerful customization, organization, and formatting features.

Here's a summary of the four views and the Works tasks for which you will use them.

View	What to Do with It
Form	Enter and view information one record at a time Design a Works on-screen form to match a printed form Print a blank form
List	View more than one record at the same time Duplicate information from record to record Enter a series of numbers, dates, and other information View the results of sorting
Query	Find and select records that match certain criteria Specify which records are to be printed in a report
Report	Print a report that organizes information into groups Perform calculations on fields, such as the average value of a coin collection

Form View and List View

When you start the database application with a new "document," Works begins in form view, because it assumes that you want to create a form to structure a new database.

You can create a form in either form view or list view, but form view is easier to work with, especially for complex forms. In form view, you can work with such features as alignment, add explanatory text, and create other details more easily than in list view.

List view, however, lets you create a simple form or put together a "quick and dirty" outline that you can later modify in form view. Moving from one view to another is easy.

As you work with a database, you'll find the method of working you like best. In general, however, you can assume that form view is particularly useful when you want to do the following:

- Cut, copy, delete, or insert whole records

- View or rearrange the structure of the form

- Insert, delete, or modify fields

List view, on the other hand, is valuable when you want to do the following:

- View or select multiple records at the same time

- Select a field and all the entries in it

- Copy, clear, or fill fields in multiple entries at the same time

Although form view is the default setting in Works, we'll start working in list view to create a simple database. After that, you'll switch to form view to modify and enhance a database form.

Using the Toolbar

What's different about the database toolbar? Six buttons that, as you can see on the next page, allow you to do the following:

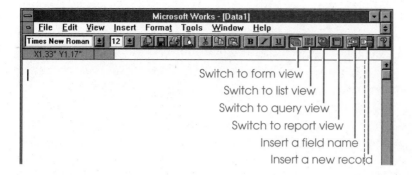

Like the other toolbars, the database toolbar has buttons that save, cut, copy, and offer you help. You can also add or delete buttons as needed.

TIP: Don't forget that Works can check your database spelling, just as it did for your spreadsheet entries. Look for the Spelling command in the same place, on the Tools menu.

For information about the Report View button, see Chapter 12, "Creating Database Reports," page 361.

Creating a Form

OK, we're ready to begin. In form view, you can design a form in any way you want, even matching the layout of a preprinted form.

Although Works lets you rearrange fields, add new ones, and delete unnecessary ones with little effort, you should plan your form. Deleting fields after you've entered data deletes the data in those fields; this can mean extra work to recover or redistribute information in each existing record.

The fields you create will eventually be your means of searching for and sorting your data, so create as many fields as you need, but not so many that searching your database becomes a chore. For example, you can create a single field for area code, exchange, and telephone number, or you can create separate fields for each. If you create a single field, you'll only be able to search for, or sort, entire phone numbers, such as 2065551000. If you create separate fields for each, you will be able to search your database by area code, exchange, or phone number.

 TIP: It's a good idea to use graph paper and plan your form before you begin to use Works; only then should you collect the data that will go in the database. That way, you can see before you start what fields need to go where and what information belongs in each field.

Think about how often you'll want to find only telephone exchanges. In the end, a compromise is best: area code in one field, and the exchange and the phone number in a second. Similarly, if you are working with names in almost any fashion, you almost always need the last name in a separate field because almost every database, at one time or another, sorts on the last name.

Creating a Form in List View

Let's start off by creating a database in list view, and then look at how list view relates to the creation of a form.

1. Open the View menu and then choose List, or click the List View button on the toolbar. You may be surprised to see how similar List View is to the spreadsheet you worked with in the last section.

   You have labels with row numbers down the left side and a (currently blank) set of column labels across the top.

   To create a field in a new document in list view, select a cell within a column, open the Edit menu, and then choose the Field Name command.

2. Works displays a dialog box like this:

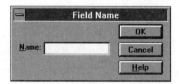

3. Type *Stock.*

4. Click OK.

   Notice that the field name appears at the head of the column, even though you selected a cell within the column. When you create or rename fields in list view, the field names appears as column labels.

5. Select a cell in the second column.

6. Open the Edit menu, and then choose the Field Name command.

7. Type *Day 1,* and then click OK.

8. Repeat the process to create fields named Day 2 through Day 5. Your screen should now resemble this illustration.

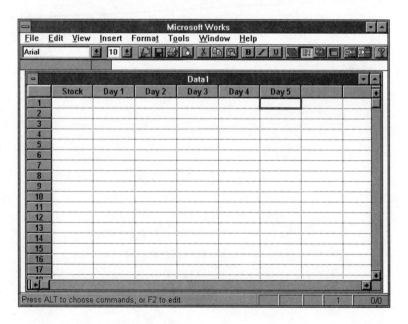

9. Now add the data into the database in the same way as you would enter data in a spreadsheet. When you are done, the database should look like this:

	Stock	Day 1	Day 2	Day 3	Day 4	Day 5		
1	A	37.5						
2	B	1.5						
3	C	28.25						
4	D	1.4						
5	E	79.75						
6								
7								
8								
9								

See Also: For information about entering data, see "Say Hello to the Spreadsheet," page 177.

TIP: As you enter data, you'll see other similarities between the spreadsheet and the database. When you enter data in the database, you will see the familiar Cancel (X) and Enter [✓] boxes, just as you did in the formula bar in the spreadsheet.

In the same way that you did in the spreadsheet, you can now use the Fill Series command on the Edit menu to fill in the remaining stock prices for days 2 through 5.

1. For stock A, select the fields Day 1 through Day 5, open the Edit menu, and then choose the Fill Series command. Change the interval in the Step by box from 1 to 1.25, and click OK.

2. Do the same for stocks B through E, varying the intervals by using *.25* for B, *.75* for C, *1.5* for D, and *.5* for E.

Now your database should look like this:

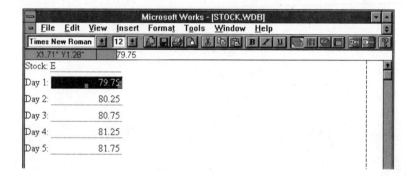

You might not realize it, but you have already created two steps on the way to a form. Now it's time to see what you've got if you look at the database in form view.

3. Open the View menu, and then choose Form or use the F9 function key or click on the Form button on the toolbar. Figure 10-2 shows what the form view looks like.

FIGURE 10-2.
The form view of the Stock database.

When you're in form view, notice that you see one complete record at a time, or all the stock prices for a complete week of five days. To see other records, use the navigation buttons at the left of the horizontal scroll bar.

See Also: For information about the navigation buttons, see "Forms, Records, Fields, and Files," page 296.

Changing Views

Most, but not all, of the functions work in both form view and list view. As you can see, you can create fields in list view and see them in form view, and you can enter data in list view and see it in form view.

You can also format fields for currency, for example, and see the same format in either view. You can't, however, assume that the same field width will carry over into both views, or that the style (such as italic) or size will transfer from one view to another.

Notice the default font and font size in Figure 10-2 (Times New Roman 12) and the field width of 20 characters Works uses in form view. If you contrast this with list view by clicking the List View button, you'll see that the defaults change. In list view, the font and size are changed to Arial 10 and the column (field) width is 10 characters.

This disparity between list view and form view occurs for a good reason. Here are some general rules about format and views:

- Additions, deletions, and changes that affect the information or structure of the database carry over from one view to the next. A cell containing 234 in one view will be a cell containing 234 in the other.

- Characteristics that are not integral to the form or data differ from view to view. Text in 15-point Times New Roman in one view might be shown as 13-point Arial in another.

You're finished with the stock database for the time being. If you haven't done so already, save it under the name *stock*, close the file, and open a new database document.

TIP: Works assigns a .WDB extension when it saves a database. When we saved this database, Works called it *stock.wdb*.

Working in Form View

Now that you've seen how easily you can create a form and a database in list view, let's work with form view, where you can visualize, organize, and modify a form to your heart's content.

Creating a Form

You can create a field anywhere in the form view window simply by pointing to the location you want and clicking the mouse button. The sensitivity of Works is remarkable. You can move the insertion point with an accuracy of a hundredth of an inch (as you can see by watching the coordinate markers). This type of mobility is valuable in most situations, but it does take patience and precision.

If you want to line up fields horizontally or vertically, Works provides an invisible grid like the one you used in Draw. With the grid turned on, Works "snaps" your fields to the gridlines, creating even spacing above and below and identical alignment from side to side.

Before you begin the second database example, an inventory form for used cars, check that the grid is turned on by looking at the Format menu. The Snap to Grid command should be checked.

To create a new field in form view (and to begin creating a new database), do the following:

1. Type the field name *Make* and end the name with a colon (:). Just as the equal sign at the beginning of a formula tells Works you're entering a formula, the colon at the end of a field tells Works that the text is a field name.

TIP: A field name in the Works database can be up to 15 characters long. You can include up to 256 fields in a single form.

2. Press Enter, or click the Enter button. Works displays a dialog box requesting the size of the field.

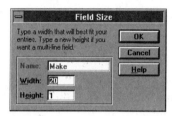

In form view, by default, Works proposes 20-character, 1-line fields. You can specify a different width and height (for multiple-line fields) in this dialog box; for now, let's use the default field size.

TIP: Remember that the Works database offers an Undo feature that can undo typing, editing, formatting, and even sorting! Use it or lose it!

3. Click OK. A dotted line appears next to the field name, and the insertion point jumps down to the next line so that you can create the next field.

4. In the fields, one below the other, type *Model:, Year:, Serial:,* and *Price:*. Remember that each time you create a new field, you must define its width as well. Accept the default width for each.

When you finish, your form should look like the one shown here.

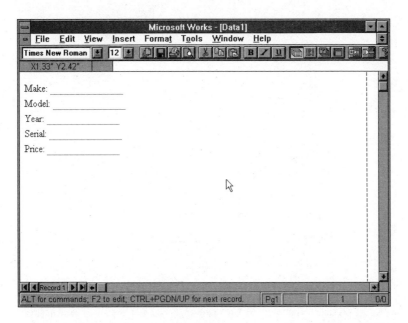

Now save the database as *cars.wdb*.

Before you move on, try the following steps and notice how the mouse pointer changes when you're working in form view.

1. Press Shift+Tab to move the highlight to the Price field.

2. Move the mouse pointer into the highlight. As you do, the mouse pointer changes to Drag. If you click, hold, and then move the mouse, the pointer changes to Move. You can then use the mouse to drag the field to another location when you're reorganizing a form. (Don't do it right now.)

3. Next move the mouse pointer to the small, light box in the lower right corner of the highlight. The mouse pointer changes to a slanting doubleheaded arrow with the word *Resize* because it is used to change the size of an object.

Formatting a Form

When you create a form, you can specify a particular font, font size, and style. To change the font, size, or style of a field label, follow these steps:

1. Select the field name.

2. From the toolbar, select the font, size, and style (italic, bold, or underline) you want to use. Keep in mind that even if you have many fonts, sizes, and styles available, you do not have to use all of them. Avoid the dreaded font junk.

You can format individual fields in a form with commands from the Format menu. Let's format the Price field for currency with two decimals by following these steps.

1. Highlight the field named Price.

2. Open the Format menu, and then choose Number.

3. Click Currency in the Number dialog box, and then click OK.

Entering and Editing Data

Now it's time to enter some data. To do this in form view, move the highlight to the dotted line next to the field name you want and simply fill out the form for each record you want to create.

To move to the first field, either click on the dotted line next to the field name Make, or use Shift+Tab to move backward in the form. (You can always use the Tab key to move from field to field.) To create the database, follow these steps.

1. Move to the first field, named Make.

2. Type *Ford.*

3. Press the tab key to move to the next field (named Year).

4. Type *Mustang.*

5. Press the tab key to move to the next field (named Model).

Continue these steps until you have the data entered as you see here.

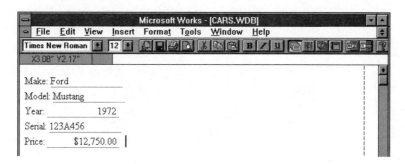

6. Start a new record by pressing the Tab key after the last field is complete.

7. Using the same steps listed above, create a record for each of the following entries. Press Enter when you finish the last record.

Make	Model	Year	License	Price
Ford	Probe	1991	234B567	$4,500.00
Chevrolet	Camaro	1974	345C567	$2,350.00
Honda	Civic	1989	231ABC123	$6,800.00
Lincoln	Mark V	1978	481DEC184	$5,000.00
Lincoln	Continental	1990	038MAR4	$17,500.00
Lincoln	Continental	1986	814AUG6	$9,000.00
Lincoln	Town Car	1988	500DOS	$17,500.00
Lincoln	Mark VII	1990	123KAY124	$18,000.00
Toyota	Celica	1988	987D789	$7,500.00

Changing Field Widths

As you enter data, Works left-aligns text and right-aligns numbers the same way it does in the spreadsheet. Most of the fields in your sample now contain left-aligned numbers in some records and right-aligned text in others.

If you get one of those dreaded ######## messages, meaning that the cell is too small to display its contents, you can change the field width. There are two ways to change field width. The first way follows the steps on the next page.

1. Highlight the Model field.

2. Open the Format menu, and then choose Field Size. When Works displays the Field Size dialog box, type *8* for the width, and click OK.

   Or you can try a faster way, described in the following steps.

1. Move the highlight to the dotted line after the Year field.

2. Point to the size box in the lower right-hand corner of the highlighted area, as shown here. Notice that the mouse pointer becomes a downward pointing arrow named Resize.

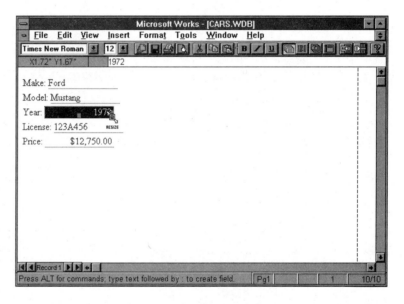

You can drag the box left or right to resize the width of a field, and you can drag it up or down to change the number of lines in a field. Let's change the width.

1. Drag the box to the left until it's slightly wider than the four digits needed for the year. If your hand slips and drags the corner downward, slide the mouse pointer up again to keep this a one-line field.

2. Now highlight the License field. Use the size box again to narrow the field to seven characters. (If you want to double-check, choose the Field Width command from the Format menu and check the width displayed in the dialog box.)

3. Change the width of the Price field to eight characters.

Your form should look a little neater now. For consistency, also narrow the Make field to about half its current width.

TIP: Keep in mind that when you change the width of a particular field on your screen, you are changing the width of that field throughout the entire database.

Here are fields and their new widths.

Make	Model	Year	License	Price
10	12	6	12	14

TIP: You can enhance a form by using the Border option on the Format menu. Just as with the spreadsheet, you can outline portions of the form to emphasize their importance.

Here's what the reformatted database looks like now:

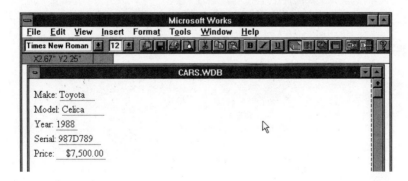

Using the Best Fit Feature

In list view, you have the greatest-of-all-time formatting helpers. To adjust the field to exactly the width that's needed, select Best Fit in the Field Width dialog box. Works will adjust the field width in a column (or an entire database) to fit the largest field. In fact, it might not be a bad idea to select all the records and do this when you are working to ensure that all the information is visible. Accessed using Format menu, the Field Width dialog box, with the Best Fit box selected, resembles this illustration:

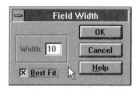

To make things even easier, you can simply double-click on the name of a field or on a row, and Works will adjust the field size and row height to fit the widest or largest entry exactly. Pretty cool.

Let's See What List View Looks Like

The form view is great for on screen forms, but when you have to see multiple records, there's nothing like the list view command. To see multiple records, click the List View button on the toolbar.

Now your database should look like this:

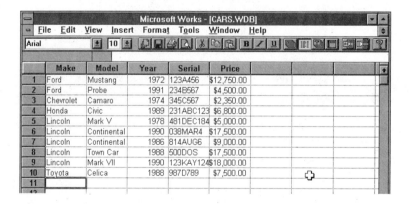

Notice again that the field widths in list view don't match the field widths in the form view. The Year field, for example, is 10 characters (the default) in list view, even though it is 6 characters in form view.

You can change the field width in list view by using the Field Width command on the Format menu or by dragging the column boundary left or right, as you did in the spreadsheet. If you widen or narrow columns in list view for printing, Works will use the widths you specified for the view from which you print.

A database in any view remains the same database, but Works is flexible enough to let you mold the fields to match the type of view you want to see and print. Remember, too, that Works can display and print a database in one font and size in form view, and a different font and size in list view. Some simple changes that made the list view more attractive are incorporated here.

Microsoft Works - [CARS.WDB]

	Make	Model	Year	Serial	Price
1	Ford	Mustang	1972	123A456	$12,750
2	Ford	Probe	1991	234B567	$4,500
3	Chevrolet	Camaro	1974	345C567	$2,350
4	Honda	Civic	1989	231ABC123	$6,800
5	Lincoln	Mark V	1978	481DEC184	$5,000
6	Lincoln	Continental	1990	038MAR4	$17,500
7	Lincoln	Continental	1986	814AUG6	$9,000
8	Lincoln	Town Car	1988	500DOS	$17,500
9	Lincoln	Mark VII	1990	123KAY124	$18,000
10	Toyota	Celica	1988	987D789	$7,500
11					

We italicized the model names, centered the year, and got rid of the two zeroes on the end of price (which are the same for all cars, so why show them?).

Splitting the Screen

The *cars.wdb* database you created is not long enough to require more than one screen to display it all, but the database, like the spreadsheet, lets you split the screen and scroll independently in two or four "panes" to view different parts of a large database.

For practice, try the following steps.

1. Be sure you're in list view.

2. Drag the split box at the top of the vertical scroll bar, and release the mouse button when the bar is about two-thirds of the way down the screen.

3. Drag the split box at the left edge of the horizontal scroll bar, and release the mouse button when the bar is about halfway across the screen.

4. Clicking in one pane and then another, scroll through your database to see different parts of the same "document." As you do, notice that the top and bottom panes on each side show the same fields, but they can show different records.

    The left and right panes can show different fields, but the same records. Notice that you do not have totally independent scrolling in each pane when you split a window four ways.

5. When you finish viewing the panes, drag the split boxes out of the document window to eliminate the splits, and scroll to the beginning of the database.

Editing a Database

Databases change. Rarely is one created that you don't add records to, delete records from, change the number and size of fields, and so on. The databases on your computer will have to be updated periodically. That's when editing becomes important.

Editing Data in Fields

Whether you're working in form view or list view, replacing data in a field is easy. You simply highlight the existing data and start typing.

When you select data in a field (not the field name) and press a key, Works takes that keystroke as a signal to replace the information currently in that field with the new information that you are entering. To see how this works, try the following:

1. In either list view or form view, move to the first record (scroll or click on the [|◀]) and click on the price for the Ford Mustang.

2. This car isn't selling, so lower the price a bit. Type *2250*, and click the Enter button or press the Enter key.

As easily as that, one entry replaces another.

If you want to delete the contents of a field without replacing it, select the data, and then choose the Clear Field Entry command from the Edit menu.

 TIP: Another way to delete data from a field is to highlight it, press the Spacebar key once, and then press the Enter key.

You can't undo a Clear command, so restore the cell data by entering it again and clicking the Enter button.

You can also edit field contents in the formula bar, much as you learned to do in the spreadsheet. The same steps work in the database as in the spreadsheet, as follows:

- To highlight one or more characters, click and then drag the mouse, or press Shift and an arrow key.

- Click anywhere in an entry to position the insertion point at that location. Using the keyboard move the insertion point one character at a time with the arrow keys. Move the insertion point to the beginning of the entry by pressing Home, or move it to the end by pressing End.

- Press the F2 key, and the insertion point will be placed at the end of the entry in the formula bar; then you will be able to edit the field contents.

- Press Del to delete characters you've highlighted.

When you need to make changes to different fields in many records, you'll probably find list view preferable to form view because it lets you see so many records at once. List view is also better when, as you saw with the stock database, you want to use the Fill commands to add the same type of information to a group of records.

Adding New Records in List View

Few databases are created and finalized at the same time. Instead, after you've created a database, you'll want to add records in either form view or list view. Your present screen should show the database in list view, so start there.

To add a new record at the end of the database, follow these steps.

1. Click in row 11 of the field named Make, and type *Ford*.

2. Using the Tab key to move from field to field, enter the following data: *Third* in the Model field; *1990* in the Year field; *XYZ123* in the Serial field; *17000* in the Price field

3. Press Enter.

You have added a new record that follows the existing 10 records. But you don't always want to add records just to the end. To add a record anywhere within the database, do this:

1. Select the row below the row where you want to add the record.

2. Open the Insert menu, and then choose Record/Field.

Here's an example of how to insert a record.

1. Click on the 8 to the left of row number 8 in *cars.wdb* to select the entire row.

2. Open the Insert menu, and then choose Record/Field. Works opens a new row at row 8, and renumbers all of the records below the new one. It assumes that you will now enter data for record #8.

3. Add the following data to the new record:

Make	Model	Year	Serial	Price
VW	Bug	1973	JKL001	$400.00

If your following along, you now have a total of 12 records.

You can create records in form view and display them in list view, and vice versa. You can create them in list view and see them, in the same order, in form view. Switching back and forth with a touch of a toolbar button is easy.

> **TIP:** Works will also insert a new record if you select a single field cell instead of an entire row, but it will not know whether you want to insert a record or a field and will ask you what you want to do through a dialog box.

Adding New Records in Form View

Adding records in form view is similar to doing so in list view. Keep the following notes in mind when adding a record in form view.

-   Click the Last record button at the left edge of the horizontal scroll bar to move to an empty form at the end of the database. Use the Tab button to get to the first field in that blank record. Add whatever records you want; Works will add them after the existing records.

-   Scroll to the record before which you want to add a new record. Open the Insert menu, select Record, and Works will add a blank row at that location. All succeeding records will be renumbered.

In what view should you add records? It really doesn't matter, so use the view that you prefer.

Deleting Records

The process of removing whole records is similar to that of adding them. To delete a record use one of these methods.

- In form view, scroll to the record you want to delete, open the Insert menu, and then choose Delete Record.

- In list view, click on the row number to select the entire record, open the Insert menu, and then choose Delete Record/Field.

You should be in form view now. To try deleting a record, do the following:

1. Use the buttons in the horizontal scroll bar to find the record for the BMW.

2. Open the Insert menu, and then choose Delete Record/Field. The record is gone, and the succeeding records are renumbered correctly.

TIP: Fortunately, deleting can be undone. Use the Undo button right after you delete a record. Remember that the Undo function works only when it is invoked immediately after the deletion is made.

Cutting and Pasting

When you remove records, remember the distinction between deleting them and cutting them. Cutting, as in other Works (and Windows) applications, removes the record from the database, but gives it a temporary home on the Clipboard. The following examples use Cut and Paste as a means of reorganizing and deleting records in a database.

TIP: Cut and Paste are also used for moving information within and among Works databases, Works applications, and other Windows-based programs. Don't forget how handy Drag and Drop is as well. This chapter covers working within a single document and application. Part 7, "Working Together," see page 466, covers ways to move your data from one document to another.

Deleting with Cut and Paste

Suppose you decide that the Toyota and the Lincoln Mark V records don't belong on this list. To cut a record in form view, follow these steps.

1. Scroll to the record for the Toyota.

2. Open the Edit menu, and then choose Cut Record.

3. Now switch to list view and try cutting there by clicking the List View button on the toolbar. The Lincoln Mark V should be record number 4, so click on the row number (not on a field) to select the entire record.

4. Open the Edit menu, and then choose Cut.

    The record for the Toyota no longer exists because it's been replaced on the Clipboard by the record for the Lincoln Mark V. You can reinstate the record for the Lincoln, however, and place it anywhere in the database.

5. Click on row number 1, open the Edit menu, and then choose Paste.

    The Lincoln is back, but in a different place. Notice that you didn't have to insert a blank record to hold the incoming information. Works makes room in both list view and form view for the material to be pasted; you don't have to worry about overwriting an existing record with the new information you paste in.

Reorganizing Fields in List View

Cutting is a useful alternative to deleting when you want to retrieve records you've taken out of a database or use the cut information in another location, either within a database or in another Works or Windows-based application. Cutting and pasting can also be an effective means of reorganizing fields in list view.

Remember, however, that you work with separate views when you work with a database. Reorganizing fields in list view does not carry over to the layout in form view, and vice versa. Try the following steps to cut and paste a field.

1. In list view, click on the field name Serial to select the entire field.

2. Open the Edit menu, and then choose Cut. The field, and all its contents, disappear to the Clipboard.

3. Now click on the blank column to the right of the Price field. You can click anywhere in the column, but you might want to form the habit of clicking the column head.

4. Open the Edit menu, and then choose Paste. Works immediately fills the selected column with the field and entries you cut, as you see here.

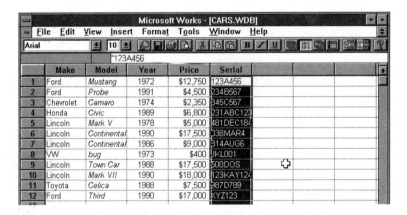

5. Click the Form View button. Notice that the Serial field remains in its original position in this view.

6. For additional practice, cut and paste the Price column to return the list view to its orginal format.

Reorganizing Fields in Form View

In the next example, you'll move the Model field to the right and the Make field down, to make room at the top of the form for some descriptive text you'll soon add.

You can move a field in form view with the Position Selection command on the Edit menu. A faster way, though, is to use the mouse.

1. Be sure you are in the form view.

2. Verify that Snap to Grid is turned on in the Format menu.

3. Point to any part of the Model field, be it the field name or the data (such as Mustang, 914, and so on), and click the mouse.

4. When the Move pointer appears, drag the entire field to the right, to about the center of the page. Notice that as you move the mouse, the outline of the field and data move with it as shown here.

5. Now click on the Make field.

6. Drag it down.

As you move the Make field, notice that an outline of the field "snaps" into place when you reach the same position on the Y axis that the Model field occupies. If Snap to Grid were not turned on, you could maneuver the outline up, down, and sideways in smaller increments. Here, however, such mobility would be a handicap, so Snap to Grid is preferable.

Adding and Deleting Fields

You can add and delete fields in either list view or form view. You might want to delete a field after you realize that you inadvertently added a field that has the same data for all records. You may want to delete a field if it is no longer meaningful to continue to have it in the database.

Deleting Fields in Form View and List View

To delete a field in form view, follow these steps.

1. Highlight the field you want to delete.

2. Press the Del key.

3. When Works asks you if you want to delete the field, confirm the deletion by selecting Yes.

   To delete a field in list view, follow these steps.

1. Highlight the field you want to delete.

2. Open the Insert menu, and then choose Delete Record/Field. Works will delete the field without asking you for a confirmation.

 TIP: If you want to delete the data in a field in list view without deleting the field name, highlight the field and press the Del key.

You can add new fields anywhere in a form—at the end, at the beginning, or between existing fields—and then edit the records to include whatever additional information you want. You can work in either list view or form view, but the better choice depends to some extent on which view you used to create the form.

Adding Fields Created in List View

If you created a form in list view, you can add fields to the end of the form or insert fields within the form in either list view or form view. It's nice to have that convenience. When you add a new field, Works always displays (and prints) the new fields to the right of previously existing fields in list view and at the bottom of the form in form view.

To add a field in list view, follow these steps.

1. Highlight the column following the last field in the database.

2. Open the Edit menu, and then choose Field Name.

3. Enter the name of the field in the Field Name Dialog box.

4. Click OK. The new field will be added.

   Adding fields in list view, however, has slight disadvantages.

   ■ If you're adding a new field between existing fields in list view, you must first insert a blank field, and then assign the field a name using the Field Name command. In form view, you insert and name the field at the same time.

   ■ In list view you can specify the width, but not the height, of a new field. This means you can add only single-line fields in list view. To change them to multiple-line fields, you must use the Field Size command in form view to make the room you need.

   ■ If you add a field in list view and then switch to form view, the new field will appear at the top of the form, superimposed on the first field in the form. Quite a mess! You'll have to move and rearrange fields to make the form usable.

Adding Fields to Forms Created in Form View

If you created a form in *form* view, you should probably add new fields in form view for one main reason: Adding new fields in list view causes Works to insert them at the top of the form, sometimes partially obscuring existing fields. When you add fields this way, you'll have to move them to new locations, so you might as well start out in form view and simplify matters.

   In the following examples, you will add new fields in both list view and form view, so you can see how each works. Start in list view with the *cars.wdb* and follow these steps.

1. In list view, click on the Price field name.

2. Open the Insert menu, and then choose Insert Record/Field. Immediately, a new blank field appears between Year and Price.

3. To name the field, open the Edit menu, and then choose Field Name.

4. Type *Color* in the dialog box that appears.

5. Click OK to name the new field. Here's what the database in list view looks like now.

Now switch to form view to see where the new field appears. Your screen should look something like this.

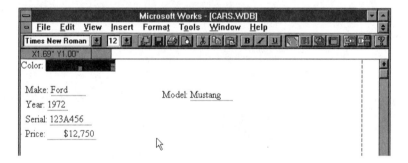

6. Drag the new field into position, placing it to the right of the Year field.

7. To make it look better, narrow the Color field to eight characters.

Reorganizing a Form in Form View

When you add a field in form view, you use the same procedure you used to create the form in the first place. Click on the position you want, type a field name, and set the field size. Where you insert the field doesn't really matter because you can move it wherever you want. You don't have to worry about aligning the field perfectly before you create it. You can always nudge the field into position after you've named and sized it.

You created a number of fields in the *cars.wdb* form, so you don't have to step through a detailed example on adding another field. Instead, try modifying your form on your own, working in form view so you can hone your skills where they'll be needed most in your own work. Let's modify the form by going through the following steps.

1. Move the Serial field to the right of the Color field, placing it under Model.

2. Now add the new fields shown in the following illustration.

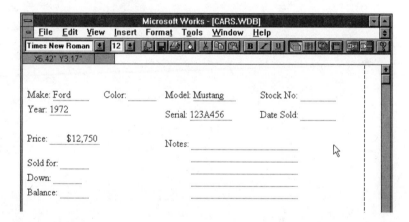

TIP: Here's a great tip. To extend the number of lines down in a field (as we did in the Notes field in *cars.wdb*), simply drag down on the resize box after highlighting the field.

For reference, the following table lists the new fields, their positions, and sizes.

Field to Add	Position	Size
Stock No	Top line, near right margin	10 characters
Date sold	Below Stock No	10 characters
Sold for	Below Price	8 characters
Down	Below Sold for	8 characters
Balance	Below Down	8 characters
Notes	Below Serial and to the right of Price	30 characters by 5 lines

3. Now switch to list view. Scroll to see how Works has added all of the new fields to the right of the existing fields.

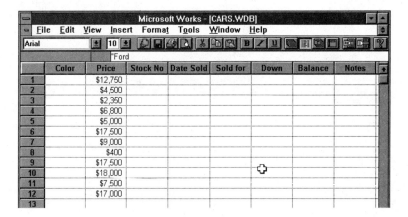

4. Finally, try a quick way to format several fields at the same time. In list view, click on the field name Sold for, and drag the highlight until it covers the Balance field.

5. Open the Format menu, and then choose Number.

6. In the Number dialog box, click Currency.

7. Click OK.

   With one command you formatted three fields. Remember this easy way to format more than one field at a time.

> **TIP:** To format more than one field in form view, click on the first field (not the field name!), and then hold down the Ctrl key as you click on each additional field to select it.

You've made some extensive additions to the form now, so its organization in form view and list view no longer matches. To avoid such mismatches, remember to think your forms through before creating them. Even though you can add, delete, and rearrange your forms, doing it right the first time will save work later.

Adding Numbers and Dates

The database, like the spreadsheet, includes three Fill commands that save time and trouble. These are Fill Right, Fill Down, and Fill Series. These commands are available only in list view, because only there can you make entries to multiple records. The Fill commands work exactly as they do in the spreadsheet.

1. In list view, click on the first cell in the Stock No field.

2. Type *1*, and then click the Enter button.

3. Extend the highlight so that it covers the cells for all records in the database (through row 12).

4. Open the Edit menu, and then choose Fill Series.

5. Click OK.

Here's what the database in list view looks like now.

	Color	Price	Stock No	Date Sold	Sold for	Down	Balance	Notes
1		$12,750	1					
2		$4,500	2					
3		$2,350	3					
4		$6,800	4					
5		$5,000	5					
6		$17,500	6					
7		$9,000	7					
8		$400	8					
9		$17,500	9					
10		$18,000	10					
11		$7,500	11					
12		$17,000	12					
13								
14								

Now with the entries still selected, format the field for leading zeros, and specify the number of digits as 8. You've now added "instant" stock numbers for the cars, with plenty of room for future additions. When car number 13 arrives, the data-entry person need only type *13* and tab to the next field.

Adding Labels and Descriptions

A label is another way to use text to identify a portion of your database. You don't use labels with name fields, but they are great for such things as including instructions or special notes on a form.

There are only three differences between a label and a field name.

- A field must always end in a colon but a label does not.

- A field name can be only 15 characters long but a label can be up to 256 characters long.

- A label cannot be displayed in list view.

TIP: If you want to include a colon in a label, begin the label with " marks, such as *"Please enter your name:.*

Let's work in form view and see how a label works.

1. Return to form view, and click at the top of the screen, about 2 inches along the X axis.

2. Type *Honest Abe's,* and click the Enter button.

   Because you didn't type a colon at the end, Works accepted the text as a label rather than as a field. Now type a longer label.

3. Click to place the insertion point slightly to the right of the first label, and type: - *We specialize in Lincolns.* Click the Enter button.

We could have created one long label, but we wanted to demonstrate how you can create labels next to each another but format separately.

When you create labels, Works lets you apply boldface and other character styles to them so they will stand out from the remainder of the form. You can also use different fonts and sizes as you see here.

```
┌──────────────────────────────────────────────────────────────┐
│ ─    Microsoft Works - [CARS.WDB]              │▼│▲│          │
│ ─  File  Edit  View  Insert  Format  Tools  Window  Help  │▲▼│  │
│ │Times New Roman│▼│ │12│▼│ │▭│▢│▤│▨│ │✂│▦│▦│ B│I│U│ │▭▭│▦│▦│▦│ │▦▦│▦│ │?│ │
│ │X6.42" Y3.25"│    │                                     │▲│  │
│                                                          │ │  │
│          Honest Abe's - We specialize in Lincolns        │ │  │
│     Make: Ford        Color: .........  Model: Mustang     Stock No: ...... 1 │ │
│     Year: 1972                         Serial: 123A456    Date Sold: ........ │ │
│                                                          │ │  │
│     Price: ...... $12,750           Notes: ............... │ │  │
│                                            ............... │ │  │
│     Sold for: ........                     ............... │ │  │
│     Down: ........                         ............... │ │  │
│     Balance: ........                              ⌐ ⌐    │▼│  │
└──────────────────────────────────────────────────────────────┘
```

We changed the font to 16-point Arial and applied bold and italics to both labels.

That's the easy way to add a label. The other way is to choose the Label command from the Insert menu. When you do this, you will see the label dialog box. Simply enter the label you want to use, and click OK.

You can use labels for other, more informative text as well. For example, you could add a label to the Notes section of your *cars.wdb* form to remind the person filling out the form to include mileage, overall condition, and any repair work done to make the car more salable. Or, if you have an employment application form on screen, you could easily provide instructions such as *"Please provide your date of birth"* with a field for date of birth following the label.

Labels are moved the same way fields are moved. Simply drag them where you want them to go. And guess what? They're deleted the same way as well. Simply highlight them and press the Del key. And guess what else? You can easily undo the mistaken deletion of a label using the Undo command or the Ctrl+Z key combination.

Making Calculations

You are already familiar with how similar the list view of the database is to a spreadsheet. These two applications also overlap considerably in their ability to perform calculations. The spreadsheet can use a formula to produce a new value. The database can also use values from one or more fields to calculate the entry that belongs in another field.

TIP: The database does not allow you to paste in a function like the spreadsheet. You have to enter the function from the keyboard.

For example, in your sample form, you created fields for the selling price of a car, the down payment, and the balance owed. Here's how you enter a function. We're in the form view.

1. Click on the Balance field.

2. Type *=Sold for-Down.*

3. Click the Enter button. You should see $0.00 in the Balance field and a formula in the formula bar, as shown here.

Works inserted a $0.00 in the Balance field because both the Sold for and Down fields in this entry are empty.

4. To verify that your formula works, click on the Sold for field, type *4500,* and click the Enter button.

5. Click on the Down field, type *1200,* and click the Enter button.

Now Works has some figures to work with, so it displays $3,300 in the Balance field.

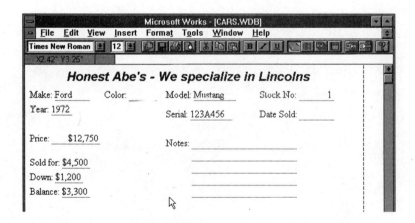

Creating formulas in the database is quite similar to creating them in the spreadsheet. However, you must type database field names to enter them into a formula in the form view. In the list view, you can point to cells to include their references, just as you do in a spreadsheet formula.

The following example returns to your simple STOCK database form to show some ways to incorporate functions in fields.

1. Save or close the *cars.wdb* database, and open the *stock.wdb* database.

2. Create the fields shown in the following illustration.

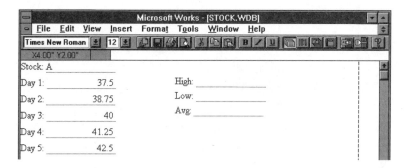

Now you can use three Works functions—MAX, MIN, and AVG—to fill in the new fields. MAX finds and displays the highest value in a set of cells or fields you specify. MIN finds and displays the lowest value. AVG calculates the average value. For each of these functions, you'll specify the fields Day 1 through Day 5 as the values for Works to examine.

3. In the High field, type *=max(day 1, day 2, day 3, day 4, day 5)*. Type the field names, including spaces, as they appear in the form. If you don't, Works will display the message *Reference not valid or wrong operand type*. Click the Enter button when you're done typing. Notice that Works displays the highest stock price in this field.

4. In the Low field, type *=min(day 1, day 2, day 3, day 4, day 5)*, and click the Enter button. Now Works displays the lowest stock price.

5. In the Avg field, type *=avg(day 1, day 2, day 3, day 4, day 5)*, and click the Enter button. This time Works calculates the average value for the five days and displays the result.

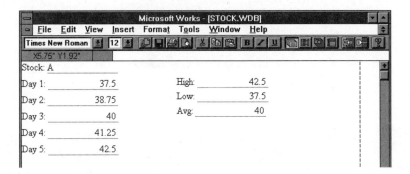

Even though you entered the functions for only one stock, Works applies them to the same fields in all records. Now click the List View button, or scroll through form view to see the other records in the database. Each record now shows the high, low, and average prices for different stocks.

Protecting Your Database

After you've gone to the trouble of building a form and entering data, you'll want to ensure that your information is protected from damage or inadvertent change.

Chapter 8, "Working with Formulas and Functions," see page 215, describes how to protect data in a spreadsheet. Protection in the database works much the same way, except that you can apply protection to forms as well as data by using the following procedure.

1. Open the Format menu, and then choose Protection. You will see the Protection dialog box shown on the next page.

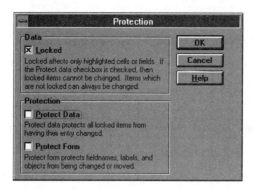

2. Now click the check boxes that correspond to what you want to protect.

Select the Protect Data option to protect any fields that were selected. Select the Locked option if you want to turn off protection, which is on by default. Turning off protection will be applied only to the selected fields. Select Protect Form if you want everything about the form protected, but you still want to make changes to the data in the fields.

TIP: It's a good idea to protect the entire form when you are sure you are finished. That way, you can still change data and even change the form should you need to later by removing the protection.

Hiding Information

While you work, you can also hide fields and records, temporarily removing sensitive or unneeded parts of your database from view.

Hiding Fields

You hide fields by following these steps.

1. Change the field width to 0.

2. When you want to redisplay the field, use the Go To command, which displays a dialog box listing the names of all the fields in your form.

3. Click on the field to which you want to move.

4. Use the Field Size command to increase the width of the hidden field.

Hiding Records

You can hide records in either list view or form view with the Hide Record command on the View menu. In list view, select the record or group of records you want to hide, and then choose the command. In form view, scroll to each individual record and hide it.

To redisplay hidden records, choose the Show All Records command from the View menu.

Don't hide records or fields unless you are sure you must. It's easy to hide records or fields, forget you have done so, and then panic when it comes time to work with the data later on.

Coming Next

This has been a full and informative chapter. Now you have the basics of creating and using a database. What's left is more advanced techniques for using the database to sort records and search for information. Let's turn our attention to those, and other database features.

11

Managing
a Database

Organizing and constructing a database requires a fair amount of time and planning, especially if you want to design a complex form or enter hundreds or thousands of records. But, as you now realize, the planning time is well spent.

Getting the information into a record is just part of using a database effectively. The methods you can use to work with and manage a database are just as important; they are the focus of this chapter.

After the database form is designed, however, you don't have to bother with sorting, alphabetizing or selecting records, because that's where Works excels. After records are entered, the database is ready for use—whenever and however you need it. How to manage these records is what this chapter is all about.

Sorting Records

After you create a database, you want to organize it so that it's easy to reference. You can do this in a variety of ways, including alphabetically by last name, numerically by serial number, chronologically by date, and so on. With Works, sorting is a breeze. As you saw in Chapter 10, page 293, Works can sort on as many as three columns or fields.

Alphabetic and numeric sorting can go either up or down. An upward, or ascending, sort goes from A to Z and from 0 to 9. A downward, or descending, sort moves in the other direction, from Z to A or from 9 to 0.

Sorting on Multiple Fields

You can sort records in either list view or form view. Of the two, list view gives you a better feel for the results because you can see a number of sorted records at one time. If you sort records in form view, Works displays only the first record in the sorted database until you scroll to see the remaining records.

We'll use the *cars.wdb* database as an example, so open it now if it is not already open. We will sort the database first by make, next by model, and then by year. Here's how.

1. Open the Tools menu, and then choose Sort Records. Works displays the following dialog box.

When you perform a sort on multiple fields, you list the most important field first (in this case, the Make field), which Works should propose. If it does not, type *make* in the 1st Field box. An ascending sort, which Works proposes, is fine, so go on to define the second sort field. You can use the Tab key to move to the next field or simply click on it using the mouse.

2. Click in the 2nd Field box, and type *model*.

3. Click in the 3rd Field box, and type *year*. The ascending sort Works proposes would list the oldest cars first, so change the sort order by clicking the button next to Descend or use the Tab key to highlight the Descend button. Now Works will list the cars from newest to oldest.

 TIP: You can either type in the name of the field on which you want to sort, or simply select it from the drop-down menu that's present in each field sort area.

4. Click OK to carry out the sort; here's what you see.

	Make	Model	Year	Price	Color	Serial	Sold for	Down
1	Ford	Mustang	1972	$12,750		123A456		
2	Ford	Probe	1991	$4,500		234B567		
3	Chevrolet	Camaro	1974	$2,350		345C567		
4	Honda	Civic	1989	$6,800		231ABC123		
5	Lincoln	Mark V	1978	$5,000		481DEC184		
6	Lincoln	Continental	1990	$17,500		038MAR4		
7	Lincoln	Continental	1986	$9,000		814AUG6		
8	VW	bug	1973	$400		JKL001		
9	Lincoln	Town Car	1988	$17,500		500DOS		
10	Lincoln	Mark VII	1990	$18,000		123KAY124		
11	Toyota	Celica	1988	$7,500		987D789		
12	Ford	Third	1990	$17,000		XYZ123		
13								
14								
15								
16								
17								
18								
19								

Microsoft Works - [CARS.WDB] — File Edit View Insert Format Tools Window Help — Arial 10 — Press ALT to choose commands, or F2 to edit. 13 12/12

If a field on which you sort contains different types of entries, such as text for some records and numbers for others, Works sorts in the following order:

- For an ascending sort, the order is text, then times (such as 12:00 A.M.), then numbers, and then dates (January 1, 1992).

- For a descending sort, the order is just the opposite. First sorted are dates, then numbers, then times, and then text.

When field entries contain mixtures of text and numbers, however, Works places combinations of numbers and text ahead of text and numbers in an ascending sort, and reverses the order in a descending sort. For example, an ascending sort of the serial numbers in the *cars.wdb* database produces 038MAR4, 123A456, 123KAY124, 231ABC123, 234B567, 345C567, 481DEC184, 500DOS, 814AUG6, 987D789, JKL001, and XYZ123.

Sorting by Case

In an alphabetical sort, Works ignores differences in capitalization, so *baby* comes before *Babylon,* but *Mars* precedes *martial.* If you create a database in which capitalization is important, you have to include more information for Works.

For example, if you want *NEW YEAR* to always precede *New Year,* create a new field and use a code, such as 1 for all capitals (NEW YEAR), 2 for initial capitals (New Year), and 3 for lowercase (new year). You can then use the case field as the second sort field. That way, you'll be sure that duplicate entries are arranged in the order you want. Here's an illustration of what we just proposed. The data in the first screen shot has not yet been sorted.

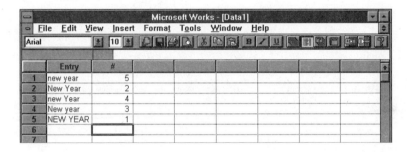

Here's the sort, first alphabetically and then by number (#).

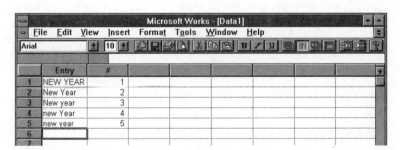

Finding Information

If you have 2,000 records (databases that size can develop faster than you think), sorting will be a help, but you probably won't want to scroll through 50 screens to find what you need.

If you need to find a particular record or group of records or all the records that match one or more criteria, Works can do this with ease. To find specific records, all you need is information (the more the better), such as some text, a unique value, or a field entry, that Works can use to separate the record (or records) you are trying to find from the entire set of records.

To find records that match certain criteria, you provide Works with a "description" of the information you seek and let Works do its work.

Finding Related Records

To find one or more records that have some information in common, use the Find command on the Edit menu. You can work in either list view or form view. Suppose, for example, you want to find all the records for Lincoln Continentals in the *cars.wdb* database. Be sure you are in list view, and do the following:

1. Open the Edit menu, and then choose the Find command. You see the dialog box shown here.

2. Type *continental* (uppercase or lowercase). Make sure that the default Match setting, Next record, is selected.

3. Click OK.

Starting from the current location of the mouse pointer, Works scans the database and moves the selection to the next occurrence of the word *continental*. If the current selection is near the end of the database, Works skips to the top and keeps going if it doesn't find a match by the time it reaches the last record.

Notice that when you carry out a Find command and specify that Works find only the next record, the entire database remains available for viewing. Now use the same dialog box, click on All records, and see what happens.

This time, the screen is considerably different. You told Works to find *continental* in all records, and Works responds by displaying *only* the records in which the text *continental* appears. This option is a great way not only to find, but also to select, particular records from the entire database.

The Find command works the same way in form view, but the result of specifying all records is less noticeable because you see only a single record at a time in form view. Let's try that by clicking on the Form View button to switch to form view. Works displays the form shown here.

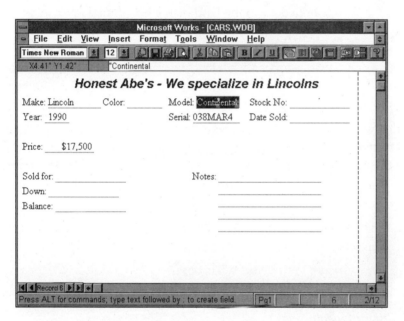

Notice that the status bar indicates that you are looking at record number 6 and that the Find command selected two records from the total of 12 in the database.

Now click the forward scroll button in the horizontal scroll bar. Works displays another record for a Lincoln Continental. Click again, and you see a blank form. Works has reached the end of the Continental records and has no more to display, given the criterion (continental) you specified in the search.

To see the entire database once again, open the View menu, and then choose Show All Records. Scroll through the records in form view, or switch to list view and you'll see that all the records are back.

TIP: When databases get large and you start using all the power that Works has to offer, you can become momentarily disoriented because the database might not appear in its entirety. If this happens, check the status bar. Then try choosing the Find command from the Edit menu to determine if you're actually looking at a set of selected records. Works continues to display the last text you searched for in the Find dialog box until you close the file or quit. If that doesn't help, use the Show All Records command on the View menu to see all the records.

Replacing Information

Just as with the word processor and the spreadsheet, the Works database has a Replace command (on the Edit menu) that allows you to first find, and then replace, a field entry. You can use Replace only in list view.

For example, let's say you want to annotate the word *Lincoln* (in the Make field) to read *Lincoln (new)*. Here's what you do:

1. Be sure you are in list view. Open the Edit menu, and then choose Replace.

2. Type *Lincoln* in the Find What box.

3. Tab to the Replace With box.

4. Enter *Lincoln (new)*.

5. Click Replace All.

6. Click OK.

The most important thing to remember about Replace is not to search to change individual letters, but to search on as much information as you can use. Always save your file before you proceed with a full-blown find-and-replace operation.

Using Wildcards

Chapter 6, see page 145, introduced the concept of using wildcard characters to find information in one or more spreadsheet cells. You can use the same characters, the asterisk (*) and the question mark (?), in the database to broaden a Find command (on the Edit menu). The asterisk, you might recall, can stand for any number of other characters, whereas a single question mark can represent any one character.

For example, specifying *m** in your *cars.wdb* database would cause Works to display all records having a field entry containing an *M* followed by any number of characters, such as Mark V, Mustang and so on. Specifying *198?* in a Find command would cause Works to display all records beginning with 198 and ending in any other character, such as 1986, 1988, and 1989.

Wildcard characters can be useful in helping you find generic information, but keep in mind that Works does not distinguish between whole words and parts of words. Use wildcard characters in the database in the same way you would use them in the spreadsheet, but always be sure to include enough specific text to narrow the selection to what you really want to find.

For example, if you were to type *c** to tell Works to find all Continentals in the *cars.wdb* database, you'd be in for a surprise. The specification is so broad that Works would include every entry in which the letter *c* is followed by one or more characters, such as the records that contain Civic, Lincoln Mark VII, and Porsche.

Queries and Query View

You can ask Works questions such as "Which cars have a price of more than $10,000?" Such a question is called a *query* in database jargon. When you want Works to apply some "judgment" to a database search, you turn to *query view*.

In appearance, query view is identical to a blank database form. In purpose, however, it is far different. Using query view, you can really give Works and your own database skills a good workout. In query view you define exactly the information you're looking for; in the process, you incorporate mathematics, logic, and relational operators, such as greater than and less than, and even logical operators, such as AND, OR, and NOT. Don't shy away from using queries because they sound intimidating. They can be very powerful and can make you a much more efficient database user.

About Queries in General

We could write an entire book on querying a database. Using a query is like using a set of super commands—using queries gives users the most control over what happens within the database. More than any of the other Works applications, databases and query view are yours to personalize. Given the way you set up your fields and the information contained in them, the type and number of questions you can ask is limited only by your imagination.

Fashioning a Query

When you use the Find command, you tell Works to search for records that contain certain information. After it finds that information, you have a group of records that are related to one another in some way.

When you use query view, you take the search process one step further. Here, Works not only finds the records you want, but lets you apply several conditions to refine the search.

You can, for example, use the Find command on a personal database to give you the names of all relatives named Hubbard. With query view, you can tell Works to narrow the field by showing you any and all relatives named Hubbard who have six or more children and are over the age of 90.

Let's state an obvious principle right now. You can only perform a query when the information the query must work with is in the database. If you don't have a field named "number of children," then you obviously cannot find relatives with a certain name and those with more than a certain number of children. Although this fact is somewhat self-evident, many people try to use the query function to make gold out of hay.

You can use the *cars.wdb* database (be sure it's open) to develop a feel for using query view. We're going to find all Lincolns that cost more than $9,000.

1. Click the Query View button to the right of the List View button on the toolbar. You can also choose Create New Query from the Tools menu in either form or list view.

    Works displays the New Query dialog box shown in Figure 11-1.

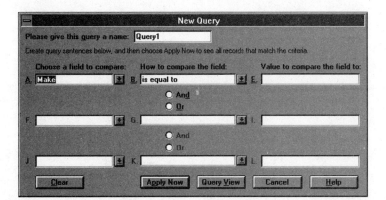

FIGURE 11-1.
The New Query
dialog box.

TIP: You can also type a query right into the formula bar in form view.

2. Give a name to the query. That way you can recall it later on by using the Query command on the View menu. If you don't give it a name, Works begins with Query1, and then names the next query Query2, and so on.

   Now you need to provide Works with three pieces of information so that it can complete the query.

   ❑ The first is the field you want compared.

   ❑ The second is how you want the field compared.

   ❑ The third is what you want the field to be compared to.

3. In the Choose a field to compare: area of the dialog box, either type *Make* or use the drop-down menu to select the field name Make.

4. In the How to compare the field: area, select is equal to from the drop-down box.

5. In the Value to compare the field to: area, type *Lincoln.*

   This query finds all cars that are Lincolns. We could have used the Find command, however, because here we have a simple condition of finding something equal to something else. We still need to demonstrate using a query with multiple conditions.

1. Select the And option.

2. In the Choose a field to compare: area, either type *Price* or use the drop-down menu to select the field name Price.

3. In the How to compare field to: area, select is greater than from the drop-down menu.

4, In the Value to compare the field to: area, type *9000.*

TIP: You are limited to eight queries for any one database, so feel free to delete those that you are finished with by using the Delete Query command on the Tools menu.

5. Click the Apply Now button and you see the results of the query, as shown here.

	Make	Model	Year	Price	Color	Serial	Sold for	Down
6	Lincoln	Continental	1990	$17,500		038MAR4		
9	Lincoln	Town Car	1988	$17,500		500DOS		
10	Lincoln	Mark VII	1990	$18,000		123KAY124		
13								

Microsoft Works - [CARS.WDB]
File Edit View Insert Format Tools Window Help
Arial   10   "Continental

As you can see, Works did its job quite well and found only those records that met the two conditions. Records 6, 9, and 10 are all records for Lincolns that cost more than $9,000.

Want to see more? How about all cars built from 1975 to the present that cost less than $6,000? Be sure you are in list view.

1. Open the Tools menu, and then choose Create New Query.

2. In the Choose a field to compare: area, type *Year* or use the drop-down menu to select the field name Year.

3. In the How to compare the field: area, select is greater than.

4. In the Value to compare the field to: area, type *1974*.

5. Select the And option.

6. In the Choose a field to compare: area, type *Price* or use the drop-down menu to select the field name Price.

7. In the How to compare field: area, choose is less than.

8. In the Value to compare the field to: area, type *$6,000*.

9. Click Apply Query.

As you can see on the next page, two records in the database (numbers 2 and 5) fit the bill.

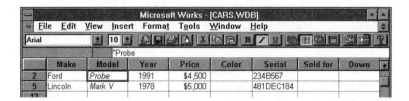

TIP: If you want to reapply the last query you created (without having to create it all over again), choose Apply Query from the View menu and double-click on the name of the query you want to apply.

Querying in Form View

Here's a slightly less elegant way to query, but one that can serve an important purpose. In Figure 11-1, you can see the Query View button at the bottom of the New Query dialog box. When you click on this button, you can see the query instructions in the appropriate fields as well as in the formula bar, as you shown here:

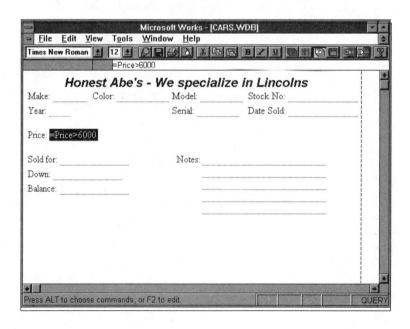

In this example, we are looking for cars that cost more than $6,000. Notice that we are still in the Query window. To see the results of the query, click on the Form or List commands on the View menu. You'll then see the results of the query.

The big advantage of using the Query View button is that once you see the instructions in form view, you can easily edit them to create a different query. For example, we could change the value 6000 to 10000 in the formula bar and only find three cars (all Lincolns) worth more than $10,000. This approach saves time and work.

Once you create a set of queries, you can select the one you need to use or edit by using the Apply Query command on the View menu. There you'll see all the queries from which you can select. To use any one, just double-click on the name; the query will be run and made available in query view for you to alter. Keep in mind, however, that once a database is closed, the queries that were created disappear and will have to be re-created if you want to use them again.

Editing a Query

Queries are great because they let you impose strict conditions on selecting records. Works also gives you a way to reuse queries—an especially important feature for complex queries.

To use a query again, you first have to duplicate it and then edit it in query view. Here's how:

1. Open the Tools menu, and then choose Duplicate Query.

2. Select the query you want to duplicate.

3. In the name box, type the name you want to use for the duplicated query. Limit the name to 15 characters.

4. Click Duplicate.

5. Click OK.

Now you can view that duplicated query and edit it as you see fit without disrupting the original one. You can, of course, edit the original one, but you will no longer have it available to use as originally designed.

Viewing Other Records

Each time you query the database, Works displays only those records you wanted to see. Where did the others go, and what if you want to see them?

Whenever you use the Find command or execute a query, Works hides all the records that don't match the criteria you specified. To see those records instead of the ones you requested, choose Switch Hidden Records from the View menu. This command causes Works to swap the two sets of records, hiding the ones you asked to see and displaying the others. You can switch back and forth as many times as you want. Each time, Works replaces the records currently on display with the alternate hidden set. Let's try this with the *cars.wdb* database.

■ Open list view, open the Select menu, and then choose Switch Hidden Records. Works displays all records other than the post-1975, under-$6,000 cars you requested in the last example.

When you work with queries, Works doesn't allow you to display both hidden and non-hidden records simultaneously. But if you want to compare two sets of records in a database, there is a way to do so. Apply your query and save the file twice. Save it once under its real name and again under a temporary name, such as *temp.wdb,* or make a duplicate and rename it, as we discussed earlier.

Now, open both files and tile the two document windows. If the records you want to see aren't displayed, switch to query view and reapply the query to each document. Switch to list view, and use the Switch Hidden Records command to display one set of records in one document window, the other set in the second window. To discard the duplicate when you no longer need it, close the extra copy of the database without saving it. When you return to Windows or the DOS prompt, delete the duplicate file to keep your hard disk uncluttered.

Here's what two such Works windows look like, showing cars priced over $6,000 and cars under $6,000.

		Microsoft Works		
File **Edit** **View** **Insert** **Forma**t **Tools** **Window** **Help**				
Arial	10			
	12750			

CARS.WDB

	Model	Year	Price	Co
1	Mustang	1972	$12,750	
4	Civic	1989	$6,800	
6	Continental	1990	$17,500	
7	Continental	1986	$9,000	
9	Town Car	1988	$17,500	
10	Mark VII	1990	$18,000	
11	Celica	1988	$7,500	
12	Third	1990	$17,000	
13				
14				
15				
16				
17				
18				
19				
20				
21				
22				

TEMP.WDB

	Model	Year	Price	Co
2	Probe	1991	$4,500	
3	Camaro	1974	$2,350	
5	Mark V	1978	$5,000	
8	bug	1973	$400	
13				
14				
15				
16				
17				
18				
19				
20				
21				
22				
23				
24				
25				
26				

Press ALT to choose commands, or F2 to edit.   1   8/12

Applying Judgment to Queries

The queries you've used so far are the type you'll most likely need on a day-to-day basis for selecting records. When you design a query with more than one field, you're entering an implied AND as part of your query, as in "Show the records for all cars built after 1975 *and* priced under $6,000.00."

AND is only one such operator that Works understands. Works also responds to OR, NOT, and even NOT EQUAL. All these operators can be used in a query. Here's what they look like and what they mean:

- The ampersand (&) for AND, as in "Find the records that match both A *and* B."

- #OR#, as in "Find the records that match A *or* B."

- The less than and greater than signs (< >) for NOT EQUAL, as in "Find the records that are *not equal* to A."

With these operators, you can go even further in your database searches by including more than a single criterion in a single query field. For example, suppose you want to see all Lincolns that were built before 1985 or cost less than $10,000.

The following approach provides you with a foundation for understanding what Works is doing. Here, you essentially formulate the query in Works language rather than your own. Remember that you can always create a new query, use up to three criteria, and include all the logical operators available in the drop-down menus. To use the query language, follow these steps.

1. Click Show All Records and switch to query view.

2. Click on the Year field.

3. Press the Del key.

4. Click the Enter button to clear the field.

5. Click in the Make field.

6. Type *=make ="lincoln"&(year<1985 #OR# price<10000)*

    Verify that you've enclosed *lincoln* in double quotation marks. (Works insists on this.)

7. Click the Enter button.

8. Switch to list view; you see the same results as if you created a new query and selected records that way.

In this example, you "wrote" your query in such a way that Works could "read" it. As always, you started the query with an equal sign to indicate you were entering characters you wanted Works to evaluate. Your first instruction was *make ="lincoln"*. Here, you specified the fields you want to search and enclosed any text in double quotation marks.

You also used parentheses. They function in queries much as they do in a spreadsheet formula. They group conditions together (year *or* price, in this example) to guarantee that Works treats the conditions as a unit. If you hadn't used parentheses, Works would interpret the query as "Search for records in which either the make is Lincoln, *and* the year is before 1985, *or* the price is less than $10,000."

The resulting display would include not only the 1986 Continental and the 1978 Mark V, but the Honda, Mustang, Porsche, and VW, all of which are under $10,000 (but are not Lincolns).

Different Types of Queries

Databases are as varied as the people who use them. Being able to find, replace, and search using all types of logical operators allows almost anyone, in any discipline, to manage a great deal of information efficiently.

Here's a summary of when to use the various conditions that you can place on specific criteria, such as greater than (>), AND (&), and exponentiation (^).

Greater than (>) and less than (<) These operators are used to find records in which a certain value is greater or less than a value you specify. Although previous examples showed how to use these operators with numeric values, you can also use them with text. Just remember to enclose the text in double quotation marks.

For example, let's say we have a database of dogs.

- Specify *>24* to find all breeds taller than 24 inches.

- Specify *"samoyed"* to list all breeds that come after samoyed in the alphabet.

Combined > and < The greater than and less than operators are used in combination to find records within a specified range. You can use them with either numbers or text, enclosing the text in double quotation marks. Because you are specifying more than one criterion, you must include the AND operator (&) to show that you want items greater than X and less than Y. We'll use the dog database again.

- Specify *>10 & <100* to find all records containing a value from 11 through 99.

- With text, specify *>"cocker" & <"doberman"* to find all breeds alphabetically between cockers and dobermans, excluding the two you use as criteria.

Logical operators The AND operator (&) is used to find records that satisfy more than one condition. The OR operator (#OR#) is used to find records that match at least one condition you specify. NOT EQUAL (<>) is used to find records that do not match the conditions you specify. You can enclose conditions within parentheses, in the same way that you group math operations, to control the way Works evaluates them.

The following examples assume you are entering a query in a field named Grade. The form includes fields for the grades, grade average, days absent, and midterm grade.

- Specify *avg >95 & absence <4* to find all students who qualify for an A. (Who have a better than 95 average and were absent fewer than four days.)

- Specify *midterm>=70&((avg>50&avg<80)&absence<8)* to find all students who qualify for a C on the basis of a 70 on the midterm and an average grade between 50 and 80, plus fewer than eight absences.

Math operators Use any of the following math operators, all of which should be familiar from the spreadsheet (and from basic math!): + (addition), – (subtraction), * (multiplication), / (division), or ^ (exponentiation). As in combined queries, use parentheses to group calculations you want to be treated as a unit. For example:

- Specify *(Price–Sold for)>1000* in the *cars.wdb* database to find all records in which the selling price was more than $1,000 below the original price.

- In a parts inventory, specify *(on hand*unit price)* to find the total value of the parts you currently have in stock.

Works functions Use built-in functions, such as AVG, MIN, and MAX, to search for records meeting criteria you have to calculate. Works includes many functions. A complete description of these functions is available in Appendix A.

Page Setup and Printing

Page setup and printing in the database will be familiar to you because they work much the same in the other Works modules. As in the word processor and the spreadsheet, you can set page margins, the orientation of the paper you are printing on, whether you want to print field names, and more.

The following sections deal with the Page Setup option on the File menu. Surprisingly, there are relatively few differences between the form view and list view Page Setup options.

Page Setup in Form View

Because the database operates in different views you have a number of choices when it comes to Page Setup. The Page Setup dialog box should be familiar because you've seen similar ones in the word processor and spreadsheet. It looks like this.

In the Margins tab of this dialog box, you can set the top, bottom, left, right, and header and footer margins.

In the Source, Size and Orientation tab, you set the source of the paper, and its size, height and width, and orientation (landscape or portrait).

In the Other Options tab, you can set the page number of the first page, set page breaks between records (or turn them off so more than one record goes on a page), print field lines, and choose to print fields plus data or data alone (some people prefer this approach because it is less cumbersome).

Page Setup in List View

The Page Setup dialog box in list view (shown below) differs only in the Other Options tab.

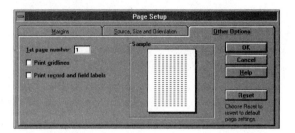

Here, you can change the 1st page number (as in form view), but you can also choose to print gridlines (regardless of how they appear on screen), and print record and field labels if you choose.

Coming Next

The database is a powerful tool for managing information. You've seen that throughout the last two chapters. In the next chapter, we'll show you how to take the records you've selected or sorted and turn them into an attractive and highly effective report.

Creating Database Reports

Databases are wonderful tools, but large ones can be a nuisance to print, especially if you want to show only selected fields and include calculations on selected data. With Microsoft Works 3 for Windows, printing reports is easy. In the same way that the word processor allows you to format a document and the spreadsheet generates charts, the database produces reports. A report is a highly flexible summary of database information that is created specifically for printing.

After you've created a database, you can generate up to eight different reports for it that include the fields and records of your choice. You can name a report, duplicate it, and delete it when you no longer need it. You can also include titles, notes, labels, and calculations in your report, as well as the usual headers, footers, and page numbers.

Although you can preview the reports you create, the Works report generator is not really meant for saving selected parts of a database for later viewing. Rather, it's an easy way to format and print the contents of a database and the results of your queries.

To begin our adventure with reports, we'll use the *cars.wdb* database that we created in Chapter 10, see page 293. Start Works and, if necessary, open the *cars.wdb* file. Maximize the document window, and then choose Show All Records to ensure that Works displays the complete database. Now let's take a brief intermission for some important information about reports and how they are structured.

The Standard Database Report

Works comes with a built-in design for a standard database report. You can customize the report before printing, but in many instances you'll find that the standard report is all you need—another major Works convenience. You can create a standard report in any Works database view, be it form view, list view, or query view.

Click the Report View button on the toolbar, or, if you prefer, open the Tools menu and choose Create New Report. In either case, you see the dialog box shown on the next page.

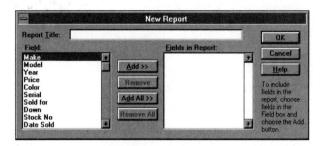

At the top of the dialog box is the Report Title box; here you type a title for your report. If you leave the space blank, the report will have no title. The two large boxes dominating the lower part of the dialog box are the areas that list the fields in your database and the fields to be used in the report.

The box on the left contains all the field names in the database you are using to create the report. The field names are listed in the same order in which they appear in the database, from left to right in list view.

The box on the right, named Fields in Report, starts out blank. Here you list the fields that you want to include in your report.

The Add and Remove buttons let you choose the fields to include in or remove from your report. When you highlight a field in the lefthand box and click Add, Works immediately duplicates the field name in the righthand box for inclusion in the report. If you make a mistake, highlight the field name in the righthand box and click Remove. Out it goes, and you're ready to continue.

Defining Report Fields

When you're creating a report, you can choose as many fields as you want, in any order you want. If you're not sure whether to include a particular field, you can select it and then remove it later.

The order in which you choose field names determines the order in which Works displays and prints them in your report; this feature allows you to arrange database fields any way you like in a report. You can, for example, list the price of a car before you list the make and model in a *cars.wdb* report. As with the initial design of a database, however, taking the time to think through how you want your report to look will save time later on.

To continue the creation of the report, let's move on:

1. Type *Honest Abe's: All cars* in the Report Title box.

2. Make is already highlighted, so simply click the Add button. You'll see the Make field jump over to the Fields in Report box.

3. Works moves the highlight to Model, the next field in the list.

4. Click Add to add it to the Fields in Report box. Do the same for Year.

5. Add Price using the same highlight-and-click technique. If you want to remove a field, simply highlight the name of the field in the Field in Report box and click the Remove button.

6. Click OK. Viola! Instant standard report? No, not quite yet.

Adding Statistics

Works is thorough and helpful; it wants to give you every chance to include useful information in the report, so it presents you with the Report Statistics dialog box, shown here.

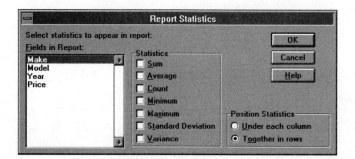

The Report Statistics dialog box reflects the sophistication of the Works report generator. Works developers knew that most reports need some statistics thrown in, so they designed this capability into the report generator.

Works displays the fields you chose to include in the Fields in Report box. The Statistics box lists a set of standard descriptive calculations from which you can choose, such as Sum, Average, Count (number of items), and others. The Position Statistics box lets you decide whether to print the statistics under each column or group them together in rows. The choice is yours; your selection might depend on how you like things to look or on how accessible you want the information to be.

You can mix and match field names and statistics. For Honest Abe's report, we'll include a count of the cars, as well as the minimum and maximum prices in the list. Take the following steps:

1. Be sure that Make is highlighted in the Fields in Report box. Click the check box next to Count to tell Works to list the number of cars.

2. Click on the Price field name to highlight it.

3. Click on the check boxes for Minimum and Maximum in the Statistics box.

4. To group the statistics in rows, verify that Together in rows is selected in the Position Statistics box.

5. Click OK.

You are still not quite finished. You've just defined the report, or created a report definition. Works displays the message you see here.

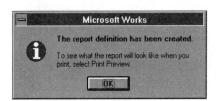

TIP: The Report Statistics box is the only place where you can change what appears in the final printed report. You cannot edit a report, because it is a printed product of the report generator. In fact, the only way you can see what a report will look like before it is printed is by using the Print Preview command on the File menu.

If you look at the screen behind this message, you might see that the "report" you've created doesn't look the way you expected. The reason: You are looking at the *report definition,* not the actual formatted report. The message tells you that the report generation process is complete and error-free, and that you can see the report itself by clicking the Print Preview button. Click OK to eliminate the message. Here's a full screen shot of the report definition.

	A	B	C	D	E	F	G
Title					Honest Abe's: All cars		
Title							
Headings	**Make**	**Model**	**Year**	**Price**			
Headings							
Record	=Make	=*Model*	=Year	=Price			
Summary							
Summary	COUNT OF Make:		=COUNT(M				
Summary	MINIMUM Price:		=MIN(Price)				
Summary	MAXIMUM Price:		=MAX(Price				

Microsoft Works - [CARS.WDB]
File Edit View Insert Format Tools Window Help
Arial   10
Press ALT to choose commands, or F2 to edit.   REPORT

Before you go any further, satisfy your curiosity by clicking the Print Preview button on the toolbar and zooming in twice to see what a standard report looks like. You should see something like the report in Figure 12-1 on the next page. And you should be proud of yourself.

If you have sorted records or added or deleted records, then your database might appear a bit different, but your report definition should have many of the same attributes.

FIGURE 12-1.
A standard
report generated
by Works.

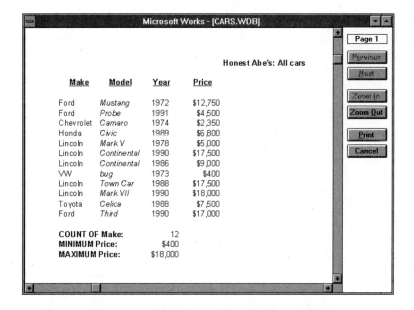

Works uses the field widths you set up in list view as the column widths when it creates a report. If your data prints completely in list view, it will also print without problem in a report. Be sure, however, to use Print Preview freely when creating a report, especially if you use different fonts and different sizes.

If any of the columns are too narrow to hold complete entries, Works truncates text at the right edge, and it displays and prints number signs (#####) in place of numbers. You can see any such problems in Print Preview, so catch them before printing to save yourself some frustration later. To widen columns, either drag the column boundary, as you do in the spreadsheet and the database list view, or use the Column Width command on the Format menu. As you know from the spreadsheet, if you click in the Best Fit check box, Works expands the column to fit all the data. Banish those #####s!

If you notice any problems with column width, fix them, and then use Print Preview to confirm that your solution worked. When you're finished, click the Cancel button to leave Print Preview. You should now be confident that you have created a usable report.

More About Report Definitions

The report definition on your screen is an outline of the report you just generated. Because Works displays the report definition rather than the report itself, you can modify a standard report without having to view or manipulate the actual records in it. For example, you can edit Honest Abe's report as you see fit. Editing in the report definition follows the same rules as editing in list view.

The parts of your report are laid out on a grid comparable to the display you see in list view. In the report definition, however, the columns are identified by letter, and the row labels (Title, Headings, etc.) tell you which elements are included in the report. Above the report definition, Works displays a formula bar that you can use for entering information and for displaying the complete contents of any cell (for example, the formula *=COUNT(Make)* in column C of the second Summary row). The box on the left end of the formula bar displays the letter of the column, but not the row name, where the highlight is currently located.

	Microsoft Works - [CARS.WDB]						
File Edit View Insert Format Tools Window Help							
Arial	10				B I U		
C	=COUNT(Make)						
	A	B	C	D	E	F	G
Title					Honest Abe's: All cars		
Title							
Headings	Make	Model	Year	Price			
Headings							
Record	=Make	=Model	=Year	=Price			
Summary							
Summary	COUNT OF Make:		=COUNT(M				
Summary	MINIMUM Price:		=MIN(Price)				
Summary	MAXIMUM Price:		=MAX(Price				

Here are the standard names for the row labels Works uses when generating a report, along with descriptions of what they do.

- *Title.* The name of your report or any other identifying text you care to include. Works boldfaces the title you type when you create a report, and centers the title above the fields in the report. Titles appear only on the first page of a printed report.

- *Headings.* Field names or other identifiers you want to use for the columns in your report. Unless you change the headings, Works uses the field names you chose, displaying and printing them in bold, underlined characters centered above each column.

- *Record.* The names of the fields to be included in the report, each in a separate column. Each field name is preceded by an equal sign, making it a formula of sorts. When generating the report, Works uses this row to find the required data for each record you chose to include.

- *Summary.* The statistics you chose to include in the report. Each summary row identifies and gives the formula for one statistic. By default, Works identifies the statistic by name and prints the text in boldface and the actual statistic in normal type.

Although you don't see them on your report definition yet, Works also recognizes two additional row types. The first is *Intr fieldname;* the second is *Summ fieldname.* You use these rows after you've sorted a database into groups (for example, by model of car in the sample database).

- *Intr* inserts rows between groups in a sorted report (Lincoln, Ford, and so on). You can use this row type to add blank space between groups or to place headings or other information at the top of each group.

■ *Summ* inserts a summary row between groups, giving you a quick means of including subtotals and other statistics for each group. Summ rows calculate intermediate statistics, such as the number of Lincolns on hand. Summary rows, on the other hand, provide statistics on the report as a whole (for example, the total number of cars in Abe's lot).

Working with Rows and Columns

You can add and delete rows and columns whenever you want to modify a report definition. You can add new field names and entries, insert extra blank lines or columns, and make room for additional titles, text, or statistics.

Adding and Deleting Columns

Adding and deleting columns in a report is similar to doing the same operations in the other Works modules. Select the column to the right of the position where you want to add a new column, and from the Insert menu choose Row/Column. To delete a column, select the actual column you want to delete, and from the Insert menu select Delete Row/Column.

Adding and Deleting Rows

Adding a row to a report differs slightly from adding rows in the other modules. You use the Row/Column command, as usual, but when working with a report definition, you always refer to rows by type. Notice that some rows in your form have titles but no column entries. Works includes these rows so the final printout (the standard by which a report should be judged) has blank spaces where Works thinks it is appropriate.

Even though the rows aren't functional in the sense that they contain information, they still belong to one row type or another. Their names indicate where blank rows will appear: one beneath the title, another beneath the column headings, and a third between the printed records and the summary statistics. If you were to type out a report based on the *cars.wdb*, you might put spaces in these positions as well, to make the report easier to read.

Suppose you want to add a subtitle to the report; as you can see, the space for the subtitle is currently blank in the report definition. Here's how to do it.

1. Click on the blank Title row to select the entire row. As in list view, when you select an entire row (or column), Works bypasses the dialog box that asks whether you want to insert a row or a column.

2. Open the Insert menu, and then choose Row/Column. Works displays a new type of dialog box, as shown here.

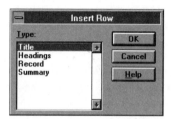

This dialog box shows the types of rows already in your report definition. The type of row you just selected (Title in this example) is highlighted. Because you selected a Title row, Works proposes adding another of the same type.

3. Click OK to add the row.

The new row appears above the one you selected. If you had chosen to add a different row type, such as Summary, Works would have inserted the row in the appropriate section of the report definition, even though you had selected a Title row before choosing the command. If you add a row in the wrong place, delete it with the Delete Row/Column command from the Insert Menu.

Modifying a Column

Now that you've added another Title row, you can enter some text in it. Let's do that now.

1. Highlight the cell in column A of the new Title row and type *March 1992.*

Unlike text, which Works displays across several empty columns, dates and other numeric information are confined to the width of the given column in the report definition. If you're still using the default column width of 10 characters, the column is too narrow to display the entire entry, so Works fills the cell with number signs (#). In Print Preview, you would also see number signs.

One solution in this case is to widen the column. You can do this by using the Best Fit option in the Column Width dialog box or by dragging the column boundary slightly to the right, increasing the width by two characters.

2. Now click the Bold button to make the text boldface.

Inserting an extra Title line might have piqued your curiosity about aligning titles. The title you originally specified is centered on the page. Centering the subtitle, however, would center it *within* column A, not *between* the page margins as you would like. You can insert the subtitle under the main title, but doing this would still not result in what you want. You'd get this:

```
Honest Abe's: All cars

March 1992
```

Widening the column a little, as you did earlier, would result in something like this:

```
Honest Abe's: All cars

        March 1992
```

Because you are working with cells in a report definition, your formatting options are not as numerous as in a truly text-based application such as a word processor. As a result, you'll sometimes need to do some tinkering to get the results you want.

In this case, for example, if you could sacrifice a centered title, you could cut the main title (Honest Abe's: All cars) to the Clipboard, reinsert it in column A, and then select Left under Alignment on the Format menu. The report would look like this.

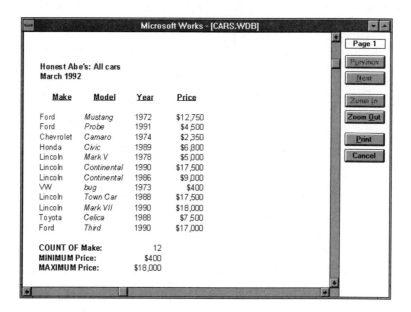

TIP: You can also adjust the vertical alignment of a text entry using the Top, Center, or Bottom options in the Alignment dialog box.

If you did want both titles centered, you could resort to a little trickery. When creating the report, you could type the subtitle in the Title portion of the New Report dialog box. After the report was created, you could then type a centered header by using the &C header code in the Headers & Footers dialog box.

In this case, you would have to do some tinkering with the formatting and, possibly, move the subtitle to the left to center it properly. You could not boldface the header, and it would appear on all pages of the report, but you would have two centered titles.

Selecting Records

After you've created a report definition, you can choose to include in it any set of records in the database by going to query view and specifying the records you want to see and print. For example, suppose you want to see a list of only Lincolns in the *cars.wdb* database. Follow these steps. (You should still have the report definition screen as the active one.)

1. Open the Tools menu, and then choose Create New Query. You'll see the New Query dialog box.

2. Specify the records you want by typing *Make* in the Choose a field to compare box; *is equal to* in the How to compare the field: box; and *Lincoln* in the Value to compare the field to box.

3. Click Apply Now.

4. Click the Print Preview button. (You can't go directly from query view to Print Preview.)

Instead of a list of all the cars in the database, you now see only the Lincolns. Works also recalculated the statistics so that they are accurate for the cars you included in the report.

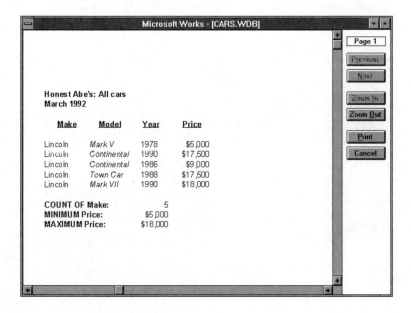

If you create a new query and specify another set of records, Works adjusts the report again to include the set you specified. Notice that even though Works includes commands for naming, duplicating, and deleting reports on the View menu, a specific query does not "stick" to a particular report. When you change the query, all of the records change to reflect the new specifications.

If you sort a database and want to keep the sorted report for future reference, you must save the database under a different name. Works saves the query and the report so you can view and print the selected records simply by opening the database under its new name and switching to report view.

Grouping Records

Displaying and printing selected records is one way to use database reporting and create a report. Another is to group records in the order you want.

In a product database, for example, you might want to print all or most of the records but group them by category, price, stock number, and so on.

You've seen how sorting works in the database. You can sort records on as many as three fields, specifying an ascending or descending sort. In report view, you can refine the output by telling Works to break up the groups, instead of listing them one after the other, and you can specify whether you want the entries grouped alphabetically, according to the first letter in the field. With the *cars.wdb* database, for example, you might want to see the cars grouped by make. To do so, follow these steps:

1. Switch to list view, and choose Show All Records from the View menu so you can view the entire database.

2. Switch back to report view by clicking on the Report View button on the toolbar.

3. Open the Tools menu, and then choose Sort Records. Works displays the following dialog box.

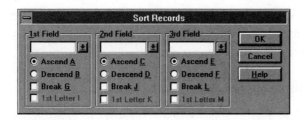

Unlike the Sort Records dialog box you used in list view, this dialog box includes a Break option and a 1st Letter option (currently dimmed) for each sort field.

The Break option tells Works to group similar entries, such as all Lincolns, together. The 1st Letter option, which is available only when the Break check box is checked, lets you group the entries alphabetically. If you don't choose 1st Letter, Works breaks the groups whenever any portion of the sort field changes (for example, Lincoln and Lincoln/New would form two groups).

To see how grouping works, continue as follows:

4. Type *make* in the 1st Field box or select Make from the drop-down menu.

5. Click in the Break check box to turn it on. You can leave the 1st Letter option unchecked. It doesn't make any difference here because the car makes will naturally list alphabetically. If, however, you specified a second sort field, such as Model, you can turn on the 1st Letter option for that field to group models alphabetically within makes.

   Under Lincoln, for example, Continentals would be in one group, the Mark V and VII in another.

6. Click OK, and then select Print Preview.

Your report has changed; see the new version below. In the next section we'll explain why and discuss how this change increases the usefulness of your reports.

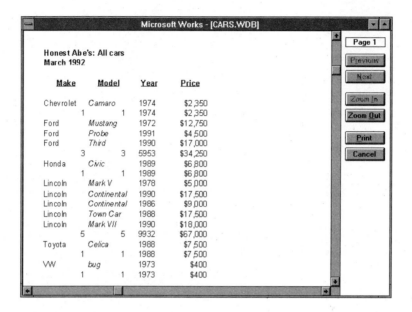

Summ Rows

You can now see in your report definition (see Figure 12-2) that Works inserted a new row, titled Summ Make.

Works creates a Summ row whenever you group records. The Summ Make row tells you that Works will insert statistics for each group within the report. By default, Works uses a COUNT function for any fields containing text entries (Make and Model, in this example), and it uses a SUM function (just like the spreadsheet and database function of the same name) to total each field containing numeric values (Year and Price).

In creating these statistics, Works uses field names, such as the COUNT of (Make), the SUM of (Price), and so on. This makes the report definition window easy to understand.

FIGURE 12-2.
The report definition after the Summ Make row is inserted.

	Microsoft Works - [CARS.WDB]						
File Edit View Insert Format Tools Window Help							
Arial	10	B I U					
A	"Honest Abe's: All cars						
	A	B	C	D	E	F	G
Title	Honest Abe's: All cars						
Title	March 1992						
Title							
Headings	Make	Model	Year	Price			
Headings							
Record	=Make	=Model	=Year	=Price			
Summ Make	=COUNT(Ma	=COUNT(M	=SUM(Year	=SUM(Price			
Summary							
Summary	COUNT OF Make:		=COUNT(M				
Summary	MINIMUM Price:		=MIN(Price)				
Summary	MAXIMUM Price:		=MAX(Price				

Press ALT to choose commands, or F2 to edit.   REPORT

You've no doubt noticed that Works, in its well-meaning but misguided default efforts, made a mistake by totaling the Year column in each group. After all, who needs a total of the years of car models? If you don't want to include a statistic that Works sets up, or if you want to delete one that's wrong, all you have to do is edit the Summ row as you would edit any other cell entry. Here's how:

1. Switch back to the report definition, if necessary.

2. Click in the cell containing =SUM(Year).

3. Open the Edit menu, and then choose Clear or press Del.

4. Switch to Print Preview, and you can see that the offending statistic is gone.

Inserting Rows and Formulas

If you prefer, you can replace the Summ rows that Works inserts with those of your own creation. You can include text and formulas. Here's an example.

1. Extend the highlight to cover columns A through D in the Summ Make row.

2. Open the Edit menu, and then choose Clear.

3. Click in the cell under =Year in the Record row.

4. Type *Subtotal:* and click the Enter button.

5. Click in the cell under =Price.

6. Type the formula *=SUM(Price),* and click the Enter button again. Your screen should resemble this illustration.

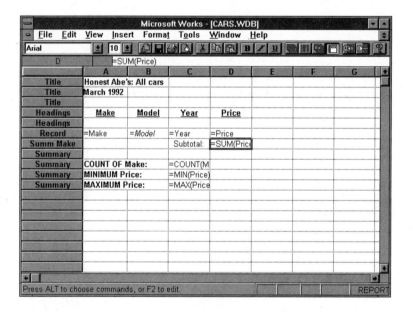

Now use the Print Preview feature to see what you've got. This time you see the Works summary replaced by subtotals of your own (see Figure 12-3).

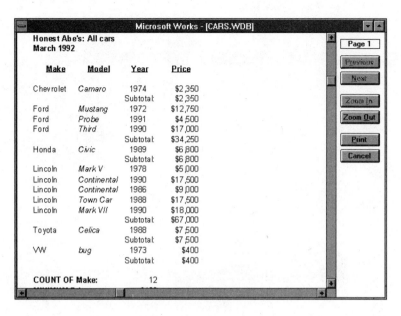

FIGURE 12-3.
Print Preview.

You can insert other row types and calculations as well. Remember, the report generator is there for you to define a report and to include the information you want. For example, now that you've created subtotals, you ought to have a total at the bottom of the report. (Remember to first access the Reports definition from the View menu.) Follow these steps.

1. Click the cell in column C of the blank row below the last summary row.

2. Type *Total:* and click the Enter button. Notice that simply entering information causes Works to add a new Summary row.

3. Type a SUM function, *=SUM(Price)*, into the cell in column D.

4. Check Print Preview. You now see a total value for all cars at the end of the report (its location here matches its location in the report generation window).

For practice, return to the report definition and format the words *Subtotal:* and *Total:* for boldface. Format the SUM cells for currency. Select your new Summary row, and insert an extra row above it to separate the row visually from the rest of the report.

Here's what the finished report looks like in Print Preview.

Working with Field Names and Field Entries

The final way to modify a basic report definition is by adding field names, field entries, and more statistics. Here you might sometimes need the *Intr fieldname* row type, described earlier in this chapter (see page 370).

Here are the definitions that Works uses:

- *Field name.* The name of a database field. When you insert a field name, Works places the name in whatever cell you selected, whatever the row type. When you preview or print the report, the field name appears as ordinary text.

- *Field entry.* The name that refers to the entries in a field (for example, =Model in the preceding examples). When you insert a field entry, you tell Works to replace that name with actual entries from the database records in the field you specify.

If you inserted =Serial as a field entry in your report, Works would replace it with the actual serial numbers of the cars listed in the report. Be sure to enter into the report generator the exact name of the field.

- *Field summary.* A statistic (Sum, Avg, Count, Min, Max, and so on) that you insert in a report in relation to a particular field. A field summary belongs in a Summ *fieldname* row. It is an easier way of inserting the type of formula you created earlier as =SUM(Price) in the Summ Make row.

You would probably want to insert a field name to add a field you didn't include in the original report definition, or to save typing time while constructing a formula or mathematical calculation or inserting text. Field entries become important only if you want to include additional data from the database. You need both field names and field entries to add extra fields to a report.

Inserting Field Names and Field Entries

You can add fields and field entries to a report whenever you want, and you can do so in any way you want. To save a little typing, however, you can use the Insert Field Name and Insert Field Entry commands on the Edit menu.

Suppose, for example, you now decide you want to include the serial number for each of the cars in your report. You realize that you should have created such a field in the original report, but Works provides you with the option to make such changes after the fact. Here are the steps you follow:

1. Click in the cell in column F of the Headings row.

2. Open the Insert menu, and then choose Field Name. Works displays the dialog box you see here.

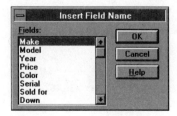

3. Click on Serial to select it.

4. Click OK.

    You can add a field name (not the field itself, yet) to any part of your report. When Works inserts the name, it doesn't add any special formatting, so you must take care of the formatting on your own.

5. Click the Bold and Underline buttons on the toolbar to make the new heading match the others.

    Now let's add the actual field.

6. Click in the cell in column F of the Record row.

7. Open the Edit menu, and then choose Insert Field Entry.

8. Select serial from the dialog box.

9. Click OK.

10. Click Print Preview. You now see all the serial numbers in the report, as shown here.

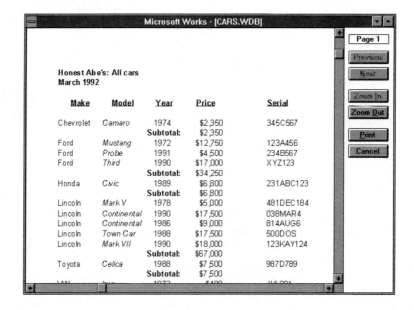

TIP: If the Print Preview screen gets crowded, use the scroll bars to move through the report.

Inserting Intr Fieldname Rows

The Intr *fieldname* row type is useful in situations such as adding extra spacing or adding internal headings between groups in a sorted database. You can also use it to insert text at the head of each group in the database.

Suppose want to repeat the headings at the top of each group in Honest Abe's report. You can do so by following these steps.

1. Click on any row title to select the entire row.

2. Open the Edit menu, and then choose Insert Row/Column.

3. Because you've grouped the database records, Works now presents you with an Intr row type, based on the first field you sorted, Make. Choose Intr Make.

4. Click OK to insert the new row. Regardless of the row you selected, Works inserts the Intr Make row above the Record row. To see what you can do with this, continue on with the following steps.

5. Click in column A of the Intr Make row.

6. Type *Make*.

7. Press Tab, and in each column repeat the heading that appears in the Headings row so you have the word Make entered across the row labeled Intr Make.

8. Use the Bold and Underline buttons on the toolbar to make the new column headings match the others.

When you switch to Print Preview, you see that each group has its own heading, as shown here.

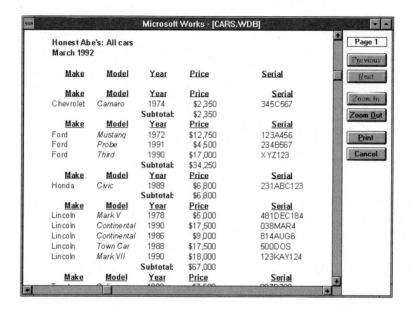

Each group of cars is now neatly laid out under its own headings. Notice, however, that Works displays two sets of headings at the top: one from the original Headings row, and the second from the *internal* headings row you just inserted. To take care of that, do the following.

1. Select the Headings row.

2. Open the Insert menu, and then choose Delete Row/Column.

3. To make your report even more attractive, select the entire Intr Make row, and insert another of its kind above it. Your report should look like the illustration on the next page.

Designers tell us that white space is as important as information in creating a report that communicates effectively. Insert rows as needed to get the spacing exactly as you want it.

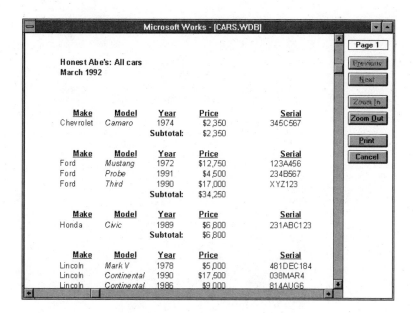

Inserting Field Summaries

You created a field summary of your own when you entered the SUM formula in the Summ Make row. Inserting summaries with the Field Summary command on the Insert menu is simpler, and is similar to choosing from the Statistics dialog box that appears when you create a report for the first time.

Field summaries, as mentioned earlier in this chapter, belong in Summ *fieldname* rows. To see how simple it is to add a summary, follow these steps:

1. Click in the cell in column A of the Summ Make row.

2. Open the Insert menu, and then choose Field Summary. Let's add a count of the number of cars in each make.

3. The field name Make is already highlighted, so simply choose the type of statistic you want. Click the button next to COUNT.

4. Click OK.

Now check Print Preview. The new statistic, which counts the number of makes (or the number of cars in each subgroup), now appears below each group.

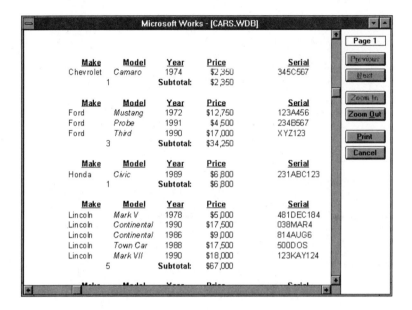

Saving a Report

When you create a report and want to save it for future reference, you can give it a name of up to 15 characters. Here's how to save a report:

1. Open the Tools menu, and then choose Name Report. When you do this, Works displays the following dialog box.

In the Reports section of the dialog box, Works lists the reports (up to eight) that you've created for this database. In this dialog box, you have one report with the default name Report1.

2. Click in the Name box, and type *Abe*.

3. Click the Rename button to change the name from Report1 to Abe.

4. Click OK.

5. Open the View menu, and then choose Report. You now see *Abe* listed at the bottom, where Works displays the names of the reports associated with the current database.

The related Delete Report and Duplicate Report commands on the Tools menu work much like the Name Report command. Delete Report, as you would expect, eliminates a report you no longer want or need. This command is useful when you want to throw away a mistake or eliminate one or more reports when you hit the eight-report limit in the report generator.

To delete a report, choose the Delete Report command, and then select the report. Click the Delete button, and then click OK.

To duplicate a report, use the same procedure but choose the Duplicate Report command. When you duplicate a report, Works gives it a default name, such as Report1. Use the Name Report command to change the name of the duplicate.

Using a Saved Report

Let's say you open a database and then want to use a report that has already been created. Do the following:

1. Open the View menu, and then choose Report. You'll see the Report dialog box.

2. Highlight the report you want to open.

3. Click OK.

Formatting and Printing Reports

You've already done a fair amount of formatting in this chapter. In addition, you know about formatting options in the word processor and spreadsheet that can be applied to the database—font, size and style, headings, headers and footers, and more.

Your most important ally in preparing a report for printing is the Print Preview button. Print Preview is an invaluable means of seeing what you'll get before you get it (WYSIWYG) in full-page displays. In fact, it's the only way you can see what a report will look like, so don't ignore it!

Basic Formatting

Take another look at Figure 12-1 on page 368. Looks like a pretty neat report, except for the poor alignment of column headings above the column entries. The column headings are centered by default, but the text entries are left-aligned and the numeric entries are right-aligned by default.

To align the column headings, the headings and entries have to match. Here's one solution. (We're working in list view.)

1. In the Intr Make row, select Make, Model, Year, Price, and Serial by extending the highlight.

2. Open the Format menu, and then choose Alignment. When you do this, Works displays the dialog box shown here.

3. Click Center.

4. In the Record row, select all the record names from =Make to =Serial. Center these as well.

Preview the report again. Here's what your report should look like.

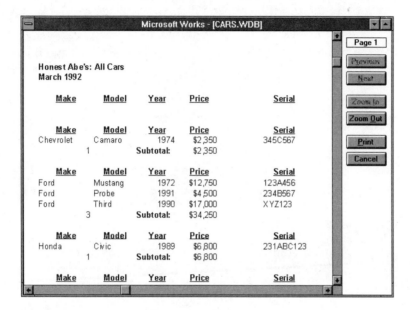

Working with Page Breaks

The report generator lets you insert and delete manual page breaks. You can insert page breaks either between rows or between columns.

Inserting a page break between rows is useful when you want to print groups on separate pages. For example, if you insert a page break above the headings or an Intr *fieldname* row in the report definition, each group starts on a new page. If you do this, the titles also print on a page by themselves, so format or position them accordingly.

A better solution is to create a blank Summ fieldname row just before the summary rows and then insert a page break before the blank row. That way, nothing is lost, things stay together as they should, and the overall report better fits your needs (with information grouped on one page).

Inserting a page break between columns is the obvious choice when you're printing a report that is too large to fit on a single sheet of paper. By inserting a vertical page break of this type, you can determine where Works will break pages between printed fields.

To insert a page break, follow these two steps:

1. Place the cursor where you want the page break to occur.

2. Open the Insert menu, and then choose Page Break. A page break appears in the on-screen report as a dashed line.

If you want to delete a page break, select Delete Page Break from the Insert menu.

 TIP: If you insert a page break at the end of the record in form view, you will have a separate page of output for each record. You can see all the pages, one by one, in Print Preview by using the Next button.

Using Page Setup

The Page Setup command in the report generator is very similar to the one in the word processor and the spreadsheet. The three options in this tab dialog box are:

- Margins

- Source, Size Orientation

- Other Options

In Other Options, a new feature is Print all but record rows. If you want to print your report *form,* including headings and summaries, but not the data entries themselves, then click on this option. It might be useful to have a hard copy of a report you find especially well designed.

Coming Next

Wow! We're done with the three main Works modules, and you now have the tools to perform 80% of the tasks that personal computers are used for. But that's not all. Now it's time to learn about the artist in you. Welcome to Works graphics.

Using Graphics

Getting Started
with Microsoft Draw

A picture really is worth a thousand words. Although your writing may be brilliant, how your document looks may often be just as important. If you need illustrations to help make a point, or to better communicate a message, Microsoft Works 3 for Windows can help. The key here is to use the Works drawing program, Microsoft Draw.

Works offers several tools, including a *clip art* library (a collection of ready-made illustrations), WordArt, and more to help give your documents the punch they deserve. For the artistically inclined, Draw offers drawing tools to create arcs, squares, circles, and more. With Draw, you can create geometric forms with ease, design your own monograms and letterheads (we'll do one here), and arrange text in circles, squares, and other patterns.

Where Is Draw, Anyway?

Unlike the other parts of Works, Draw is not directly available on the Startup screen you are familiar with, nor is it on any Works menu bar. You access Draw through the Works word processor or the Works database (in form view), using the Insert menu.

Typically, Draw is used in two ways:

- You create a document or a database, use the Drawing command on the Insert menu to place a drawing in the document or database, and then use Draw's tools to modify the drawing.

- You create a drawing from scratch and then place it into the document or database.

When you insert a drawing into a document, Works inserts it at the current position of the insertion point. At any time, you can go back, select the drawing, and modify it.

Before we jump into Draw, let's be sure we have enough room on screen to do what we want—to create a stationery letterhead. Do the following:

1. Open the word processor.

2. Be sure that the insertion point is at the beginning of the document (in front of the first character of the first paragraph).

3. Press Enter to create a blank paragraph, and then move the insertion point up to the new paragraph.

To start Draw, open the Insert menu, and then choose Drawing. The Microsoft Draw window appears.

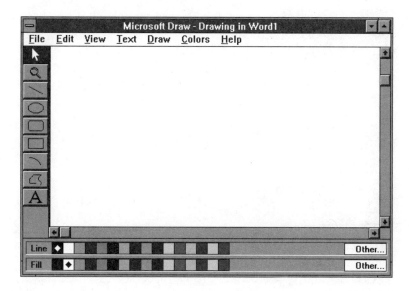

The blank workspace filling most of the window is the canvas on which you will draw. On the left side is a *toolbox* containing the various drawing tools; across the bottom is a *color palette* showing available colors for drawing lines and filling shapes.

As usual, the title bar and control buttons are at the top of the screen, and the menu bar is just below the title bar. Notice that the name of your word processing document appears in the title bar. That's Draw's way of telling you that any drawing you create will be inserted into a Works document. Notice, too, that Draw includes a Help menu.

Draw: Basic Training

To create an image with Draw, you must first know what tools are available and how to use them. The key thing about Draw is that you can't practice enough. Be patient, practice, and have fun; you'll find Draw to be as valuable as any other Works feature.

We'll start by checking the contents of the Toolbox.

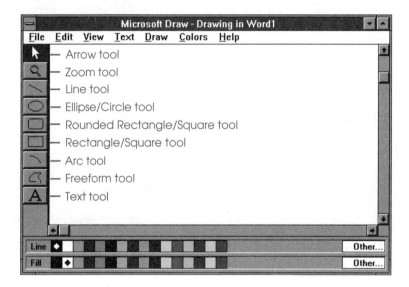

The top two items, an arrow and a magnifying glass, are "management" tools. The arrow lets you select and manipulate shapes (called *objects* in Draw). The magnifying glass lets you zoom in and out to change the displayed size of an object. The rest of the tools create objects.

Drawing an Ellipse

Let's get started. First be sure that in the Microsoft Draw window a diamond shape appears next to both Line and Fill on the Color Palette (at the bottom of the window).

Now let's draw.

1. Click on the Ellipse/Circle tool (fourth from the top) and move the pointer into the blank workspace.

Notice that the pointer becomes a set of cross hairs. As you create objects, you'll use the center of the cross hairs to mark your starting point.

2. To draw an ellipse, hold down the left mouse button and drag the mouse. Release the button when you've drawn an egg shape a few inches across, as you see here.

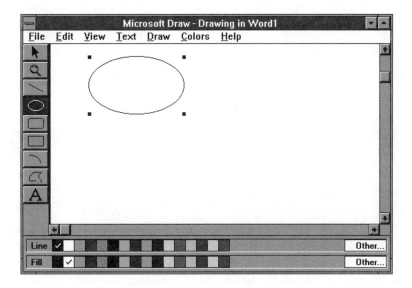

What Is an Object?

In Draw, an object is a shape or an image that can be manipulated independently of other objects. For example, if you create a drawing that consists of three squares, a triangle, and some text, each of these elements is a separate and independent element of the drawing. They can be acted on alone or together. Even though they are independent, they can all be used to create a drawing that is greater (in impact and meaning) than the sum of its parts or elements.

The ellipse that you just created is an object. So will be the other shapes you create throughout this chapter. Just as you can edit a document created with the word processor, you can change objects as well.

Changing the Size of an Object

When you released the mouse button in the previous example, four small black boxes appeared outside your ellipse. These boxes, called *handles,* appear at the corners of an invisible box that Draw places around each object you create. You see the resize handles only when the object is selected, as your ellipse is now. To select an object, simply click anywhere inside it. To deselect it, click anywhere outside the object.

You can drag one of the resize handles to change the size (or shape) of an object. Here's how to do it.

1. Select the Arrow (the object manipulation tool) by clicking on the Arrow in the Toolbox or by clicking in any blank portion of the workspace.

2. Place the pointer anywhere in the ellipse and click to select it again.

3. Point to one of the handles and press the mouse button. Notice that the arrow pointer changes to an arrowhead. Drag the handle in any direction. As you drag the handle, an outline of the ellipse will follow the handle to show how its changing positions affect the shape of the object. When you've created an ellipse you like, release the mouse button.

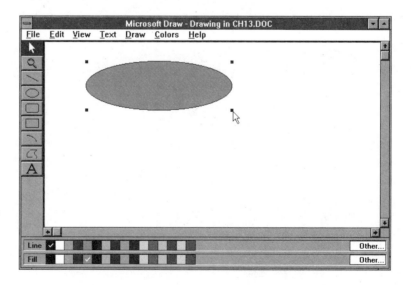

Practice changing the shape of the ellipse. This technique applies to all objects. Simply select and drag when you want to change the size.

Handling an Object

You've now seen why Draw refers to shapes as objects. When you manipulate a shape, Draw treats it as an independent unit. Consequently, you can place objects on top of each other, group them together, and manipulate them singly or together. Let's look at some of the possibilities.

1. Click on the Rectangle/Square tool.

2. Place the cross hairs on your ellipse and draw a rectangle that extends beyond the border of the ellipse, as you see here.

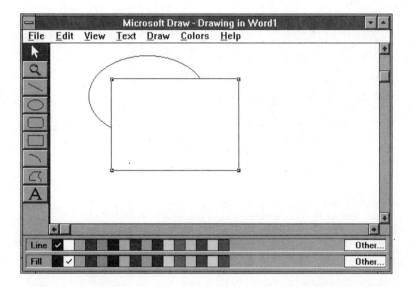

When you're finished, the rectangle is on top of and partly covers the ellipse. Now let's move the rectangle.

3. Select the rectangle with the Arrow tool.

4. Drag the dotted outline of the rectangle until it is completely off the ellipse.

When you release the mouse button, notice that Draw has completely separated the two shapes. Both the ellipse and the rectangle are whole and unchanged, and look like this.

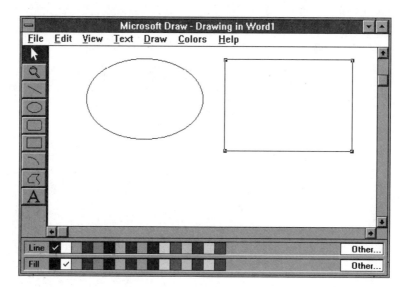

Selecting Multiple Objects

Objects stand alone and are independent of other objects. When you want to do something to an object, you must first select it. In Draw, if you want to do the same thing to more than one object at a time, you can do that as well. Here's how to select multiple objects:

1. Be sure you have chosen the Arrow tool.

2. Place the pointer in a blank area of the workspace above and to the left of both the ellipse and the rectangle.

3. Hold down the left mouse button and drag the mouse. As you drag the mouse, a dotted rectangle will form. This dotted outline is the *selection rectangle*. You use it to select a group of objects.

4. Expand the selection to include both the ellipse and the rectangle
   you drew, as you see here.

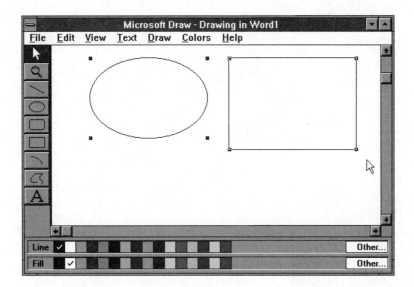

 TIP: It's very important when selecting objects, especially
lines and arcs, to click right on the object. If you don't, the
object will not be selected and you won't see the object's
handles.

When you release the mouse button, resize handles appear around
both objects to indicate that they are selected. They are still separate objects,
but the selection rectangle tells Draw you want to work with both at the
same time.

Surrounding objects by using the Arrow tool is one good way to select
them. If objects are scattered all around a window, however, selecting them
using this method is impractical. An alternative way follows.

1. Select the first object.

2. Press the Shift key; while holding it down, choose another object.
   You can select as many objects as necessary.

If you want to deselect a particular object, simply press the Shift key and click on that object. If you want to deselect all the objects, click outside of an object.

Managing Multiple Selections

Once you've selected a group of objects, you can move, color, copy, or delete them. Try moving and coloring the two objects we created by following these steps.

1. Place the pointer on either object (both of which you simultaneously selected earlier).

2. Press the left mouse button and drag slowly. As you drag the mouse, dotted outlines of the two objects follow the mouse pointer. When you release the mouse button, the ellipse and the rectangle move to new positions, maintaining their original relationship to one another.

3. Point to the part of the color palette labeled Fill. The current fill color (probably white) is indicated by a check mark.

4. Click on any other color. After you select a color, a check mark appears on the color in the palette, and Draw fills the shapes with the color you select. You can fill with other colors with just a click.

 TIP: If the only thing that changed was the color of the object's border, then you clicked in the Line area and not in Fill. Try again.

To see how managing multiple objects differs from managing individual objects, try this.

1. Click in any blank area of the workspace to deselect the objects. Be sure you click well outside of the objects you have created.

2. Click on the rectangle to select it.

3. Click on a different fill color in the palette.

This time only the rectangle changes color.

> **TIP:** If you've been wondering about the difference between the Line and Fill palettes, then select an object and select white for the fill and a bright color, such as red, for the line. Fill refers to the internal color of an object and line refers to the border.

Combining Objects

Objects are, by definition, independent of one another. But separate objects can be combined to create one object. Try grouping the ellipse and the rectangle as follows.

1. Select both objects as you did before, using the selection rectangle. Notice the positions of the resize handles.

2. Open the Draw menu, and then choose Group or use the keyboard shortcut, Ctrl+G. To ungroup the objects, you can use the Ungroup command on the Draw menu or the Ctrl+H key combination.

    When you carry out the command, a single set of four resize handles appears around both objects. Draw is now prepared to treat the two objects as one. When you click on one, the other is selected as well.

3. Point to one of the resize handles and drag it.

    When you release the mouse button, Draw adjusts the sizes and shapes of both objects, once again maintaining their original relationship to one another.

Working with Patterns and Lines

Works provides additional options for changing the look of objects. You can fill a shape with a pattern as well as a color, and you can change the style and thickness of a line.

As you can see here, we have created several different shapes (and some shapes within shapes) containing different patterns and using lines of varying thickness.

FIGURE 13-1.
Examples of
Pattern and Line
Style options.

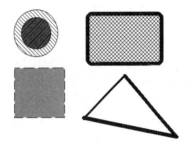

Here's how to fill an object.

1. Select the object.

2. Open the Draw menu, and then choose Pattern.

3. Click on the pattern you want from the choices shown here.

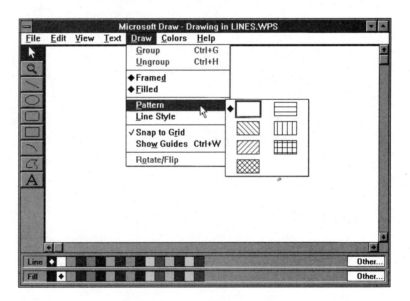

The circle within a circle you see in Figure 13-1 was created by drawing a smaller circle within a larger one and then using the Pattern and Line Style options, with different fill colors. See if you can produce it!

Here's how to change the style of a line.

1. Select the object.

2. Open the Draw menu, and then choose Line Style.

3. Click on the style you want to use. You can apply a style to a straight line or to a line that constitutes an object, such as those in Figure 13-1.

Now let's turn to the actual nuts and bolts of creating an image. Let's pretend you are in the umbrella sales and repair business and you want to design a logo.

Using Draw

Drawing programs are among the most enjoyable, and often the most frustrating, computer applications. On one hand, you have instant shapes in a variety of colors. On the other hand, your efforts may not produce the image you have envisioned. Not everyone is a Michelangelo, so we'll keep this illustration simple. Keep in mind that ClipArt is easy to use and can be modified as well.

See Also: For information about ClipArt, see Chapter 14, "Special Touches: ClipArt, Note-It, and WordArt," page 425.

We need a clean screen, so start again with Draw in the word processor application.

1. If necessary, from the Edit menu choose Select All or use the keyboard shortcut, Ctrl+A.

2. Press the Del key (the keyboard shortcut), or choose the Clear command from the Edit menu to clear the screen. You're ready to start again.

3. Maximize the Draw window and verify that the scroll boxes are at the top and left edges of the scroll bars.

4. Open the Draw menu, and then choose Show Guides (or use the Ctrl+W key combination).

When the full window reappears, Draw displays two dotted guidelines in the center of the screen. These guides are comparable to the movable straight edges on drafting equipment. They indicate your position relative to the top lefthand corner of the drawing. Because the guides are movable, and because objects "snap to" them like filings to a magnet when you move the objects close enough, you can use the guides to help position text and images with a high degree of precision.

To use the guides, place the pointer on the vertical guide and press the left mouse button.

A decimal number appears above a right-pointing arrow to tell you how far the guide is from the left edge of the drawing area and in which direction Draw is measuring. The same type of information appears when you point to the horizontal guide and press the left mouse button.

To move a guide, point to it and drag it in the direction you want it to go. To start off, however, leave the guides where they are.

Creating a Drawing

This is the drawing and text you're going to create.

POB 395
Williams, MA 06475
Phone (823) 657-5866
Fax (823) 657-4744

RAINGEAR

The drawing area available to you is much larger than the visible screen area, but to simplify matters and to ensure that your drawing will fit neatly on your stationery, let's create the drawing within a single window. At the same time, we'll make the objects large enough to manipulate easily, which will result in a larger drawing than you really need. In the future, you will probably want to create drawings closer to the actual size you need. But for this example, you'll find a larger drawing easier to work with.

The outline of an umbrella will be the centerpiece of the logo. You'll use the Arc tool to make an outline. Follow these steps to prepare for the drawing.

1. Open the Draw menu.

2. If a diamond-shaped mark appears next to the Filled command, click on it to turn the option off. If a diamond-shaped mark does *not* appear next to the Framed command, click on it to turn it on.

Creating an Object Outline

If you've ever tried drawing the two halves of a heart, a butterfly, or a pair of scissors, you know that it can be very difficult to make both halves identical. With Draw, the process is much easier because you can use the tools to create regular shapes. To use an even faster method, however, make half of the drawing, copy the object, and then flip it to create a mirror image.

You'll need five curves across the bottom edge of the umbrella, so let's start there. Later you can make the top curve of the umbrella fit exactly in one try. Here goes.

1. Select the Arc tool from the Toolbox.

2. Place the center of the cross hairs about a quarter of an inch above the intersection of the two guides.

3. Press the left mouse button and drag to create a small arc extending from the starting point to the horizontal guide, as you see here. Be sure that the arc is still selected and that its handles are showing.

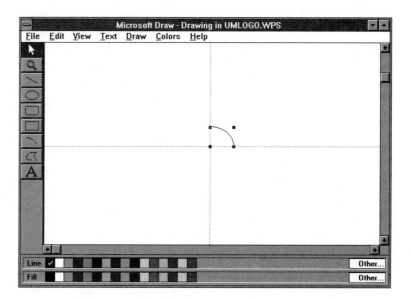

Now you can make Draw do most of the work.

4. Copy the arc to the Clipboard using the Copy command on the Edit menu.

5. Open the Edit menu, and then choose Paste. You'll see another arc appear on the screen. What you did was paste the selected object to the Clipboard and then copy it back to the drawing. This is the way Works duplicates an object.

Flipping an Object

The arc doesn't do much for you as is, so you have more work to do.

1. Open the Draw menu, and then choose Rotate/Flip. A menu opens offering you four choices: Rotate Left, Rotate Right, Flip Horizontal, and Flip Vertical.

2. To make a side-to-side mirror image of the arc, choose Flip Horizontal.

3. Click in a blank area of the window to deselect all the objects.

4. Select the new arc by placing the pointer on it, and then drag the arc into position next to the original, as you see here.

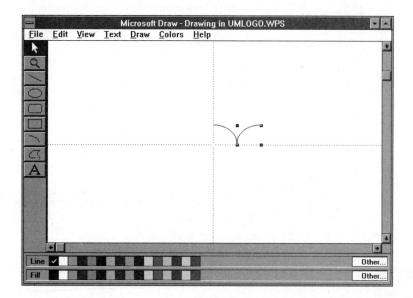

5. The original arc you copied is still on the Clipboard because you haven't replaced it yet. Paste another copy onto the screen (using Paste from the Edit menu or the Ctrl+V key combination).

6. Drag the new copy, without flipping it, and place it next to the first arc you pasted.

7. Now that you have a complete curve, use the Arrow tool to select both pasted halves.

8. Open the Draw menu, and then choose Group to make the two halves into a single object.

9. Open the Edit menu, and then choose Copy to copy the curve to the Clipboard.

10. Finally, paste the copy into the workspace, positioning it like this.

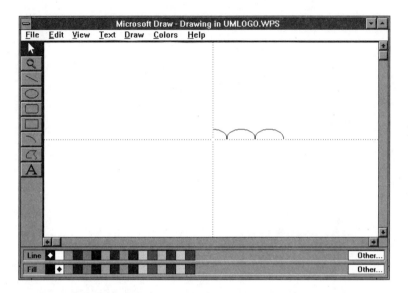

Positioning Objects

This process is a bit long, but hang in there. The results will be worth it. Now let's draw the rest of the umbrella.

1. Choose the Arc tool again.

2. Position the cross hairs about an inch and a half from the top of the window and draw a new arc extending to the outside edge of the smaller curves you made.

3. The next few steps require some precision, so let's get a closer view. Open the View menu and choose 200% Size. Your image will double in size in the window.

4. Choose the Line tool.

5. Make part of the umbrella's handle by drawing a short vertical line slightly to the right of the umbrella's center. You might have trouble positioning the line accurately if Draw is snapping the line to the guides. If so, turn off the Snap to Grid option on the Draw menu.

   Once you draw the line, your screen should look like this (at 200%).

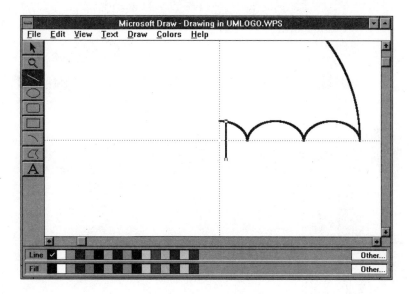

6. You need another vertical line about a half inch below the one you just drew. You can gauge one-half inch using the guides. Draw another vertical line just below the first one.

   That's half your umbrella. Now make the other half by flipping the image.

7. First, return to full view (Full Size on the View menu).

8. Select the entire umbrella.

9. You now want to work with all the pieces as a single object, so from the Draw menu choose Group.

415

10. Now copy the group to the Clipboard and then paste it back into the workspace. You need to make a duplicate of the first half and then align it with the original.

11. Open the Draw menu, choose Rotate/Flip, and then choose Flip Horizontal to flip the copy.

12. Drag the rest of your umbrella into position. Remember to grab one of the lines on your drawing to move the new group. Now admire your work.

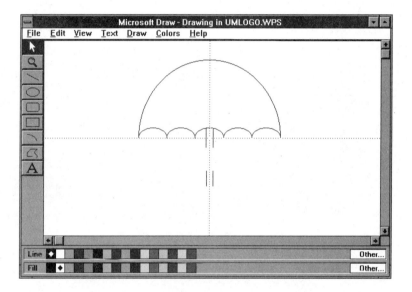

Adding Text to a Drawing

Now we'll add text to the drawing. To do this, you need to use the Text tool and an appropriate font and font size.

1. Open the Text menu, and then choose Font.

2. Select any font you want from the drop-down menu. We'll use Arial.

3. Open the Text menu, choose Size, and select 18.

4. Choose the Text tool (the A icon in the Toolbox). Move the cursor to an area in the workspace with plenty of room. Click. Notice that the pointer is now an I-beam, as it is when you are working with the word processor.

5. Type *RAINGEAR* in all capital letters. Your screen should look like this.

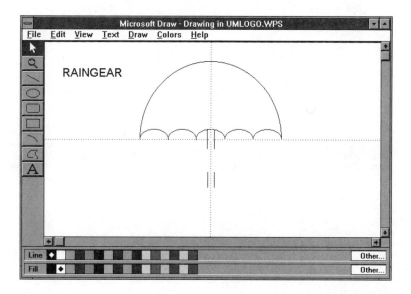

6. Press Enter. Notice that the text is surrounded by handles. Yep, it's another object! Draw treats all the letters as a single object because you typed them all at the same time.

7. Drag the text object into position, centering it under the umbrella, as you see on the next page.

8. Italicize the selected text by choosing Italics from the Text menu. Notice that you can choose other options as well, such as Bold and Underline.

9. If you haven't done so already, get rid of the guide lines (on the Draw menu) by deselecting Show Guides.

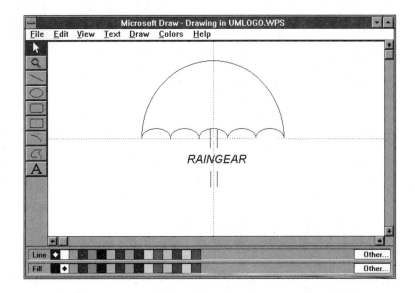

Finishing Up

Once you finish the logo, group the pieces to create a single object (use Select All from the Edit menu). This allows you to move, copy, or even delete it as a single item. If you want to work on a part of the logo later, you can choose the Ungroup command from the Draw menu and "deconstruct" the object into its separate parts.

As a last step, we need to add some information about the Raingear company, specifically the address, phone number, and fax number. We could have added this information in the word processor, but adding it now is easier and gives you more control over placement.

We will place the text so the finished logo looks like the one shown on the next page.

Enter this text in 8 point type:

POB 395

Williams, MA 06475

Phone (823) 657-5866

Fax (823) 657-4744

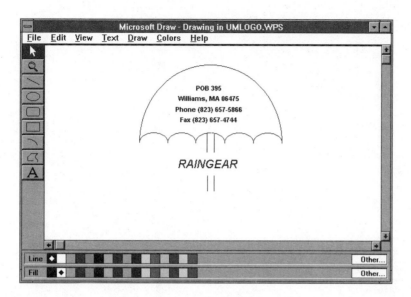

Now select all of the text and make it boldface. Select the individual text objects and place them as you wish. You can see how we did it. You should be very proud of what you've created.

Back to the Word Processor

Since your drawing can't exist independently of the word processor or the database, let's return to the word processor.

In Draw, open the File menu, and then choose Exit and Return to [name of the word processor file].

Draw displays a dialog box asking if you want to update the word processor file. When Works updates, it inserts the drawing into the document. This is what you want, so click Yes; your drawing appears at the top of the document, as you see on the next page (in Print Preview).

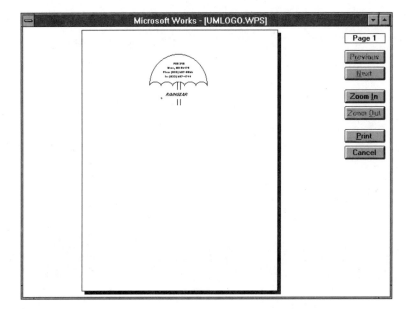

Notice that Works inserted your art work at the current position of the insertion point in the document. No problem. Simply return to the document (press Cancel in Print Preview) and click on the Center Align button on the toolbar. Print Preview shows you a perfectly created and centered logo. Congratulations!

Scaling a Drawing

If you want, you can use the resize handles in Draw to shrink a picture after it is placed in a document. Simply drag on either side to increase or decrease the horizontal or vertical size, or on one of the corners to increase or decrease both simultaneously.

This is a more than adequate way to size, but it's not very precise. If you want to be precise, you can go to the Picture/Object command on the Format menu. Here's how to do it:

1. Select the drawing, if necessary, by clicking on it once.

2. Open the Format menu (in the word processor), and then choose Picture/Object. Works displays the following dialog box.

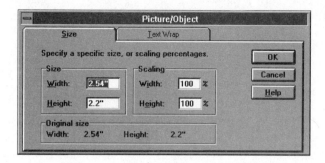

You can use the Size tab in this dialog box for one of several different adjustments in the format of the object.

■ You can adjust both the height and the width.

■ You can adjust the scale of both the height and width. How does scale differ from size? Size is the actual measured size of the object, which in this case is expressed in inches. Scale is a percentage of the original size of the drawing.

If you keep a drawing within the bounds of a single Draw screen, Works can usually import it into a document at or near its full size. Works scales down drawings larger than a single screen to fit within the margins of the page. For the umbrella logo you created, Works did not need to scale down the drawing when importing it.

Scaled or not, once a drawing is in your document, you can decide on a specific size that suits your preferences. For this example, you can scale the drawing to 75 percent of the original.

1. Type *75* in both the Height and Width boxes of the Scaling area of the Size tab.

2. Click OK.

When Works displays the drawing again, check the edges to be sure you haven't lost any of the drawing. If you specify a larger size than Works can accommodate, it clips the drawing at the edges; this most often occurs with text. If this happens, increase the scale of the drawing until all of it appears.

When you scale a drawing, you can specify different percentages to alter the ratio of height to width. If you do, however, be sure to preview the result before printing. Uneven scaling can be desirable in some situations, but in others you might find squares printing out as rectangles or pies turning into eggs!

 TIP: A drawing can be positioned by using the Left Align, Center Align, or Right Align buttons on the toolbar, or by using the Paragraph command on the Format menu and clicking on the Indents and Alignment tab.

Text and Objects

In the example we have been working with, text will follow the object since the logo goes at the top of the page. But suppose you want to have an object embedded in text. How do you combine the two?

One of the best ways to integrate text and objects is to wrap the text around the object, as you see here.

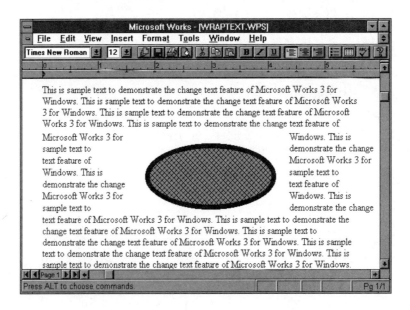

Here's how you do it.

1. Click on the object you want to wrap text around.

2. Open the Format menu, and then choose Picture/Object.

3. Click on the Text Wrap tab.

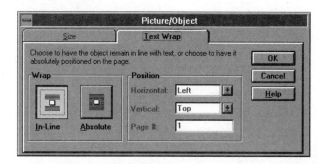

4. Select Absolute. This option keeps the text object in place while the text flows around it, as you see above. The In-Line option increases the spacing above and below the graphic as necessary.

5. In the Horizontal list box, select Left, Right, or Center depending on the position you want to place the object in relation to the right and left edges of the page.

6. In the Vertical list box, select Top, Center, or Bottom depending on where you want the object to appear between the top and bottom edges of the page.

7. Click OK.

TIP: You can switch to Page Layout view to work with absolute objects. Page Layout view is extremely useful because you can position inserted objects and pictures by dragging them to any location on the page.

Correcting a Drawing

Sometimes, perhaps often, you won't be satisfied with a drawing when you print it. You can easily return to Draw and to the drawing you want to fix.

1. Open the word-processed document containing the drawing. Remember that the drawing becomes part of the word-processed document.

2. Double-click on the drawing.

That's it. When you double-click, Works starts Draw and displays the drawing you've indicated in the Microsoft Draw window. You can move back and forth between Draw and Works whenever you want. To get back to the word processor, simply open the File menu, and choose Exit and Return to [your document].

To see how attractive a letter can look using this logo, take a look at this preview screen.

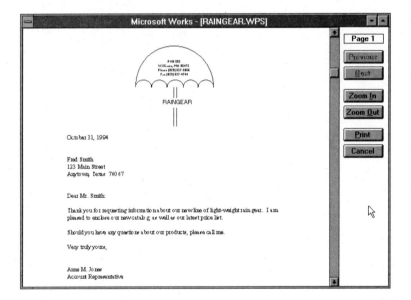

Coming Next

Draw is a simple yet powerful tool. However, it is only one of the graphics tools in Works. In the next chapter you'll find out about ClipArt, Note-It, and WordArt.

Special Touches: ClipArt, Note-It, and WordArt

You already know how Microsoft Works 3 for Windows can help you produce stunning documents, informative spreadsheets, and well-organized databases. But you might not know about Works' special flourishes. Each of these—ClipArt, Note-It, and WordArt—adds a special look to a Works document that will set it apart from the rest.

In this chapter, we'll describe what these tools are; in Chapter 17, see page 493, we'll discuss in detail how to insert these special flourishes into your Works documents.

A Look at ClipArt

Works comes with a library of about 100 different ClipArt graphics, ranging from a silhouette of a cat to a recycling symbol, as shown here.

These pictures are stored in a directory named *clipart* within the main directory, *msworks*, that the Works Setup program creates for you.

Want to see some samples? Simply open the Insert menu, and then choose ClipArt. If this is the first time you are using ClipArt, Works must generate a ClipArt gallery. If the gallery has already been created, you'll see the Microsoft ClipArt Gallery, as shown on the next page.

As you can see, the gallery is organized by general categories of images, such as animals and business scenes. To see any one set of images, click once on the category name. To insert an image into a document, double-click on the image and it will appear at the location of the insertion point in the document.

In the illustration on the next page, All Categories is highlighted (meaning all images are listed).

To explore the ClipArt gallery click below the scroll box in the vertical scroll bar to scroll the list one "boxful" at a time.

Using ClipArt Options

The ClipArt feature goes far beyond letting you see and insert images into documents. When you choose the Options button in the gallery window, you see four different options (shown here) that you can use to extend ClipArt's usefulness.

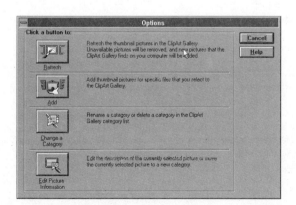

The Refresh option automatically adds to the gallery any pictures that are located on your computer. If you created an image in another application, Works finds it and adds it to the gallery. It also removes the corresponding thumbnail from the gallery if you remove the image from the computer.

When you choose the Refresh option, Works displays the dialog box you see here; it looks for pictures on the drives you select, and automatically adds them to the gallery. You'll be surprised at how many images you have on your computer in formats that Works can accommodate.

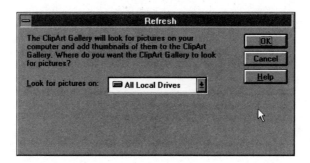

As Works scans the selected drives, it looks for pictures to add. When it finds them, it stops and asks you if you want to categorize each one or if you simply want the whole group added, to be named later on. Once you have identified the pictures you want to add, Works takes over and adds them.

TIP: If you have several Windows-based applications on your hard drive, be careful about refreshing non-selectively. You'll get every icon and bit-mapped image floating around.

428

The Add option allows you to add a thumbnail sketch to the gallery. This option is a better alternative to Refresh when all you want to add is a specific image or a collection of images.

The Change a Category option allows you to rename or delete a category of ClipArt. This feature is useful when you need to rename a category to better reflect its contents.

Finally, the Edit Picture Information option edits the description of a picture and can move the picture to another category.

Finding ClipArt

If you have a special request for a particular type of ClipArt, you can use the Find button in the Microsoft ClipArt Gallery to help you search. For example, let's say you're looking for a graphic that has to do with sports, specifically a soccer ball.

To find an image with a particular description, follow these steps.

1. Click Find in the Microsoft ClipArt Gallery. When you do this, you see the Find Picture dialog box.

2. Use the drop-down menus, or enter information in only one of the text boxes to help you locate the image you want to find. You can search on only one criterion.

For example, in this search we are looking for any images with the word soccer in the filename. We could have searched particular directories or even searched by description. But we thought it best and fastest to search this way. Once the search is finished, only those images that meet the criteria appear in the gallery. You've found your image!

TIP: A picture must be part of the gallery for Works to find it. If you have added pictures, don't forget to select Refresh so that the images become part of the gallery.

Using Note-It

In addition to drawings, Works also lets you embed the electronic equivalent of self-sticking notes in word-processed documents.

Note-It is useful for drawing a reader's attention to comments, notes, questions, and even editorial judgments in a word-processed document or database. Note-It places a picture in the document window, such as a balloon [💬], a check mark [✓], or a folder [📁]. When you double-click on that picture, you see the contents of the note.

The example we'll show you is the insertion of a note (using the check mark) to call attention to an answer on a multiple-choice test that needs to be changed. By the way, this test format is a Works template modified to fit the material covered on the test.

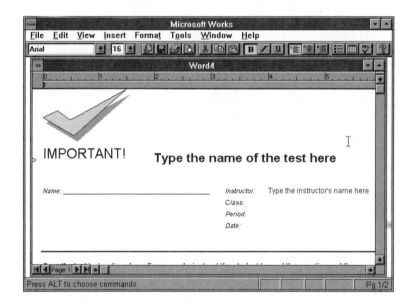

Here's how you do it.

1. Open up the database or word processor document.

2. Place the insertion point where you want the Note-It to appear. In this example, it goes at the beginning of the document.

3. Open the Insert menu, and then choose Note-It. When you do this, you see the Microsoft Note-It dialog box shown here.

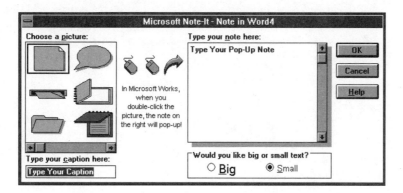

4. Click on the picture you want to use. We selected the big check mark from the 58 available pictures. Use the horizontal scroll bar at the bottom of the Choose a picture box to see them all.

5. In the Type your caption here box, enter the caption you want to use for the note.

TIP: Don't want a caption? Don't enter one. Works Note-It will work anyway.

6. Select the size of text you want in the note (Big or Small).

7. Click OK to return to the original document, where you will see the Note-It picture. To see the contents of a note, as shown here, double-click on the Note-It picture.

Please review this format before the scheduled meeting next Tuesday.

Working with Note-It Objects

Note-It produces objects that, like other Works objects, can be edited, resized, moved, and deleted. To edit a note, select the note and then choose Microsoft Note-It Object from the Edit menu. Now you can edit the contents of the note. Press OK when you are finished.

To change the size of the note, simply select it and drag it by any one of its handles, just as you did when you learned how to resize a drawing in the last chapter.

To move a note, simply drag it to a new location. Keep in mind that the content of the note will remain the same. Moving it to a new location separates the note from the context within which it was created, thus potentially diminishing the note's meaning.

To delete a note, select it and press the Del key.

 TIP: If you insert a note into a database, keep in mind that the picture representing the note will be the same size as the height of the database field. For example, a check mark or a balloon will be reduced to fit the field size. You can either increase the field size (which might look awkward) or resize the picture. The latter approach is usually the best.

Working with WordArt

If you like ClipArt and Note-It, you'll love WordArt. Why? Because it provides you with almost unlimited tools to modify text, with effects such as the following.

With WordArt, you enter text, then the design in which you want the text to appear, and then the size and font. The text is inserted into a document as an object; like any other object, it can be resized, moved, and edited. WordArt is a separate program that is integrated into Works. Consequently, you will not find any WordArt help on the main Works menu. Instead, you must open the WordArt menu, as explained below.

Creating WordArt

Let's work through an example: creating the stationery, shown here, for a surfing shop. Here's how we did it.

1. Open the Insert menu, and then choose WordArt. When you do this, you see the dialog box and text area shown in Figure 14-1 on the next page.

If you want, you can now select Help and get help only on WordArt.

FIGURE 14-1.
The dialog box
where you
enter text.

2. In the Enter Your Text Here dialog box, enter the text you want to format as WordArt. We entered *Surfin' USA*.

3. Click on the Shape Name box, on the left end of the WordArt toolbar (see page 436), to open the drop-down menu shown below. We selected the Wave 1 option. (The name appears in the Shape Name box after you select the option.)

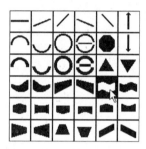

4. Select the font you want to use. We used the default Arial.

5. Select the font size you want to use. We selected 30 point. The default, Best Fit, fits the WordArt to the size of the WordArt box you first created; this may result in very small text. You can size the WordArt box by dragging its handles. When you increase the size of the font, the size of the box adjusts automatically.

   If you do increase the font size, you might see a dialog box asking you if you want to resize the WordArt object. Click Yes.

6. To make the heading stand out even more (and look sufficiently wavy), we made it bold and italic by using the buttons on the WordArt toolbar.

7. When you finish using WordArt, click where you want to work next.

   In this example, the WordArt appears as shown here.

8. Click on the Center Align button on the toolbar to center the object.

9. Add the rest of the address, as shown on page 433. We used Arial 10 point.

   To make Works work even better for us, we saved this as a custom template named *surfin*. The stationery is designed; the template is available. When someone wants to write a letter, he or she only has to call up the template and go to work.

See Also: For more information about custom templates, see "Using Document Templates," page 76.

Customizing WordArt

We just showed you one of many different WordArt designs. WordArt has an entire toolbar all its own that can accomplish all kinds of changes. Here's a guide to the WordArt toolbar, and what each box and button does.

— Plain Text ⬆	Shape Name	Click on the box to select a shape from the list. For example, if you choose a semicircle, the WordArt text curves.
Arial ⬆	Font Name	Click on the box to select a font from the list.
Best Fit ⬆	Font Size	Click on the arrow to select a font size from the list. When you select the Best Fit option, your application selects a font size that best fills the area you've drawn for your WordArt.
B	Bold	Click on the Bold button to thicken the WordArt.
I	Italic	Click on the Italic button to add a slight slant to the WordArt letters.
Ee	Even Height	Click on the Even Height button to make all letters the same height regardless of capitalization.
◁	Flip	Click on the Flip button to turn the WordArt on its side.
⿻	Stretch	Click on the Stretch button to the spread text both vertically and horizontally to fill the area you've drawn for your WordArt.
▣	Align	Click on the Align button to position text in the area you've drawn for your WordArt. If you don't select an alignment, the WordArt is automatically centered.

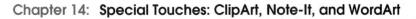	Spacing Between Characters	Click on the Spacing Between Characters button to see options for adjusting the amount of space between characters. Spacing Between Characters is often referred to as "kerning" or "tracking."
	Rotation	Click on the Rotation button to see options for turning the WordArt text.
	Shading	Click on the Shading button to see options for choosing a pattern or color for the WordArt text.
	Shadow	Click on the Shadow button to see options for choosing a shadow for your WordArt text.
	Border	Click on the Border button to see options for choosing a border thickness for your WordArt text.

Many of these have their own dialog boxes with straightforward options that can help you produce highly customized effects. For example, here we rotated the WordArt 20 degrees.

And here, we used one of several available shadow effects.

Finally, as another example, here's the text with some extra space between the characters and some light shading.

TIP: When you are done with WordArt, simply click where you want to work next. Be sure that you don't accidentally click on the Enter Your Text Here dialog box, on a button on the WordArt toolbar or in a dialog box, or on the WordArt you've created.

Inserting Symbols

You just learned how to create all types of interesting text effects. You can also insert a variety of different symbols into your documents, such as ®, $\frac{1}{2}$, and ä. Here's how to do it:

1. Open the Insert menu, and then choose WordArt.

2. In the Enter Your Text Here dialog box, place the insertion point where you want the symbol to appear.

3. Click Insert Symbol. The following dialog box appears.

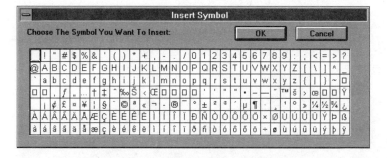

4. Select the symbol you want to use in the WordArt.

5. Click OK. The symbol is inserted in the WordArt you are creating.

Coming Next

Now you're an artist. Using these tools, plus Microsoft Draw, you can create anything you can imagine. Simply take your time, save often, and practice. You'll find that Draw, ClipArt, Note-It, and WordArt are useful, fun and helpful. Now we'll move on to Works Communications—the gateway to the world of telecommunications.

Using Works
Communications

Chapter 15   Getting in Touch

Getting in Touch

All good things come to an end, but it's especially important to log off correctly from Works Communications. Doing so ensures that when you log on the next time, Works Communications is ready to go.

Around the block, around the country, and around the world —someday, perhaps, around the universe. With your computer and Microsoft Works 3 for Windows, you can reach all these places with a few clicks of a button.

The word processor, spreadsheet, and database modules of Works allow you to choose the Dial This Number option on the Tools menu and dial any number. Dialing a phone number is only one way that Works and your computer can help you connect to and communicate with other computers. Another, much more powerful way is through *telecommunications,* which lets you become part of the large and growing group of people who rely on computer-to-computer hookups to gather information, transfer files, bat ideas back and forth, and keep in touch with one another. If you think telecommunications is just for sophisticated PC users, think again. Even the most naive user can take advantage of bulletin boards such as CompuServe or America On Line and find out the closing price of Marvel Stock (44), the weather in Seattle (rainy—surprised?), and how many games back the Yankees are (1 ½).

Communicating with Computers

Before you can use your computer for any type of communications, it must be set up to use your phone line to "hook up" with another computer. Your version of Works uses Works Communications to do this.

This chapter will explain some telecommunications terminology, help you develop an understanding of how Works Communications works, and show you how to use the module. All you need is your computer, a phone line, a modem, and Works.

After you've installed a modem, computer communications boils down to several operations that you perform in sequence. Here are the general steps:

1. Set up your computer and modem to communicate.

2. Dial the phone number to connect to the other computer.

3. Log on to identify yourself.

4. Telecommunicate!

When you finish communicating, you log off to tell the remote computer that you're finished. Then you disconnect or hang up so neither you nor the other computer leaves the phone line open.

What You Need to Go On Line

You need four things to get started in the telecommunications business:

- A computer (almost any kind will do)
- A modem
- Communications software
- An open phone line

You already have the computer (or are about to buy one). In any telecommunications activity, the computer acts as a sender and receiver of information.

The second thing you need is a modem, a piece of hardware that handles the three C's of remote computing: calling, connecting, and communicating. Although your computer can "think" for itself perfectly well, without a modem it cannot pass information to other computers through the phone lines.

The word *modem* is short for *modulate/demodulate,* which describes exactly what a modem does. To send information, a modem *modulates* the electrical signal output from a computer, in a sense embedding the data in a sound wave that can travel over a telephone line much as radio stations "embed" music in their AM and FM signals. When receiving information, the modem *demodulates* the incoming carrier wave, retrieving the bits of data and reconstructing them in a form the computer can use.

No matter how sophisticated any part of your telecommunications system is, if your modem doesn't do the job, you're stuck. For example, some modems have filters that screen out some of the noise that invades every line. When you're talking, this interference, which sounds like static, is simply a nuisance. But when you're telecommunicating, it can be a disaster because it corrupts transmissions; what you send either does not get to its destination or what gets there does not match what you've sent.

The third thing you need is communications software (included in Works), which performs the translation between the information as it appears to you and as it is sent.

Finally, you need a telephone connection to where you want to send (or from where you want to receive) information; in other words, you need a phone line. It may be a dedicated line just for telecommunications or a regular line that you also use for talking on the phone. If you have only one line for both voice and data, your voice line will be tied up when you are transmitting. Most people who are really serious about telecommunications end up with two phone lines.

TIP: If you have Call Waiting you should disable it before you log on. Do that by lifting the receiver, pressing the ∗ button, and pressing 70. If that doesn't work, check with your phone company.

The Language of Communications

When you connect your computer to another computer via a modem, you must ensure that the two computers "speak" the same language, transmit at the same speed, and follow the same rules of etiquette. If you don't, one computer might transmit in a "dialect" the other one can't understand. Or it might transmit too quickly for the other one to follow.

Rules of etiquette in telecommunications are needed for the same reasons they are needed in everyday life: to avoid conflicts. These rules of etiquette prevent both computers from trying to transmit at the same time and essentially trying to shout each other down.

Works Communications and comparable communications programs are your means of ensuring that communications sessions proceed smoothly. Works Communications takes care of all aspects of a communications session, from making the initial connection to making sure that both computers talk in a way that the other understands.

Although you won't actually connect to another computer in this chapter, you can start Works Communications to see the menus and commands described in this chapter. Works Communications is right there on the Startup screen. To start it, simply click on the icon that represents the module.

Starting Works Communications

To start Works Communications, click on the Communications button on the Startup screen. When you do this, the Modem Setup dialog box appears, as shown in Figure 15-1.

FIGURE 15-1.
The Modem Setup
dialog box.

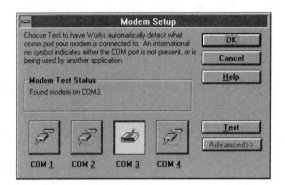

The first thing to do is to have Works test all the possible communication ports through which your modem might be able to operate, and identify the one to which the modem is connected. This makes things very easy for you, especially if you never took Modem 101 in school.

When your modem was installed, one of four ports was identified as the one to use for telecommunicating. You can find out which one by referring to your modem documentation or by asking the people who configured and sold you the modem (which probably came as part of your computer). But Works actually does this for you.

Here's how to get started.

1. Click Test in the Modem Setup dialog box. After a moment or two, you'll see which communication port your modem is connected to.

2. Click on the modem icon. In our example above, it's COM 3.

3. Click OK.

The Easy Connect dialog box appears. You don't have to use this feature, but it does allow you to connect to frequently dialed numbers with one click since Works remembers the important setup values. When you save the session (upon logging off) Works saves the number for you so that all it takes is a click later on to get started.

Let's say you regularly send files from your New York office to a branch of your business in Los Angeles. You might want to enter the number of the LA branch in the Easy Connect dialog box. Or, you might be a fan of GEnie, another bulletin board. You type the number in, Works saves the session settings, and GEnie is only a click away.

For now, we'll click on Cancel because we don't want to start communicating right away. That's what would happen if we entered a number and clicked OK.

Once you click on Cancel, you see the Communications window, named Comm1 as you see here.

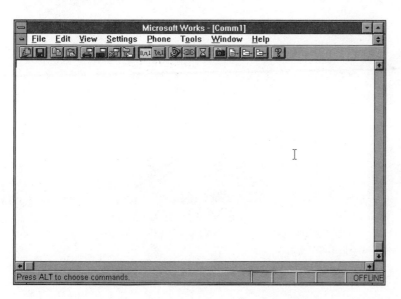

The Communications Toolbar

Like all the other toolbars we have discussed, the Communications toolbar offers buttons galore to make your work easier and more efficient.

As we explained in Chapter 3, you can add buttons for commands you use often and remove buttons that you never use. In either case, you are familiar with many of the buttons you see here (such as Save and Copy), but there are new ones as well:

Here's what each button does.

Startup Dialog. Displays the Startup dialog box, which gives you access to files, templates, and Works Wizards.

Save. Saves the active file with its current name.

Copy. Copies highlighted text and stores it on the Clipboard.

Paste. Inserts Clipboard contents into the Communications window at the insertion point.

Communication Settings. Adjusts communication settings.

Terminal Settings. Adjusts terminal settings.

Phone Settings. Adjusts phone settings.

Transfer Settings. Changes transfer options.

8-N-1 Settings. Changes communication settings to 8 data bits, no parity, and 1 stop bit.

7-E-1 Settings. Changes communication settings to 7 data bits, even parity, and 1 stop bit.

Easy Connect. Connects to another computer using an existing phone number.

Dial/Hangup. Disconnects from the computer to which you are connected.

Pause. Temporarily suspends communications.

Capture Text. Saves incoming text as a file.

Send Text. Sends text from an ASCII file to another computer.

Send Binary File. Sends a document as a binary file to another computer.

Receive Binary File. Receives and saves a binary file sent to you by another computer.

Learning Works. Provides access to Cue Cards, Help, the Tutorial, and WorksWizards.

Getting Ready to Communicate

Setting up for communications means telling Works Communications about your modem, specifying the phone number of the computer you want to call, and ensuring that both computers will use the same communications settings when sending and receiving data.

Most, if not all, of the information you need for setup should be listed in the documentation for your modem and for the remote computer. If you're connecting two independent personal computers, such as yours and someone else's, be sure to use the same settings for both.

To set up for communications, you use the aptly named Settings menu, shown here.

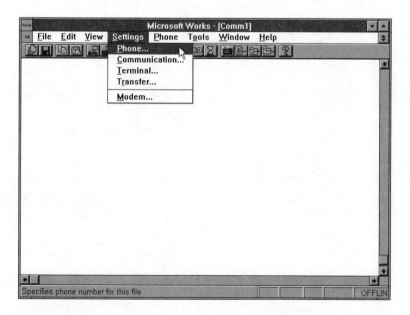

If you've never tried communications, some of the terms you see here and in command dialog boxes might look a bit unfriendly, but don't let them intimidate you. Works Communications, and popular telecommunication services such as CompuServe, wouldn't exist if you needed a Ph.D. in nuclear physics to get started.

We'll take it nice and slow, step by step, from the beginning.

Dialing Up

Once your modem has been identified, you can adjust all the important settings using the Settings menu. Open the Settings menu and choose Phone, Communication, Terminal, or Transfer to reach these tabs in the Settings dialog box.

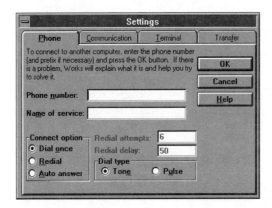

You can also click on each particular tab in the Settings dialog box.

The following sections describe what each tab does.

The Phone Options

The Phone tab allows you to enter the phone number you want to use and the name associated with the phone number, as well as information about the type of phone you have (tone or pulse) and connection options (such as dialing only once or redialing until a connection is made). You can even specify how long you want to wait between tries.

> **TIP:** An important character to remember when entering numbers is the comma. Use a comma to tell Works Communications to pause for two seconds before dialing the next digit. For example, if you dial 9 for an outside line, you can type the phone number as *9,18005551000* to have Works Communications pause after the 9. If you use Call Waiting, you can help your communications session go smoothly by disabling the feature temporarily. (See the TIP on page 447.)

The Communication Options

The Communication tab allows you to set the communication port, the speed at which you send information (the baud rate), and specific settings (such as parity) that allow your computer to speak intelligibly to another computer. Below you can see what the Communication tab in the Settings dialog box looks like.

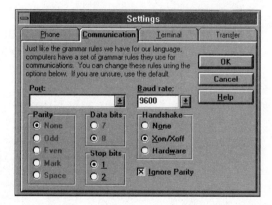

This is an important group of settings, without which you cannot connect to another computer. The Communication settings determine how fast your modem sends and receives data, the type of error checking it uses, and the number of bits (binary 1s and 0s) it uses to represent each character. You also use this tab to specify which *connector* or *port* your modem uses for sending and receiving information. Even if all your other settings are perfect, indicating the wrong port is like answering the phone that isn't ringing.

The Communication tab proposes standard settings for communications parameters, so you might not need to tinker with these at all. If you do, however, you should be able to find the appropriate settings in the documentation for your particular computer. Here's what all these settings mean:

- *Port* identifies the port to which your modem is connected. COM 1 is the first serial port (or the only one if you have a single serial port), COM 2 is the second serial port, and so on up to COM 4, the last possible serial port you can have.

- *Baud rate* determines the speed of transmission. Your modem is rated for a certain speed, such as 1200, 2400, 4800, 9600, 14400, and so on. Faster modems can speak with slower ones, but slower ones need an exact match or need to connect to a slower modem to communicate successfully. Works Communications goes up to 19200.

  This parameter is sometimes called *bps,* which is short for *bits per second,* as in "a 1200bps modem." Technically, bps describes transmission speed more accurately than does the older term *baud rate.*

- *Data bits* refers to the number of binary digits used to represent each character. During transmission, each data bit is sent as a high or low "blip" in a data stream. Most transmissions use either 7 or 8 data bits. You can use the two toolbar buttons (8-N-1 Settings and 7-E-1 Settings) to switch settings here if necessary.

- *Stop bits* tells the receiving computer where each character ends. Stop bits are timing intervals between characters.

- *Parity* indicates a form of error checking to determine whether a character has been transmitted correctly.

- *Handshake* keeps the temporary storage location (such as downloaded text) from overflowing with possible loss of data while you're transferring a file. Xon/Xoff, a standard handshaking method, causes Works Communications to send a signal to the remote computer that pauses transmission when the buffer (a reserved portion of memory) is full. You might have to choose either Hardware or None if the remote computer uses a different type of handshaking or none at all.

The Terminal Options

Terminal emulation refers to the way your computer behaves while connected to another computer. Back in the early days of communications, large computers dealt with specific types of *terminals,* which were smaller units with far less "brain power" than the mainframes that accepted their output and fed them input. Here are the terminal options available in the Settings dialog box.

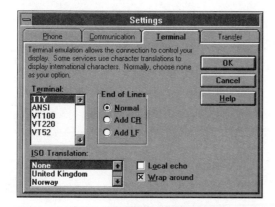

When you're using a personal computer to communicate, you often have to tell it to emulate a particular type of terminal, by sending and receiving formatting codes and displaying characters as the terminal would do. Again, your documentation should tell you which type of terminal to emulate. Works Communications proposes TTY as the default.

The Terminal command provides you with options to define the type of computer terminal you want to emulate. Some computers require that a particular type of terminal be used, in addition to special software. The Terminal options allow you to select the type of terminal you need to emulate as well as set other important parameters for the emulation.

Here's an explanation of the various options available in the Terminal tab of the Settings dialog box:

- *Terminal* matches the type of computer you have with the type of computer you are communicating with.

- *End of Lines* allows you to change the format of incoming text. Select Add CR (for carriage return) if there are lines of text that don't begin at the left edge of your screen, or Add LF (for line feed) if lines of text are overwriting each other.

- *Local echo* displays the characters you type. Communications is unlike other Works modules in that you don't always see what you type. Turn on Local echo if your typing doesn't appear on the screen.

- *Wrap around* wraps text to the next line at the window's edge.

- *ISO Translation* is used to specify a different country if you are going to send and receive information in a different language. The country you choose determines the characters Works Communications uses. Your choice must be one that the remote computer can recognize.

The Transfer Options

Finally, the Transfer tab gives you a choice of four protocols or agreements between computers on how data should be sent. Here are the various options.

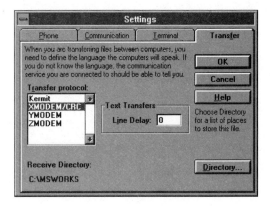

Xmodem/CRC is the most common; it is very reliable, but slow. Ymodem is faster than Xmodem/CRC (since it sends more information at a time), but it does not work well if your phone connection is not good. Zmodem is even faster than Ymodem and is as reliable as Xmodem/CRC. It is a good choice, but less common than X or Y. Finally, Kermit (not related to the frog) is the slowest of the four, but the most reliable. Because of this, it is often used to communicate between different types of personal computers.

> **TIP:** When you type a phone number, type all of the numbers you would dial, including such digits as 9, if you need an outside line, and 1, if you're calling out of your local dialing area. You can use parentheses, spaces, or hyphens to separate the parts of a phone number, but they're not necessary.

The Modem Options

A modem is a modem is a modem. Right? Wrong. Modems vary by make, model, and speed, and by the types of commands they use to start and end phone connections. To help Works Communications determine which port the modem is connected to, use the Modem command on the Settings menu. Choosing Modem brings up the Modem Setup dialog box, which you saw in Figure 15-1 on page 448.

Works tests the different communications ports for you and indicates the one to which the modem is connected.

Saving Your Settings

Even though it is unlikely, you may need to make a variety of adjustments before you are able to communicate using Works. After you have finished all that work, the last thing you want to do is have to do it over again.

Luckily, you can save the settings in a file by choosing the Save command from the File menu. When you choose this command, Works Communications displays a familiar-looking Save As dialog box, which asks you to type a name for the settings file and, if you want, to specify a drive or directory. Although the file you save isn't one that you can display and work with as you can a letter or other document, Works Communications saves it with the extension *.wcm*.

The next time you want to connect with the same computer, simply choose the Open command from the File menu and specify the filename; Works Communications reads all your settings, including any phone number, and is ready to go.

Connecting!

After your computer and modem are set up and ready to communicate, you can go online by simply choosing Dial on the Phone menu. After you choose Dial, Works Communications displays a small dialog box showing the number it is calling. The dialog box also shows the time remaining until Works Communications stops trying to connect if the remote computer doesn't answer.

What happens next may be disconcerting, but it means things are probably going well. You're likely to hear a high-pitched sound from your PC speaker, which means that the modem is trying to connect. Then you'll hear other sounds, including some loud hissing. Finally, when you do connect, your modem may provide an audio signal of several beeps.

After you've established a connection, the remote computer might ask you to log on. For example, CompuServe asks you for your ID number as well as your password. The service you use provides you with both.

Sending a File

Works Communications provides you with a ready means of transferring your Works files from place to place simply by establishing a phone connection between your computer and the remote computer. No need to send that document through the mail; simply send it as an electronic file and it's there in minutes.

Computer files can travel in either of two forms: as *text files* or as *binary files*. Text files are also known as ASCII files. ASCII, short for American Standard Code for Information Interchange, is a set of codes used to translate letters, numbers, and punctuation marks into a form that all computers can handle. ASCII files can contain tabs, carriage returns, and other simple formatting, but they cannot include any unusual or program-specific formatting, such as superscripts, italics, or graphics.

Binary files, on the other hand, can contain all manner of codes and unusual characters. Program files, such as Works itself, are always binary files. Document files you create with Works are also binary files, although you can save them as a Text or Text (DOS) file in the Save File as Type portion of the dialog box.

It doesn't matter which type of file you want to send; the procedures are the same. To send a file, first get ready by doing the following:

1. Connect the sending and receiving computers.

2. Open the Settings menu, and then choose Transfer; or click on the Transfer Settings button on the toolbar [ ]. The Settings dialog box, with the Transfer tab active, appears.

3. In the Transfer protocol box, select the protocol you want to use.

4. Click OK.

To send the file, do the following:

1. Open the Tools menu, and then choose Send File; or click on the Send Text [ ] or Send Binary File [ ] button. The Send File dialog box appears.

2. In the File Name box, select the file you want to send. You can easily get to other directories through this box as well, by clicking through different locations on the disk.

3. Click OK.

Although you will not see the file itself being transferred, you can tell that Works is working because a little indicator on the screen tracks the progress of the transfer.

Receiving a File

You can receive text from, as well as send text to, another computer and then save it to your disk. This is often referred to as downloading; sending a file to another computer is called uploading.

As with sending a file, during receiving (downloading) the contents of the file are not displayed on either computer's screen. Works displays a status box that indicates how much of the file has been received.

To receive and save a file, follow these steps:

1. Open the Tools menu, and then choose Receive File, or click on

   the Receive Binary File button [ ] on the toolbar. Works shows you the Receive File dialog box.

2. Enter the name of the file you are going to receive.

3. Click OK.

As with sending a file, a status box keeps you informed about the file transfer.

> **TIP:** If you want to cancel the transfer of a file before the job is done, click the Cancel button, and then click OK.

Once the file has been transferred, you will probably want to save it. To save a file that has been downloaded, follow these steps:

1. Click on the Transfer Settings button [ ] on the toolbar.

2. If you want to save downloaded files in a directory other than the one shown under Receive Directory, choose the Directory button.

3. Choose the options you want.

4. Click OK.

5. Click OK again. The text that was downloaded to your computer from another computer is saved as a file using the name you specified.

Capturing Text

As text rolls by in a communications session, another way to save that text is to capture it to a file. Works automatically captures up to 256,000 lines of text during a communications session in the buffer. It asks you at the end of your session if you want to save the text by giving it a filename or by adding it to the end of an existing file.

You only need to use the Capture Text command if you want to name the file or specify which file the text should be added to. You must choose this command before you receive the text you want to save. Only the text that is received after you choose the command is saved.

To capture text and save it as a file, follow these steps.

1. Open the Tools menu, and then choose Capture Text.

2. Select the drive on which you want to save the text as a file.

3. Select the directory in which you want to save the text as a file.

4. Type a name for the file. Works saves all captured text as an ASCII (text) file. This is the only file type available for captured text.

5. Click OK.

   If the file has already been created (in Works), you have a few choices.

   ▪ You can choose Replace to replace the existing file.

   ▪ You can choose Append to add the downloaded text to the end of the file.

   ▪ You can choose Cancel (or press Esc) to cancel the operation and return to the dialog box to type another filename.

While Works captures text, you'll see the word CAPTURE displayed in the status line.

If, in the middle of a session, you want to stop the capture process, select End Capture Text from the Tools menu.

Using Scripts

A script is a saved set of commands that Works can invoke at any time. Think of a script as a tape recording of instructions. When you create it, you describe each instruction. When you are finished, you can play the instructions back to help you accomplish a particular task.

Recording a Script

You can record a sequence of steps for a particular task in Works Communications, such as logging on.

Here, we'll create a script for a sign-on sequence so each time you want to log on, you can simply select the name from the Tools menu and be in business.

1. Open the Tools menu, and then choose Record Script.

2. You'll see the Record Script dialog box, as shown here.

3. Click OK. Works displays Recording a script in the status line.

4. Log on to the computer or information service as you usually do, by typing your ID and password, or by choosing Easy Connect (from the Phone menu).

5. When you finish recording all the steps, choose End Recording from the Tools menu.

Works saves the recording in exactly the sequence that you specified. The next time you choose the same computer's name from the list at the bottom of the Phone menu, or open the same Communications file, Works asks if you want to connect. Click OK to use the recorded log-on to connect to the other computer.

You can also record tasks other than logging on. To do this, follow these steps.

1. Open the Tools menu, and then choose Record Script.

2. Select the Other option in the Record Script dialog box.

3. In the Script Name box, type a script name of 15 characters or less.

    For example, if you are going to record the steps to view stock market quotes, you might name the script *View Quotes.*

4. Click OK.

5. Perform the exact steps needed to accomplish the task.

6. When you have finished recording all the steps, choose End Recording from the Tools menu. Works saves the recording for you to play back later.

TIP: To cancel a recording in progress, choose Cancel Recording from the Tools menu or press the Esc key. Works stops the recording and does not save it.

Playing Back a Script

A script is only useful when you play it back. Here's how to do this.

1. Open the File menu, and then choose Open Existing File.

2. Select the Communications file you want to open.

3. When Works asks if you want to connect to the other computer, click OK.

    Works uses your recorded log-on to connect to the other computer.

    To play back a recording for other tasks, select the name of the script from the list at the bottom of the Tools menu.

Logging Off

You must take care of two simple but important tasks when ending a communications session: logging off and then hanging up.

If you're communicating with a remote computer that requires you to log on, remember to end your session by logging off. Logging off is never difficult—it can be as simple as typing *bye*. Regardless of how it's done, logging off tells the remote computer that you're officially checking out. Be sure to log off if you're connected to a computer on which you pay for connect time. If you hang up without logging off, you might end up paying for time you didn't use.

Your final step in ending a communications session is to choose the Hang Up command from the Phone menu. Hanging up disconnects you from the remote computer, the same way you end a phone call by hanging up the phone.

Coming Next

That's the end of Part 6 and your primer on connecting to other computers using Works. Now we'll move to the most advanced material in this book, sharing information created with different modules. It might be advanced, but it's not difficult. It even turns out to be a real time saver, and best of all—fun!

Working Together

16

Sharing Information

You've learned the basics of using Microsoft Works 3 for Windows to create documents, spreadsheets, and databases, and then using Works Communications to send any one of these files anywhere you want. You've even learned how to use Microsoft Draw to jazz up a document with drawings and clip art, and you've used the spreadsheet's charting feature to produce a graph. These are some of the ways of using the different parts of Works in an integrated fashion.

More often than not, real-life work requires that you be able to combine information of different types and even from different sources. Besides drawings and charts, you might need to include rows and columns of spreadsheet values in a financial statement created with the word processor, or you might need to move inventory balances from a database file into the spreadsheet where you track your need for new materials.

In this chapter, we'll show you how to move data easily from one part of Works to another. We'll use all four of the Works modules in the examples that we provide.

Let's begin with the following examples.

1. Start Works, if necessary.

2. Create a new word processor document, open the View menu, and turn on All Characters if it's not already checked. Don't enter any information.

3. Maximize the module window, but *not* the document window. Leaving the document window at its default size makes it easier to switch quickly from one document window to another by clicking on a title bar.

4. Click on the Startup Dialog toolbar button to return to the Startup window and create a new spreadsheet and a new database. Again, do not maximize the document windows. And don't enter any information yet.

5. In the Word1 window, type *This is word processing.*

6. In the Sheet1 window, type the following values in columns A and B:

	A	B
Row 1	100	200
Row 2	300	400
Row 3	500	600

7. In the Data1 window, create three fields named *Last:, First:,* and *Middle:,* and type the following data to create three sample records:

Last	First	Middle
Agassiz	Louis	
Audubon	John	James
Darwin	Charles	Robert

From Here to There and Back

You can select and move (or copy) information from any Works module to any other Works module. For example, with a few clicks, you can go from the spreadsheet to the word processor and back again.

Although the Works spreadsheet and database are valuable modules, the word processor is more flexible in terms of accepting data from other modules, including programs other than Works that run under Windows 3.1.

Within any of the four Works modules, you can cut and paste or copy and paste freely to move information around. Between the word processor and the spreadsheet (not the database), you can also use a more sophisticated *Paste Special* procedure that lets you create a link between the copied information and the original information in the spreadsheet. After you create such a link, Works can update the information in the word processor whenever you change the same or related information in the contributing spreadsheet.

Knowing roughly what Works does when you use data-transfer commands will make you feel more confident about moving data from place to place. All you need is a basic understanding of the three data-transfer mechanisms Works supports: cut and paste (or copy and paste), linking, and embedding. We'll deal with cut and paste in this chapter and linking and embedding in the next.

Cutting, Copying, and Pasting

Both cut and paste, and copy and paste, use the Clipboard as a temporary storage place for information you want to duplicate or move. The two procedures differ in a way you might remember from our earlier discussions.

Cut and paste moves the information from one location to another, whereas copy and paste duplicates it. Other than this, cut and paste and copy and paste work in exactly the same way. In general, here are the steps you follow in any cut and paste or copy and paste operation.

1. Select the information you want to place in a different document.

2. Cut or copy the information to the Clipboard.

3. Select the location in the receiving document where you want to paste the information.

4. Paste the contents of the Clipboard into the receiving document.

Because Works is both integrated software and a Windows-based program, you can use the Clipboard as a way station whether you're moving information within a document, between documents in the same module (such as the word processor), or between documents in different applications. For example, if you want to move the information from the Works spreadsheet to Microsoft Access (a separate database program), the cut and paste procedures are exactly the same as if you were moving it within the same module.

Cut and paste and copy and paste are simple ways to move data from one module to another. Because modules differ in the way they treat data, however, you will see some differences in the way Works handles the information.

Cut and Paste Results

Here are brief descriptions of the results when you cut and paste data between Works modules. The examples describe the process of transferring data between the modules.

- *Spreadsheet to word processor:* If you paste the contents of multiple cells into a word-processed document, Works arranges the incoming data into a tablelike format.

- *Database to word processor:* If you paste one or more records into a word-processed document, Works arranges the data in rows and columns separated by tabs.

- *Word-processed table to spreadsheet:* If you paste a table separated by tabs into a spreadsheet, Works places each table entry in a separate cell.

- *Word-processed table to database:* If you paste a word-processed table separated by tabs into the database, Works reads across the table and turns each row of entries into a separate database record.

If you're working in list view, Works places each entry in a separate cell. If necessary, Works also creates fields with default names (Field 1, Field 2, Field 3, and so on) for the entries. If you're working in form view, you can paste the table into a blank form with the Paste Record command, and Works creates default field names and fills in as many blank forms as rows in the table.

- *Word-processed text to spreadsheet or database:* If you paste a string of text such as words, a sentence, or a paragraph, into either the spreadsheet or the database, Works inserts the entire block into the highlighted cell or field.

- *Database to spreadsheet:* If you paste database records into a spread-sheet, Works inserts field entries in columns and records in rows.

The following sections show some examples that demonstrate these guidelines.

Pasting from the Spreadsheet

The first example is a transfer of information from the spreadsheet to the word processor.

 TIP: There's a good deal of cutting, copying, and pasting throughout this chapter. Don't forget to use the toolbar icons to save yourself some time and effort.

You've already created the worksheet and the word processor document, so follow these steps:

1. Select cells A1 through B3 in the spreadsheet.

2. Open the Edit menu, and then choose Copy. This copies the contents of the selection to the Clipboard.

3. Switch to the word processor document (using the Window menu).

4. Place the insertion point in a blank new paragraph below the sample text in your word processor document.

5. Open the Edit menu, and then choose Paste Special. When you do this, you see the Paste Special dialog box, shown here.

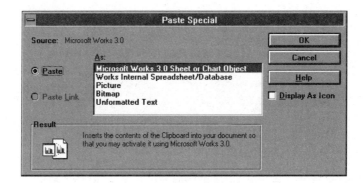

The Paste Special dialog box lets you specify a format for the spreadsheet data you paste into the word processor. As you can see, you can paste the data as an object (which cannot be edited) or in one of several other formats, including unformatted text. The familiar Paste command on the Edit menu pastes information as an object that cannot be edited.

6. Select Unformatted Text in the Paste Special dialog box.

7. Click OK.

The word processor screen now looks like this.

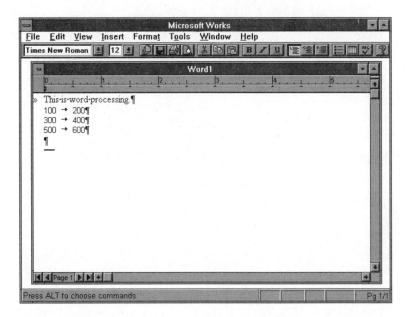

Works pastes in the values you copied to the Clipboard, adding tabs to align the cell contents in your word processor document. The (→) represents a tab. By default, Works sets the tabs 0.5 inches apart. You can alter these settings by dragging the tab markers to the left or right on the ruler, as you learned in Chapter 5.

Pasting from the Database

Pasting from the database to the word processor is similar to pasting from the spreadsheet. Here's an example for you to follow:

1. Switch to the database document using the Window menu.

2. Click the List View button on the toolbar to see your records in list view.

3. Select all three records in the database.

4. Open the Edit menu, and then choose Copy.

5. Return to the word processor document.

6. Place the insertion point after the spreadsheet data that you pasted.

7. Open the Edit menu, and then choose Paste.

Now you have a word processor document with data from both the spreadsheet and the database plugged in; it looks like this.

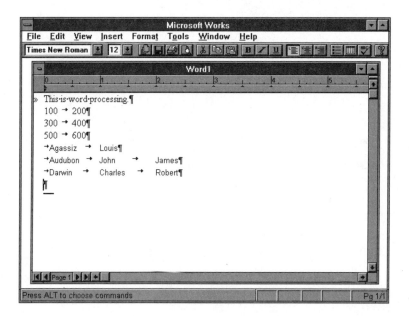

When you paste from the database, Works again separates fields with tabs. Notice that even the format is maintained when you paste. For example, the different fonts used to create these individual files are maintained in the final document.

Formatting Pasted Data

After you've pasted spreadsheet data or database records into a word processor document, you can select the information and format it in any way you like as long as you did not transfer it as an object.

For example, you might want to format the current word processor document as described here.

1. Select the copied spreadsheet values.

2. Use the toolbar to format them in a font and size you like, such as Arial 10.

3. Click the Center Align button on the toolbar to center the data.

4. Select the three database records.

5. Use the Border command on the Format menu to draw an outline border around them.

6. Narrow the border by dragging the right margin marker on the ruler to the left.

Your screen should now look like the screen on the next page.

Pasting from the Word Processor

Although you're more likely to paste from the spreadsheet or the database to the word processor than the other way around, you can move text from a word processor document into either a spreadsheet or a database. To see how this works, do the following:

1. Select the original text, *This is word processing,* in the word processor document.

2. Open the Edit menu, and then choose Copy.

3. Switch to the database window.

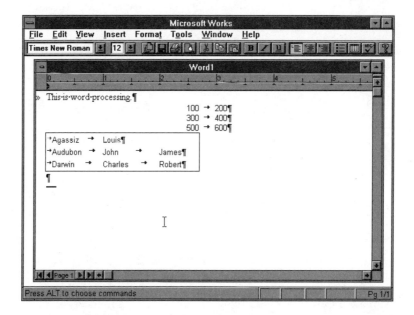

If you're in list view, choose the cell in row 4 of the field headed First, and choose Paste from the Edit menu.

If you're in form view, move to a new record, highlight the dotted line for First:, and choose Paste from the Edit menu.

When you paste a block of word-processed text in list view, Works inserts the text in the field you selected. If you are in list view and select a cell that does not have a field name, Works pastes the text into the selected cell and gives the column a default name, such as Field 5.

In contrast, when you paste word-processed text in form view, Works pastes the text into the first field, regardless of the field you selected. If you select a blank part of the form, Works still pastes the Clipboard information into the first field.

To see what happens when you paste from the word processor into the spreadsheet, follow these steps.

1. Switch to the spreadsheet, and click on cell A4 to select it.

2. Open the Edit menu, and then choose Paste. You don't have to copy the data again from the word processor because the text you copied earlier is still on the Clipboard.

   As in the database list view, Works pastes the incoming text into the cell you selected.

Pasting Tables to the Spreadsheet

Now let's see what happens when you move a table from the word processor to the spreadsheet. First, we need to start from scratch with a new table so you can easily distinguish old data from new. Here's how to do it.

1. Switch to the word processor.

2. Place the insertion point at the beginning of a new paragraph.

3. Click on the ruler to set left-aligned tabs at 1 inch and 2 inches.

4. Type the following, pressing the Tab key between entries.

   ```
   Quarter        Two bits      $0.25
   Dollar         Buck          $1.00
   Ten Dollars    Sawbuck       $10.00
   Thousand       Grand         $1000.00
   ```

5. Select all the text you just typed.

6. Open the Edit menu, and then choose Copy.

7. To move the table into the spreadsheet, switch to Sheet1.

8. Click on cell D1 to select it.

9. Open the Edit menu, and then choose Paste.

   Your screen should look the one shown on the next page, with the table created in the word processor nicely formatted in the spreadsheet.

	A	B	C	D	E	F	G	H
1	100	200		Quarter	Two bits	$0.25		
2	300	400		Dollar	Buck	$1.00		
3	500	600		Ten Dollars	Sawbuck	$10.00		
4	This is word processing			Thousand	Grand	$1,000.00		
5								
6								
7								
8								
9								
10								
11								
12								
13								
14								
15								
16								
17								
18								

As you can see, each table entry becomes a cell entry in the spreadsheet.

Pasting Tables to the Database

Your database document already contains a form and a few records, so to see how Works moves the table you created into a database, start with a blank database document and follow these steps.

1. Open the File menu, and then choose Create New File, or click on the Startup Dialog button on the toolbar.

2. Click Database to open a new document.

3. Create three fields named *Name*, *Slang*, and *Amount* in the Data2 window.

4. Select the Name field.

5. Open the Edit menu, and then choose Paste.

Here's what the screen should look like.

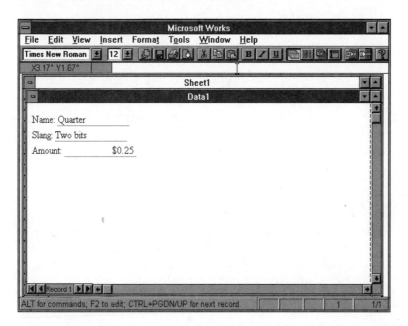

Now here's the interesting part: You see only the entries in the first row of your word-processed table.

6. Click the next button (the one with the right-pointing arrowhead) in the horizontal scroll bar. Works displays a form containing a record for the second row of your table. Scroll through form view some more, or switch to list view, and you'll see that Works pasted the entire table into the database as field entries for four separate records.

If you had pasted the table into a blank form, you would see pretty much the same thing, except Works would assign default names to the three fields corresponding to the columns in your table. You could change these default names by selecting each and typing a new name.

Creating a Form Letter

Let's apply some of the techniques you just learned to a common task involving the word processor and the database: writing personalized form letters.

To produce a form letter, you need two preexisting Works documents. First, you need a basic letter and second, a database of names and other information that you'll call on to personalize the letter.

After you've created these two documents, you can put the form letter together on your own or with the help of the Quick Database WorksWizard. The WorksWizard ensures that the form letter is constructed correctly. But doing it on your own is not so difficult and allows you much more flexibility.

To create a form letter, start with a word-processed document containing the text for the body of the letter. To turn the document into a form letter, you insert *placeholders* that show Works where you want the personalized information to appear. Each placeholder is the name of an existing field, such as First Name, in a database you've already created. On screen, a placeholder is distinguished from surrounding text by chevrons that look like this: ≪ and ≫.

A Real-Life Exercise

Using the Form Letter WorksWizard is easy as long as your database fields match the fields used by the Address Book WorksWizard, and as long as you don't want to include more than the address or the address and a salutation.

If you want to use different field names in your database, or if you want to insert personalized information in the body of your letter, you must create your own form letter and insert different fields using the Field command on the Insert menu. This command lets you select existing fields in a database and insert placeholders wherever you want in a document.

The basic steps for creating a form letter are as follows.

1. Create the database with all the fields you want included.

2. Tell Works which database you want to use.

3. Create the letter you want to use, with the placeholder names (corresponding to the database field names) inserted in the letter.

4. Print the word processor file, and the form letters will print with the personalized information from the database integrated into the text.

Let's write a personalized form letter that notifies job applicants about the time and place of their interview.

1. Create the database using eight fields:

Last Name

First Name

Street

City

State

Zip

Date of Appointment

Time of Appointment

We separated the name into first and last so we can sort on the Last Name field separately if we want to. Your database should look like the one below.

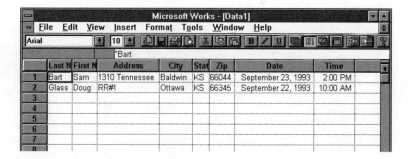

2. Switch to the word processor.

3. Open the Insert menu, and then choose Database Field. When you do this, you see the Insert Field dialog box, as shown below.

4. Click on the Database button.

5. Select the database you want to use.

6. Click OK. The list of fields in the database appears, as you can see in the Insert Field dialog box shown here.

7. Click on Close.

8. Type the date at the top of the blank word processor document.

9. Insert fields in the letter by moving the insertion point where you want the applicant's first name to appear, and type *Mr.* (they're both men!). So far, your letter looks like this:

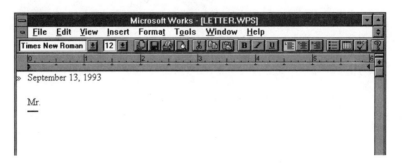

10. Now for the fun. Enter the second field (which is First Name), and then choose Database Field from the Insert Field menu.

11. Click on the field name *First Name*.

12. Click Insert. You can also simply double-click to insert a field. When you do this, you see the field name First Name entered into the letter between the chevrons, << and >>. Here is what the form letter looks like so far.

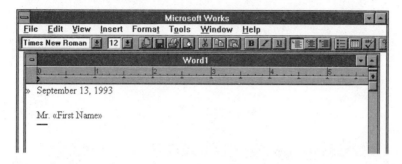

13. Now you need to enter text, plus additional fields, until your letter looks like the one shown below. Notice that you can insert commas and spaces as you see fit, such as between the City and State fields.

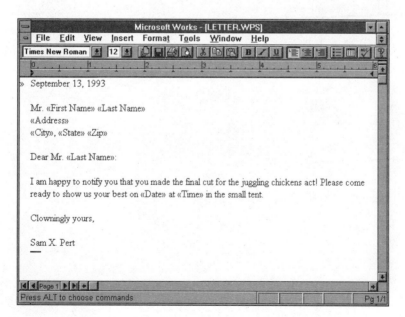

Notice that we used the Last Name field twice, once in the address and once in the greeting. You can use any field as often as you want.

TIP: If you want to get fancy and format inserted text from the database, simply make your format changes in the letter and Works will print it that way.

To see what your integrated and highly personalized letter looks like, use the Print Preview option on the File menu. As you can see here, the information from the database has been successfully integrated. If you click on the Next button in Print Preview, you see the next completed form letter.

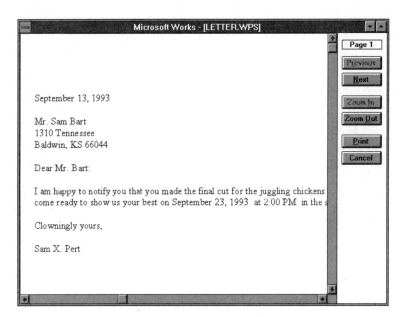

See Also: For information about selecting specific records to merge by using a query, see "Queries and Query View," page 348.

Recycling Databases and Letters

You can reuse information in a letter or database as the need arises. A letter file can also be called a template (or boilerplate), and you can use it with several different databases. For example, you might have other applicants to interview. Simply save the letter for later use, and select a different database next time.

You can also use the same database to print envelopes. Because you only need the first three fields for envelopes, you can create a "letter" merge to print envelopes with only the first three fields from the database that contains mailing address information. The lesson here? Don't throw anything away. You might find that the file you deleted containing 150 names and addresses would come in handy about now.

Mailing Labels and Envelopes

Printing mailing labels and envelopes is just like printing form letters. You use both the word processor and a database of names and addresses. You use the word processor to create a document containing the database fields you want to print, and you use the database to supply the information you need.

You can print only selected records, rather than the entire database, by using a query. The main difference between printing addresses and printing letters is in the layout, margins, and page sizes you specify for the labels or envelopes.

Mailing Labels

Using mailing labels is easier than you might think, because Works does most of the work for you. Although a mailing-label document doesn't look much like a document in the traditional sense, it's your starting point for printing labels. The document itself is simply a set of database fields you use to print the labels. Take the following steps.

1. Open a new word processor document.

2. Open the Tools menu, and then choose Envelopes and Labels.

3. In the Envelopes and Labels dialog box, click on the Mailing Labels tab.

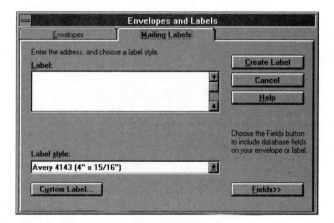

4. Click on the Fields button.

5. Click on the Database button.

6. Select the database you want to use from the Choose Database dialog box.

7. Click OK.

8. Select the first field to appear on the label by double-clicking on it or by highlighting it and clicking on the Insert button. When selected, it appears in the Label text box. You'll notice that we also typed the word *Mr.* to appear in each label.

9. Complete the Label box as you see here.

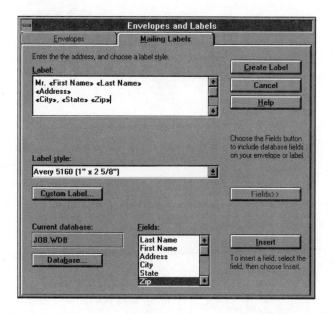

10. Select the type of label you want to use from the Label style drop-down menu.

11. Click Create Label.

12. Open the File menu, and then choose Print Preview. Works will ask you what database you want to use.

13. Select the database you want.

Here's what labels for the two records in our database look like. Just as they should!

Envelopes

The process for creating and printing envelopes is exactly the same as for creating mailing labels, except for the dialog box you use. The Envelopes tab of the Envelopes and Labels dialog box, shown here, requires you to identify the type of envelope you want to use, as well as design an address using the Fields button.

After you click on the Create Envelope button, the envelope looks like the Print Preview shown here.

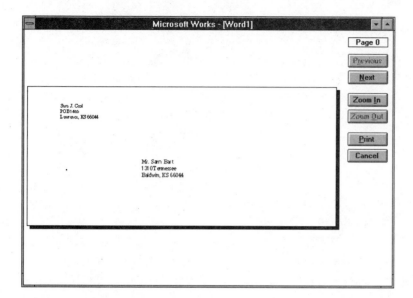

Coming Next

Works can connect documents so that when you change one, the other responds in kind. That's what we'll turn our attention to next.

17

Linking and Embedding

inking and embedding are two ways that Works can help you update and incorporate information quickly and easily. *Linking* means establishing a connection between an object, such as a chart, and a Works document or database file. When you create such a link, changes you make in the original document are automatically reflected in the word-processed document, spreadsheet, or database. Basically, linking means that when you update the original, you also change a copy of the original, no matter where the copy is located. *Embedding* means inserting an object in the word processor. With embedding you can create an object, or change an existing one—but only in the word processor.

The primary difference between linking and embedding is the location of the original information. With linking, the original information resides in its own separate document. With embedding, the original information resides in the word-processed document.

For example, a chart created with the spreadsheet is *linked* to a word-processed document, because the original chart resides in the spreadsheet, not the word processor. If you *embed* a spreadsheet table into a word-processed document (using the Insert menu), the table stands alone and is not connected to any other application.

In this chapter, we'll go through some simple examples of linking and embedding.

Linking Objects

You link information from a *source document* (where the object is created) to a *destination document,* where the object is pasted. You can also link the object from the source to several different destinations.

For example, if you link a chart created with the spreadsheet to a word-processed document, Works writes an internal note to itself, linking the information even after you've closed the document or quit Works.

Because the link is permanent, it ensures that any changes you make to the chart or to the data in the spreadsheet are automatically reflected in the word-processed document. You can link the same chart to a database as well.

To show you how easy linking is, let's look at a simple but very useful example: between a chart created with the spreadsheet and a document created with the word processor.

Before we begin, remember the following rule: When you create information in one Works application to be linked to another application, you must save and name the source document (the file that contains the information to be linked).

Linking with the Spreadsheet

Linking spreadsheet data is a bit like copying and pasting. You select and copy a chart to the Clipboard as usual, but then you paste it into a word-processed document using the Paste Special command instead of the Paste command. The Paste Special command (available in the word processor, spreadsheet, and database) establishes a link between the original document (and module) and the pasted copy. With this link, the copied information has a direct line to the source document, and Works can update the copy whenever you change the original.

To try out linking, close all the files you are working with; you're going to create new ones. Let's say that you have completed a report that contains text and a chart showing how a widget company has done over the past two years.

Enter the text as shown here. We saved it under the filename 1993rpt. The word processor extension is .WPS.

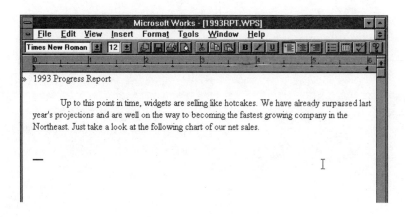

Now use the following data to create a spreadsheet and save it under the name *1993DATA*. Since this file was created in the spreadsheet, Works gives it the extention .WKS.

	A	B
1	Quarter 1	34
2	Quarter 2	38
4	Quarter 3	45
5	Quarter 4	52

Now create a simple line chart that looks like the one below, and save the spreadsheet after the chart is created.

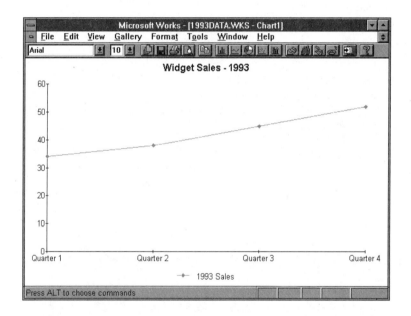

For information, see Chapter 9, "Creating Charts," page 251.

We now have a source document (the chart) and the destination document (the word-processed report). Let's go to work.

First, we'll insert the chart into the word-processed document by following these steps:

1. Open the spreadsheet that contains the chart you want to link.

2. Switch to the word-processed document.

3. Move the insertion point to the location where you want the chart to appear.

4. Open the Insert menu, and then choose Chart. When you do this, you see the Insert Chart dialog box, as shown here.

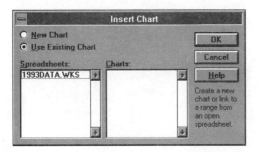

5. Click on the Use Existing Chart button.

6. In the Spreadsheets box, click on the name of the spreadsheet that you used to create the chart. When you do this, Works lists the charts that are attached to that spreadsheet.

7. In the Charts box, highlight the name of the chart you want to insert.

8. Click on OK. As you can see on the next page, the chart is inserted into the word-processed document.

By inserting the chart into the word-processed document, you linked the data in the spreadsheet (which you used to create the chart) to the chart that appears in the report.

Want proof? Switch to the spreadsheet and change the value of any of the data points. Now go back to the report. Notice anything different? That's right—any change made to the original data in the spreadsheet is reflected in the chart in the report.

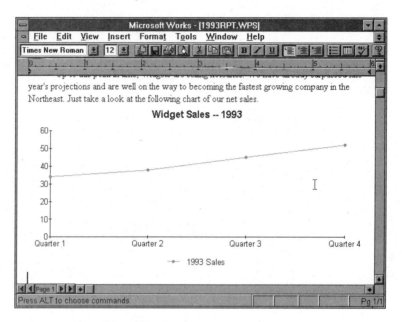

Verifying the Link

Let's say that you get some new report figures and you want to update the spreadsheet on which the chart (now in the final report) is based. Remember that even if the report is not opened, the link still exists, meaning that any change made to the spreadsheet is reflected in the chart, which, in turn, is reflected in the report.

Let's see what happens when you change the spreadsheet and save it without ever opening or doing anything to the report to which the chart is linked.

1. Save and close all open Works files.

2. Open the spreadsheet named 1993DATA.WKS.

3. Change the value in cell B2 to 55.

4. Save the spreadsheet.

5. Now open the document named 1993RPT.WPS.

   Before Works opens the document, it first displays the this dialog box.

This gives you the opportunity to update the document before you open it.

6. Click Yes, and a few moments later the report appears, complete with updates based on the linked spreadsheet data.

 TIP: You can open the source document that you used to create an object by double-clicking on the object. For example, if you double-click on a chart, the spreadsheet module opens.

Editing a Linked Object

The easiest way to edit a linked object is to first double-click on that object. For example, if you are working in a word-processed document that contains a chart that needs to be changed, simply double-click on the chart. Any changes you make are reflected in the chart as it appears in the word-processed document.

TIP: The Paste Special command on the Insert menu allows you to paste linked information into a word-processed document as an object, database, spreadsheet, picture, or bitmap, or as unformatted text. Depending on what you want to do with the information, you can select the appropriate alternative.

Editing a Link

In addition to editing linked data, you might sometimes want to edit the link itself. For example, you might want to save a spreadsheet under a new name or in a different directory. You do this type of editing with the Links command on the Edit menu. Let's explore that now.

1. If the spreadsheet document is open, close it.

2. If necessary, highlight the linked data in the word-processed document. Choose the Links command from the Edit menu.

   Works displays the Links dialog box, as shown here.

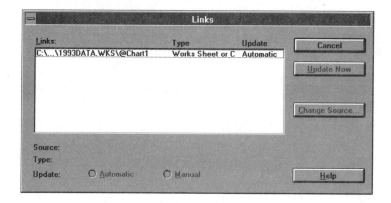

In the box labeled Links, Works identifies the source document, the type of document it is, and whether the update is automatic or manual. The other options are as follows.

- You can select an Automatic update (which Works does without waiting for your OK) or a Manual update (which Works does only if you to tell it to). The Manual update is a good idea when you want to see what the destination document looks like before you make the changes.

- You can click Update Now to update highlighted information.

- You can click Change Source to change the identification of the source document. For example, you can change the drive letter or directory if you have moved the file.

Embedding Objects

Embedding allows you to create and modify objects within the word processor. Unlike linking, you don't leave the word processor module to do any of your work.

The best way to show you how to embed objects is to work through some examples. You already know how to insert a drawing (see Chapter 13, page 397, for a review), and you also know how to use ClipArt, WordArt, and Note-It. These objects are all embedded, as you learned in Chapter 14, page 425. In this section, we'll show you how to embed and work with a chart in a word processor file. We'll also show you how to create objects within a word-processed document.

Creating and Embedding a Spreadsheet

You can create and embed a spreadsheet within a word-processed document without ever leaving the word-processed document.

The scenario: You are in the middle of a report and want to insert information to be arranged in a spreadsheet format. The report looks something like what you see here.

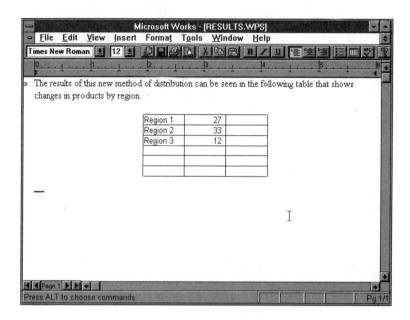

Here's how we prepared this report. Remember, embedding can only take place in the word processor, so that's where you start.

1. Place the insertion point where you want to embed the spreadsheet. In this example, some text was entered and then the insertion point was centered so the spreadsheet would be centered as well.

2. Open the Insert menu, and then choose Spreadsheet/Table. When you do this, you see the Spreadsheet/Table dialog box, shown here.

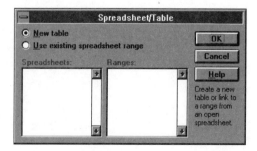

3. Click on New table. If you already created a spreadsheet you want to use, you would click Use existing spreadsheet range; that range would form the basis for the inserted spreadsheet/table.

4. Click on OK. When you do this, Works places a mini-spreadsheet right into the word processor document. It contains only three columns and five rows, but you can use the standard drag techniques to increase its size.

5. Enter the information you want in the spreadsheet.

6. Click anywhere outside the spreadsheet or press the Esc key to return to the word processor. The table appears as shown below. You'll notice that like any object (the table is an object), it can be dragged, moved, and resized. And like any object, when you double-click on it, the original application used to create the object is revealed as you see below (along with the appropriate toolbar!). When you are done making any changes, simply click once again in the word processor window and your document returns to normal.

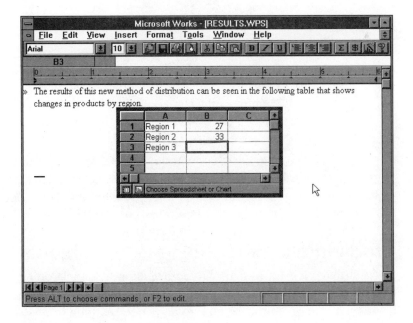

Creating and Embedding a Chart

If you can embed a new spreadsheet/table combo, isn't charting just one step away? It certainly is. The spreadsheet toolbar contains all the buttons and other features that you became familiar with in Chapter 8, page 215.

You can create a chart from an existing spreadsheet by clicking on the New Chart button on the toolbar. The figure below shows a pie chart that was created by highlighting the information, clicking on the New Chart button, and selecting 3-D Pie from the New Chart dialog box.

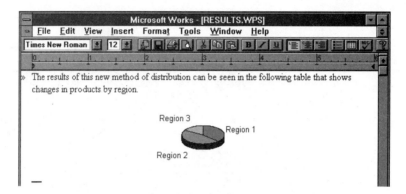

It's that simple to embed a chart into a word processor document. As you can see, the buttons for switching from a spreadsheet to a chart and back again are at the bottom of the chart object area. Simply click whichever one you want when you want to work on the chart. Clicking outside the chart produces just the chart itself as an object.

If you want to create a chart without first creating a spreadsheet, you go through the same procedures we listed above, including embedding the table and then generating the chart. Works will remind you that before you can create a chart, you first must have data on which to base the chart.

Creating and Embedding Other Objects

Now all that's left to your becoming a linking and embedding expert is knowing how to embed other types of objects into a word processor document. What might these other objects be? Anything from a sound to a picture created with Paintbrush.

To insert other types of objects, follow these steps.

1. Place the insertion point where you want to insert the object.

2. Open the Insert menu, and then select Object. When you do this, you see the Insert Object dialog box, as shown here.

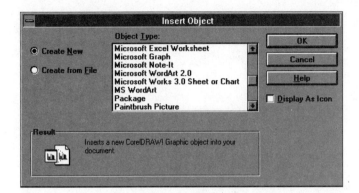

As you can see, you can select the type of object you want to insert. You can also specify whether you want the object to be a new creation or you want to create the object from an existing file.

For example, if you click on the Create New button and click Microsoft Note-It from the Object Type box, Works gives you the Note-It dialog box. (Choosing such object types as ClipArt, Drawing, Note-It, and WordArt from the Insert Objects dialog box is just like selecting the menu command from the Insert menu.

3. Click to indicate whether this will be a new object or if you want to import one from an existing file. If you want to use an existing file, Works asks you to identify the complete path to the file.

4. Click on the type of object you want to insert.

5. Click on OK.

Works takes over from there and inserts the identified object.

That's All!

Ta-da! You're done with *Running Microsoft Works 3 for Windows*, but we certainly hope that you are not done running Works. We hope this book has helped you master some of the important basic techniques for using Works.

P
A
R
T

8

Appendices

A

Built-In Spreadsheet and Database Functions

One of the best things about Works, and what helps make it such a workhorse, is the 76 built-in functions you can use instead of defining your own formulas to do the same work.

Every function has a name and must be typed in the following format:

```
=FunctionName(Argument0,Argument1,...ArgumentN)
```

FunctionName is the name of the function. Function names are shown in capitals in this appendix.

Argument0,Argument1,... ArgumentN represent arguments or values used in the calculation. Arguments can be numbers, cell references, range references or names, field names, or other functions. Regardless of form, however, all arguments must represent numbers. For example, if cell B3 is included as an argument, B3 must contain a numeric value.

All functions, like all formulas, begin with an equal sign (=) to indicate that they are to be calculated rather than interpreted as text or values. Arguments, if used, are always enclosed in parentheses. If a function takes multiple arguments, the arguments must be separated by commas.

People tend to shy away from using functions because they feel intimidated by them and think that functions are too complicated. Our advice is to try them! What can you lose? You'll be amazed at how much time you can save and how much more powerful a tool Works becomes.

Works organizes these 76 functions into eight categories, as follows:

- Date and time functions

- Financial functions

- Informational functions

- Logical functions

- Lookup and reference functions

- Math and trigonometric functions

- Statistical functions

- Text functions

The following descriptions provide a reference to the Works functions, organized by category.

Date and Time Functions

DATE(*year,month,day*)

DATE converts a date to a constant number between 1 and 65534, representing the days from January 1, 1900, through June 3, 2079. The values for *year*, *month*, and *day* must be numbers.

For example, =DATE(1992,1,20) returns 33623 for January 20, 1992. *Year* can also be a number from 0 (for 1900) through 179 (2079), *month* can be 1 through 12, and *day* can be 1 through 31. If the *day* or *month* are outside the normal ranges, the function corrects for the error. It does not return ERR.

DAY(*datenumber*)

DAY returns the number of the day of the month for the date specified as date. Using the preceding DATE example of 33623 for January 20, 1992, =DAY(33623) returns 20. Date can be entered either as a number between 1 and 65534 or as a date surrounded by single quotation marks, for example, =DAY('1/20/92').

MONTH(*date*)

MONTH returns the number of the month for the date specified as date. Date can be entered either as a number between 1 and 65534 or as a date surrounded by single quotation marks, for example, =MONTH('1/20/92').

YEAR(*date*)

YEAR returns the number of the year for the date specified as date. Date can be entered either as a number between 1 and 65534 or as a date surrounded by single quotation marks.

TIME(*hour,minute,second*)

TIME converts a time to a number between 0 and 0.99999, representing the hours, minutes, and seconds between 12:00:00 a.m. and 11:59:59 p.m.

MINUTE(*time*)

MINUTE returns the number of the minute, from 0 through 59, for the time specified as time. Specify time as a number between 0 and 0.99999, representing the times between 12:00:00 a.m. and 11:59:59 p.m., or enclose the time in single quotation marks.

SECOND(*TimeNumber*)

A function that converts a number for the second of the time represented by TimeNumber. Second returns a value in the range of 0 to 59.

HOUR(*time*)

HOUR returns the number of the hour of the day (0 through 23) for the time specified as time. Specify time as a number between 0 and 0.99999, for example, =HOUR(.9876), representing the times between 12:00:00 a.m. and 11:59:59 p.m. or enclose the time in single quotation marks.

NOW( )

NOW returns a serial number representing the current date and time. The number returned consists of an integer plus a decimal fraction. The integer is the serial number representing the date; the fraction is the serial number representing the time.

Financial Functions

CTERM(*interest rate,future value,present value*)

CTERM calculates the number of compounding periods required for an investment to grow from the specified present value to the specified future value, given a fixed interest rate per compounding period.

DDB(*cost,salvage,life,period*)

DDB uses the double-declining balance method of calculating depreciation of an asset. Cost is the original cost of the asset. Salvage is the expected value at the end of the asset's life. Life is the number of years or other time periods the asset is expected to be usable. Period is the time period for which you want to calculate the depreciation.

The function calculates depreciation for a given period according to the formula

$$\frac{(value*2)}{life}$$

FV(*payment,rate,term*)

FV calculates the future value of an annuity in which equal payments earn a fixed rate per term, compounded over the specified number of terms.

The function assumes that the first payment is made at the end of the first period and calculates future value according to the formula

$$\frac{Payment*((1+Rate)^{Term}-1)}{Rate}$$

IRR(*guess,range*)

IRR gives the internal rate of return (profit) on the series of cash flows represented by range. Guess is an estimate of the yield. Range is the reference to the cell range containing the values to be calculated.

NPV(*rate,range*)

NPV returns the net present value of a series of payments at a fixed interest rate per period. Rate is the interest rate per period. Range is the range of cells containing the values to calculate. If the interest rate is annual, but the payment periods are more frequent, divide the rate by the number of periods (such as 12).

The function uses the formula

$$NPV = \sum_{i=1}^{n} \frac{Payment[i]}{(1+Rate)i}$$

PMT(*principal,rate,term*)

PMT calculates the payment per period on a loan or investment with a fixed interest rate over the specified term.

Principal is the amount of the loan or investment. Rate is the interest rate. Term is the length of the loan or investment. The rate and the term must correspond to the same periods. If the rate is annual, but the payment is monthly, divide the rate by 12.

The calculation is based on the formula

$$PMT = \frac{present\ value * rate}{(1-(1+rate)^{-term})}$$

PV(*payment,rate,term*)

PV calculates the present value of a series of equal payments earning a fixed rate of interest over a specified term.

Payment is the amount per period. Rate is the interest rate. Term is the number of periods. The function assumes that the first payment is made at the end of the first period.

The calculation is based on the formula

$$PV = \frac{payment * (1-(1+rate)^{-term})}{rate}$$

RATE(*future value,present value,term*)

RATE returns the fixed interest rate per period needed for an investment to grow from its present value to an expected future value in the number of terms specified.

Future value is the value expected at the end of the term. Present value is the current value of the investment. Term is the number of periods to be considered.

The calculation is based on the formula

$$Rate = \left(\frac{future\ value}{present\ value}\right)^{\frac{1}{term}} - 1$$

SLN(*cost,salvage,life*)

SLN calculates the straight-line depreciation for an asset. Straight-line depreciation assumes a linear reduction in value, so the depreciation amount is the same for any period.

Cost is the initial cost of the asset. Salvage is its estimated salvage value. Life is the number of periods the asset is expected to remain useful.

The calculation is based on the formula

$$SLN = \frac{cost\text{-}salvage}{life}$$

SYD(*cost,salvage,life,period*)

SYD calculates depreciation of an asset according to the sum-of-the-years-digits method, in which the greatest allowances for depreciation are made in the earliest years in the life of the asset.

Cost is the initial cost of the asset. Salvage is the estimated salvage value of the asset. Life is the estimated useful life of the asset. Period is the period for which depreciation is to be calculated.

The calculation is based on the formula

$$SYD = \frac{(cost\text{-}salvage)*(life\text{-}period+1)}{\left(\frac{life*(life*+1)}{2}\right)}$$

TERM(*payment,rate,future value*)

TERM calculates the number of periods required for an annuity to grow to the specified future value at a fixed interest rate and a fixed payment per period.

Payment is the amount per period. Rate is the interest rate. Future value is the desired future value. If the interest rate is annual, divide the rate by 12 for a monthly payment period.

Informational Functions

ERR( )

ERR returns the value ERR. This function is usually used to display ERR in a specified cell under a specified condition. ERR takes no argument.

For example, =IF(A1<0,ERR(),A1) displays ERR if the value in cell A1 is less than 0; otherwise, the IF function that contains the ERR function displays the value in cell A1.

ISERR(*x*)

ISERR determines whether the argument is the error value ERR. If the argument produces ERR, the function returns 1. Otherwise, the function returns 0. The ISERR function can be used to control the propagation of the ERR error message through related formulas in a spreadsheet.

For example, =IF(ISERR(C15),0,C15) returns 0 if cell C15 contains an error, but otherwise returns the value in cell C15.

ISNA(*x*)

ISNA determines whether the argument is the value N/A (not available). This function is similar to the ISERR function in helping prevent the propagation of one value (N/A) throughout related formulas in a spreadsheet.

NA( )

NA returns the value N/A (not available). Works treats N/A as a numeric, not text, value. See also ISNA.

Logical Functions

AND(*logical0,logical1,...*)

AND gives 1 (True) if all of the arguments are TRUE (nonzero), and it gives 0 (False) if one or more arguments are FALSE (zero).

For example, if the range B1:B3 contains the values TRUE, FALSE, and TRUE, then =AND(B1:B3) equals 0 (False).

FALSE( )

FALSE returns the value 0, meaning False. This function is the complement of TRUE().

For example, =IF(A1>0,TRUE(),FALSE()) returns 1 (True) if the value in cell A1 is greater than 0; otherwise, the IF function returns 0 (False).

IF(*condition,true value,false value*)

IF returns one of two results, depending on the outcome of a specified condition. Condition is the condition to evaluate and is often an expression that includes an operator such as greater than (>), less than (<), or equal (=); true value is the value that is returned if the outcome of the condition is true. False value is the value returned if the outcome of the condition is false.

NOT(*logical*)

NOT reverses the value of its argument. If logical is FALSE, NOT returns 1 (True). If logical is TRUE, NOT returns 0 (false).

For example, =NOT(1+1=3) equals 1 (True).

OR(*logical0,logical1,)*

OR gives 1 (True) if one or more of the arguments are TRUE. It gives 0 (False) if all of the arguments are FALSE.

For example, =OR(1+1=1,2+2=5) equals 0 (False).

TRUE( )

TRUE returns the value 1, meaning True. See also FALSE.

Lookup and Reference Functions

CHOOSE(*x,option0,option1,...optionN*)

CHOOSE uses the value of x to return the value of the option whose position in the list of arguments corresponds to x.

For example, in the function =CHOOSE(2,20,30,40,50) the function returns 40, because its position corresponds to 2 (20=0, 30=1, 40=2, 50=3).

COLS(*range reference*)

COLS returns the number of columns in a range. For example, =COLS(A1:C1) returns 3 because the range covers three columns—A, B, and C.

HLOOKUP(*search value,range,row*)

HLOOKUP uses a search value to retrieve an entry from a predefined table. Search value is a value in the top row of the table. Range is the range comprising the table. Row is the number of rows that the function is to go below the search value to retrieve the desired entry.

For example, if a table in cells A1 through C4 contains the following:

	A	B	C
1	1	2	3
2	10	20	30
3	70	80	90

the formula =HLOOKUP(2,A1:C4,2), returns 50. The function first reads across the top row of the range defined by A1:C4.

INDEX(*range,column,row*)

INDEX returns the value of the cell at the intersection of the specified column and row. Column and row numbers begin with 0, so the intersection of column 0 and row 0 is the first value in the specified range.

ROWS(*range*)

ROWS returns the number of rows in a range.

VLOOKUP(*search value,range,column*)

VLOOKUP uses a search value to retrieve an entry from a predefined table.

For example, if a table in cells A1 through C4 contains the following:

	A	B	C
1	2	20	60
2	3	30	70
3	4	40	80

the formula =VLOOKUP(2,A1:C4,2), returns 60. The function first reads down the leftmost column of the range defined by A1:C4. When it finds a number equal to the search value, it goes across the specified number of columns (2) and retrieves the value in the cell at that location. The function returns 0 if the target cell contains text.

Math and Trigonometric Functions

ABS(*x*)

ABS gives the absolute value of x. For example, ABS(-3)=3. X can not be 0.

ACOS(*x*)

ACOS gives the arccosine (inverse cosine) of the angle whose cosine is x. X must be a value between -1 and +1. The function returns a value between 0 and p radians (0 through 180 degrees).

ASIN(*x*)

ASIN gives the arcsine (inverse sine) of the angle whose sine is x.

X must be a value between -1 and +1. The function returns a value between $^{-\pi}/2$ and $^{\pi}/2$ (90 degrees through 90 degrees).

ATAN(*x*)

ATAN gives the arctangent (inverse tangent) of the angle whose tangent is x. The function returns a value between $^{-\pi}/2$ and $^{\pi}/2$ (90 degrees through 90 degrees).

ATAN2(*x-coordinate,y-coordinate*)

ATAN2 gives the arctangent of an angle defined by x and y coordinates. X is the x coordinate and y is the y coordinate. Otherwise, the function returns a value between $^{-\pi}/2$ and $^{\pi}/2$ as shown in the following table:

If x is	If y is	Function returns
+	+	0 through $^{\pi}/2$
–	+	$^{\pi}/2$ through π
–	–	$-\pi$ through $^{-\pi}/2$
+	–	$^{-\pi}/2$–0

COS(*x*)

COS gives the cosine of x, an angle expressed in radians.

EXP(*x*)

EXP returns the value of the constant 2.71828..., the base of the natural logarithm raised to the power of x.

INT(*x*)

INT gives the integer part of the value x. The INT function truncates the decimal portion of a number without rounding up or down.

For example, =INT(3.14) and =INT(3.99) both produce the same value, 3.

LN(*x*)

LN gives the natural logarithm (base e, the constant 2.71828) of x.

LOG(*x*)

LOG gives the base 10 logarithm of x.

MOD(*numerator,denominator*)

MOD gives the remainder of numerator divided by denominator. For example, =MOD(10,3) produces 1 because 10 divided by 3 has a remainder of 1.

PI( )

PI returns the value of pi rounded to nine decimal places (3.141592654).

RAND( )

RAND returns a random number. The number is a decimal fraction from 0 up to, but not including, 1.

ROUND(*x,number of places*)

ROUND rounds the value x to the number of places specified.

SIN(*x*)

SIN returns the sine of x, an angle expressed in radians.

SQRT(*x*)

SQRT returns the square root of x.

TAN(*x*)

TAN returns the tangent of x, an angle expressed in radians.

Statistical Functions

AVG(*range0,range1,...rangeN*)

AVG gives the average of the values in the ranges listed as arguments.

Range0,range1,...rangeN are sets of values. They can be entered as numbers, cell or range references, or formulas. Text is always treated as 0. Blank cells are also treated as 0 if they occur in cell references; in range references, they are ignored.

COUNT(*range0,range1,...rangeN*)

COUNT returns the number of cells in the ranges specified.

Range0,range1,...rangeN can be numbers, cell or range references, or formulas. The function counts cells containing not only numbers, but text and the values ERR and N/A, which are returned by other functions. Blank cells are counted only if they occur in cell (not range) references.

MAX(*range0,range1,...rangeN*)

MAX returns the largest (maximum) value in the referenced ranges.

Range0,range1,...rangeN can be numbers, cell or range references, or formulas. The function ignores blank cells in range references, but treats them as 0 in cell references.

MIN(*range0,range1,...rangeN*)

MIN returns the smallest (minimum) value in the referenced ranges.

STD(*range0,range1,...rangeN*)

STD calculates the population standard deviation of the values in the specified ranges.

Range0,range1,...rangeN can be numbers, cell or range references, or formulas. Blank cells are ignored in range references but treated as 0 in cell references. To calculate the standard deviation of a sample, use the formula STD(ranges)*SQRT(COUNT(ranges)/(COUNT(ranges)1)), where ranges include range0,range1,...rangeN for the functions involved.

SUM(*range0,range1,...rangeN*)

SUM totals the values in the specified ranges.

Range0,range1,...rangeN can be numbers, cell references or ranges, or formulas. Blank cells are ignored in range references and treated as 0 in cell references. For examples, refer to Chapter 7.

VAR(*range0,range1,...rangeN*)

VAR calculates variance, the degree to which the values in the specified ranges deviate from the mean for all values.

Range0,range1,...rangeN can be numbers, cell or range references, or formulas. Blank cells are ignored in range references and treated as 0 in cell references. To calculate sample variance, use the formula VAR(ranges)*(COUNT(ranges)/(COUNT(ranges)1)), where ranges includes range0, range1,...rangeN, as described above.

Text Functions

EXACT(*text value0,text value1*)

EXACT compares two strings of characters and gives 1 (true) If They are exactly the same, 0 (False) If They are not.

For example, if cells A9 and G9 contain Buy and cell D9 contains Sell, then:

=EXACT(A9,G9) equals 1 (true)

=EXACT(A9,D9) equals 0 (False)

=EXACT("Fred",D9) equals 0 (False)

FIND(*find text,search text,offset*)

FIND finds one string of text within another string of text and returns the number of the character at which FindText occurs.

For example, if cell A10 contains the text *Gertrude Stein*, then:

=FIND("Stein",A10,0) equals 9

=FIND("eat","The Beatles",4) equals 5

=FIND("Hello","Goodbye",0) equals ERR

LEFT(*text value,length*)

LEFT gives the first (or leftmost) character or characters in a text string. Length specifies how many characters you want LEFT to extract. For example, if cell A1 contains Madonna, then =LEFT(A1,1) equals M.

If cell F19 contains #NEW8778, then =LEFT(F19,4) equals #NEW.

LENGTH(*text value*)

LENGTH determines the number of characters in a string of text. When the LENGTH function counts the number of characters, it also counts blank spaces and punctuation marks. For example, if cell B5 contains the text London, England, then =LENGTH(B5) equals 15.

LOWER(*text value*)

LOWER converts all uppercase letters of text in TextValue to lowercase. TextValue references the cell that contains text.

For example, if cell B12 contains the text K.D. Lang, then =LOWER(B12) equals k.d. lang.

MID(*text value,offset,length*)

MID gives a specific number of characters from a text string, starting at the position you specify. TextValue references a cell that contains text. Offset is the position of the first character you want to extract from TextValue. Length is the total number of characters you want MID to extract.

For example, if cell B12 contains the text Paul Newman, then =MID(B12,0,4) equals Paul.

N(*range reference*)

N gives the entry in the first cell in a range as a value. If the first cell contains text, N gives the value 0 (zero). RangeReference is a cell or range reference, or a range name.

For example, if cell B25 contains the text PAID and cells B26 and B27 contain $45.00 and $36.00, respectively, then =N(B25:B27) equals 0 (zero).

PROPER(*text value*)

PROPER capitalizes the first letter of each word and any text that follows any character other than a letter in a text string. TextValue references the cell that contains the text.

For example, =PROPER("This is a title") equals This Is A Title.

REPEAT(*text value,count*)

REPEAT repeats text as many times as you specify. TextValue can be a reference to a cell that contains text.

For example, if cell A3 contains Sales, then =REPEAT(A3,2) equals SalesSales.

REPLACE(*old text,offset,length,new text*)

REPLACE exchanges one string of text for another. OldText references a cell that contains text. Offset is the number of the character within OldText at which to begin replacing OldText characters with NewText. NewText is the text that you want to replace OldText with. NewText can be a reference to a cell that contains text.

For example, the following formula replaces the five characters after the fifth character in OldText with NewText. =REPLACE("abcde-fghijk",5,5,"*") equals abcde*k.

RIGHT(*text value,length*)

RIGHT returns the last (or rightmost) character or characters in a text string. TextValue references to a cell that contains text. For example, if cell D5 contains the text Sale Price, then =RIGHT(D5,5) equals Price.

S(*range reference*)

S gives the text in the first cell in a range. RangeReference is a cell or range reference, or a range name.

For example, if cell C10 contains the text string CA and cells C11 and C12 contain 95678 and 90266, respectively, then =S(C10:C12) equals CA.

STRING(*x,decimal places*)

STRING gives the value converted to text with the specified number of decimal places. X references a cell that contains a value. DecimalPlaces is the number of decimal places you want Works to display for the value that is converted to text.

For example, if cell B3 contains the value 345, then =STRING(B3,2) equals 345.00 (as text).

TRIM(*text value*)

TRIM removes all spaces from TextValue except for single spaces between words.

For example, if cell E2 contains the text Monthly   Status   Report, then =TRIM(E2) equals Monthly Status Report.

UPPER(*text value*)

UPPER converts text to uppercase.

For example, if cell A4 contains the text sell and cell B4 contains the text buy, then =UPPER(A4) equals SELL.

VALUE(*textvalue*)

VALUE gives a number entered as text as its corresponding numeric value.

For example, if cell K5 contains $554.00 entered as text (that is, when you highlight the cell, $554.00 is displayed in the formula bar with a double quotation mark preceding it), then =VALUE(K5) equals 554 as a value, not text.

Keystroke Shortcuts

Windows Keystrokes

To	Press
Switch to the next pane	F6
Switch to the next document window	Ctrl + F6
Switch to the previous pane	Shift + F6
Switch to the previous document window	Ctrl + Shift + F6
Switch to the next application window or minimized window	Alt + Esc
Switch to the next application window, maximizing icons	Alt + Tab
Switch to the previous application window	Shift + Alt + Esc
Switch to the Task List	Ctrl + Esc
Close the active document window	Ctrl + F4

Choosing Menus and Commands

To	Press
Save a document	Ctrl + S
Get Help	F1
Activate the menu bar	F10
Choose the application window Control menu	Alt + Spacebar
Choose the document window Control menu	Alt + -
Choose the Charts menu	Alt + C
Choose the Edit menu	Alt + E
Choose the File menu	Alt + F
Choose the Format menu	Alt + T
Choose the Gallery menu	Alt + G
Choose the Help menu	Alt + H

Choose the Tutorial	Shift + F1
Choose the Insert menu	Alt + I
Choose the Options menu	Alt + O
Choose the Select menu	Alt + S
Choose the View menu	Alt + V
Choose the Window menu	Alt + W
Print a document	Ctrl + P
Close any open menu	Esc
Open the Font box on the Toolbar	Ctrl + F
Open the Font Size box on the Toolbar	Ctrl + Z
Switch between form view and list view	F9
Quit Works	Alt + F4

Changing the Appearance of Cells

To	**Press**
Make text bold	Ctrl + B
Make text italic	Ctrl + I
Make text subscript	Ctrl + =
Make text superscript	Ctrl + Shift + +
Underline text	Ctrl + U
Remove all font styles	Ctrl + Spacebar
Repeat format	Shift + F7

To Change Cells/Fields to	**Press**
Format with commas	Ctrl + Comma
Currency format	Ctrl + 4
Percent format	Ctrl + 5

530

Formula Bar Operations

To	Press
Confirm information in a cell or field	Enter
Confirm information in a range of cells	Ctrl + Enter
Change information in a cell or field	F2
Activate and clear the formula bar	Backspace or Shift + Backspace or DEL

Inserting Information

To Insert	Press
A tab stop	Tab
A new paragraph	Enter
A page break	Ctrl + Enter
The current date	Ctrl + ;
The current time	Ctrl + Shift + ;
An optional hyphen (in the Word Processor only)	Ctrl + -
A nonbreaking hyphen (in the Word Processor only)	Ctrl + Shift + -
A nonbreaking space (in the Word Processor only)	Ctrl + Shift + Spacebar
An end-of-line mark (in the Word Processor and Database form view only)	Shift + Enter
Create Autosum total (in the Spreadsheet only)	Ctrl + M

Line and Paragraph Spacing

To	Press
Single-space lines	Ctrl + 1
Double-space lines	Ctrl + 2
Space lines 1.5 lines apart	Ctrl + 5
Reduce space before a paragraph	Ctrl + 0 (zero)
Add space before a paragraph	Ctrl + O (letter O)

Moving Around in a Document

To Move	Press
To a bookmark	F5
To the next bookmark	Shift + F5
To the beginning of the line	Home
To the end of the line	End
To the beginning of the document	Ctrl + Home
To the end of the document	Ctrl + End
Up one line	↑
Down one line	↓
To the previous paragraph (in the Word Processor only)	Ctrl + ↑
To the next paragraph (in the Word Processor only)	Ctrl + ↓
Left one character	←
Right one character	→
To the previous word (in the Word Processor only)	Ctrl + ←
To the next word (in the Word Processor only)	Ctrl + →
To the top of the document window	Ctrl + PgUp
To the bottom of the document window	Ctrl + PgDn

To Scroll	Press
Up one window	PgUp
Down one window	PgDn

Moving Around in a Dialog Box

To	Press
Move forward through options	Tab
Move backward through options	Shift + Tab
Open a list box	↓
Confirm an option or carry it out	Enter
Cancel the changes and close the dialog box	Esc

Changing Information

To	Press
Copy a selection	Ctrl + C
Paste a selection	Ctrl + V
Cut a selection	Ctrl + X
Delete a selection	DEL or Backspace
Delete character to the left of the insertion point	Backspace
Delete character to the right of the insertion point	DEL
Undo changes in the Word Processor	Alt + Backspace
Repeat a search	F7
Edit a cell	F2
Copy the values of above a cell	Ctrl + '
Copy a screen image	Print Screen
Copy an image of the active window	Alt + Print Screen
Paginate a document	F9
Calculate a spreadsheet	F9
Go To	F5

Highlighting in the Word Processor

To	Press
Extend a selection	F8
Quit extending	Esc
Collapse a selection	Shift + F8

To Highlight	Press
A word	F8 twice
A sentence	F8 three times
A paragraph	F8 four times
A document	F8 five times
The previous character	Shift + ←
The next character	Shift + →
The previous word	Ctrl + Shift + ←
The next word	Ctrl + Shift + →
To the beginning of line	Shift + Home
To the end of the line	Shift + End
To the beginning of the document	Ctrl + Shift + Home
To the end of the document	Ctrl + Shift + End
To the previous line	Shift + ↑
To the next line	Shift + ↓
To the previous paragraph	Ctrl + Shift + ↑
To the next paragraph	Ctrl + Shift + ↓
To the previous window	Shift + PgUp
To the next window	Shift + PgDn
To the top of the window	Ctrl + Shift + PgUp
To the bottom of the window	Ctrl + Shift + PgDn

Moving Around in a Spreadsheet

To Move	Press
To the next named range	Shift + F5
To the previous cell in a range	Shift + Enter
To the next cell in a range	Enter
To the beginning of the row	Home
To the end of the row	End
To the beginning of the spreadsheet	Ctrl + Home
To the end of the spreadsheet	Ctrl + End
Up one cell	↑
Down one cell	↓
Left one cell	← or Shift + Tab
Right one cell	→ or Tab
Up to the first or last cell of a range	Ctrl + ↑
Down to the first or last cell of a range	Ctrl + ↓
Left to the first or last cell of a range	Ctrl + ←
Right to the first or last cell of a range	Ctrl + →

To Scroll	Press
Up one window	PgUp
Down one window	PgDn
Left one window	Ctrl + PgUp
Right one window	Ctrl + PgDn

Highlighting Spreadsheet Information

To Highlight	Press
A row	Ctrl + F8
A column	Shift + F8
An entire spreadsheet	Ctrl + Shift + F8

Left one cell	Shift + ←
Left to the first or last cell of a range	Ctrl + Shift + ←
Right one cell	Shift + →
Right to the first or last cell of a range	Ctrl + Shift + →
Down one cell	Shift + ↑
Up one cell	Shift + ↓
Down to the first or last cell of a range	Ctrl + Shift + ↑
Up to the first or last cell of a range	Ctrl + Shift + ↓
To the beginning of the row	Shift + Home
To the end of the row	Shift + End
To the beginning of the spreadsheet	Ctrl + Shift + Home
To the end of the spreadsheet	Ctrl + Shift + End
Up one window	Shift + PgUp
Down one window	Shift + PgDn
Left one window	Ctrl + Shift + PgUp
Right one window	Ctrl + Shift + PgDn

To	**Press**
Cancel a selection	Esc

Moving Around in a Database or Report

To Move	**Press**
Left through the database or report	←
Right through the database or report	→
To the previous unlocked field	Shift + Tab
To the next unlocked field	Tab
To the beginning of the database (the first field or record)	Ctrl + Home
To the end of the database (the last field or record)	Ctrl + End

Up one field	↑
Down one field	↓
Up to the top or previous record	Ctrl + ↑
Down to the last or next record	Ctrl + ↓

To Move in List View	**Press**
To the beginning of a record	Home
To the end of a record	End
Left to the first field	Ctrl + ←
Right to the last field	Ctrl + →

To Move in Form View	**Press**
To the left margin of a form	Home
To the right margin of a form	End
To the previous record	Ctrl + PgUp
To the next record	Ctrl + PgDn
Up one page	PgUp
Down one page	PgDn

To Scroll in List View	**Press**
Up one window	PgUp
Down one window	PgDn
Right one window	Ctrl + PgDn
Left one window	Ctrl + PgUp

To Scroll in Form View	**Press**
Horizontally one window to left	Ctrl + ←
Horizontally one window to right	Ctrl + →

Highlighting Database Information

To Highlight	Press
A record (in list view)	Ctrl + F8
A field (in list view)	Shift + F8
An entire database (in list view)	Ctrl + Shift + F8
Left one field	Shift + ←
Right one field	Shift + →
A record, to the first field entry	Ctrl + Shift + ←
A record, to the last field entry	Ctrl + Shift + →
Up one field	Shift + ↑
Down one field	Shift + ↓
A field, up to the first record	Ctrl + Shift + ↑
A field, down to the last record	Ctrl + Shift + ↓
To the beginning of a record	Shift + Home
To the end of a record	Shift + End
To the beginning of the database	Ctrl + Shift + Home
To the end of the database	Ctrl + Shift + End
Up one window (in list view)	Shift + PgUp
Down one window (in list view)	Shift + PgDn
Left one window (in list view)	Ctrl + Shift + PgUp
Right one window (in list view)	Ctrl + Shift + PgDn

To	Press
Cancel a selection	Esc

Moving Around in Communications

To Move	Press
To the beginning of the line	Home
To the end of the line	End
To the beginning of the buffer	Ctrl + Home

To the end of the buffer	Ctrl + End
Up one line	↑
Down one line	↓
Left one character	←
Right one character	→

To Scroll	**Press**
Up one window	PgUp
Down one window	PgDn

Highlighting in Communications

To	**Press**
Extend a selection	F8
Quit extending	Esc
Collapse a selection	Shift + F8

To Highlight	**Press**
To the beginning of the line	Shift + Home
To the end of the line	Shift + End
To the beginning of the buffer	Ctrl + Shift + Home
To the end of the buffer	Ctrl + Shift + End
To the previous window	Shift + PgUp
To the next window	Shift + PgDn
To the top of the window	Ctrl + Shift + PgUp
To the bottom of the window	Ctrl + Shift + PgDn

C

Installing Microsoft Works for Windows

What You Need to Run Works

Works runs on most personal computers, but Works does take lots of room on your hard drive. Here's exactly what you will need to make Works go for you.

- A personal computer with at least a 386 microprocessor and at least 4 megabytes of RAM. The more RAM you have above 4 megabytes, the faster Works will run.

- A VGA monitor or better.

- At least 15 megabytes of hard disk space for a complete installation; 4 megabytes for a minimum installation .

- Microsoft Windows 3.1 already installed on your system; Works will not run without it.

Although you don't need a mouse or a trackball or a pointing device, one is recommended.

Installing Works

Installing Works is an absolute cinch. Just follow these instructions step by step, and you will soon be up and running.

1. Be sure that your computer is turned on.

2. Start Windows. This is most often done by entering

   `win`

   in the directory in which Windows is located. If Windows is already running, close all applications so that only the Program Manager is active and open.

3. Insert the Works Setup disk into the disk drive. Remember to close the disk drive door if necessary.

4. In the Program Manager window, choose the Run command from the File menu.

5. If your Works Setup disk is in drive A, enter

   `a:\setup`

   in the Command Line text box.

If your Works Setup disk is in drive B, enter

`b:\setup`

in the Command Line text box.

These commands let Windows know in what drive the setup information is located.

6. Click OK.

    After you click the OK button, a series of screens will follow that will guide you through Works' installation.

Changing the Installation

You might want to add or remove particular features from Works depending upon your work habits and the capabilities of your computer system. To modify the setup file, follow these steps:

1. Open the Microsoft Works for Windows group in the Program Manager.

2. Double-click on the Microsoft Works Setup icon.

3. Click on the Add/Remove button to open the Maintenance Installation dialog box.

4. To add or remove entire sets of features, such as all the proofing tools, click on the corresponding check box in the options list. To add or remove only certain features in a set, select the set and click the Change Option button. If you want to add items, check the boxes corresponding to the items. If you want to remove items, click on the boxes so they are empty.

5. Continue adding or removing items from groups as needed.

6. When you're done, click on the Continue button.

Removing Works

If you want to remove Works from your hard disk, here's how to do it:

1. Open the Microsoft Works for Windows group in the Program Manager.

2. Double-click on the Microsoft Works Setup icon.

3. Click on the Uninstall All button. Works wants you to be sure about your decision, so it will prompt you to respond Yes and to confirm your command.

4. Click Yes.

5. Follow the instructions you see on the screen as Works is removed from your hard disk. Along the way, you will probably see a Works message asking you if you want to remove a file that might be shared with another application or document. If you have any doubt as to the file's importance, don't remove it.

Index

Special Symbols

+ (addition operator), 220, 221
& (ampersand), 220, 221, 355
/ (division operator), 220, 221
= (equal-to operator), 220, 221
^ (exponent operator), 220, 221
> (greater-than operator), 220, 221
>= (greater-than-or-equal-to operator), 220, 221
< (less-than operator), 220, 221, 355
<= (less-than-or-equal-to operator), 220, 221
* (multiplication operator), 220, 221
<> (not-equal-to operator), 220, 221
| (pipe), 220, 221, 355
- (subtraction operator), 220, 221
~ (tilde), 220, 221

A

ABS function, 520
Absolute references, 229, 232–33

Accessories group, 11
   activating, 14
   minimized, 12
ACOS function, 520
adding text, 103
Add Legend command, 271
addition operator (+), 220, 221
Addresses, 44–45, 178
Align button, 436
aligning text, 121, 123–24
Alignment
   command, 374, 390
   dialog box, 374
All Characters command, 97, 470
All command, 214
Alt key, 14
ampersand (&), 220, 221, 355
AND function, 517
AND operator, 355
applications combining data, 53
application window, 7, 94
   arrangement of documents, 25
   Control-menu box, 33
   word processor, 33–35

JoAnne Woodcock, currently a master writer for Microsoft Press, is author of *The Ultimate MS-DOS Book* and the *MS-DOS 6 Companion*, as well as *Running Microsoft Works 3 for Windows*, the *Concise Guide to MS-DOS 5*, and the *Concise Guide to Microsoft Works for Windows*—all published by Microsoft Press. She is also the coauthor of *Running UNIX* and *Microsoft Word Style Sheets* and a contributor to the *Microsoft Press Computer Dictionary*.

Neil J. Salkind teaches child development at the University of Kansas, and has written college level textbooks, as well as more than 30 books on computer software and hardware. His book *Getting Started with the Apple Macintosh* (Microsoft) won the Best Book of the Year award from the Computer Press Association. When he's not writing, he's collecting first editions, participating in Masters swimming, or juggling.

The manuscript for this book was prepared and submitted to Microsoft Press in electronic form. Text files were prepared using WordPerfect 5.0 for Windows. Pages were composed by Benchmark Productions, Inc. using Ventura Publisher for Windows 4.1, with text in Garamond and display type in Avant Garde Demi. Composed pages were delivered to the printer as electronic prepress files.

Cover Designer
Rebecca Geisler-Johnson

Cover Color Separator
Color Service, Inc.

Interior Graphic Designer
Kim Eggleston

Illustrator
Mark Monlux

Principal Typographer
Benchmark Productions, Inc.

Principal Editorial Compositor
Andrew Williams

Principal Proofreader
Andrea Mulligan

Principal Word Processor
Jennifer Noble

Indexer
Sharon Hilgenberg

Printed on recycled paper stock.

Build Your Spreadsheet Expertise

Build Your Word Processing Skills

Toolbars

To quickly and easily carry out common activities, simply click on a button on one of the Works toolbars.

Communications Toolbar

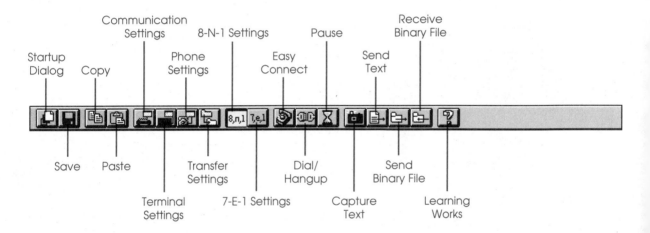

Database Toolbar

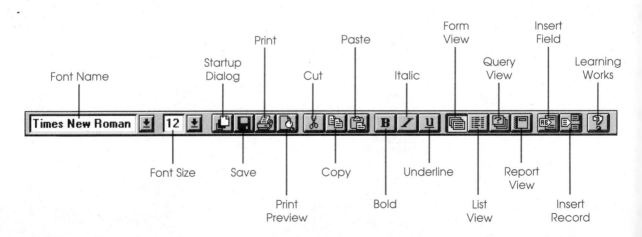